JOHN PAUL JONES

JOHN PAUL
JONES

A RESTLESS SPIRIT

PETER VANSITTART

ROBSON BOOKS

This edition first published in Great Britain in 2004 by Robson Books, The Chrysalis Building, Bramley Road, London, W10 6SP

An imprint of Chrysalis Books Group

British Library Cataloguing in Publication Data
A catalogue record for this title is available from the British Library.

ISBN 1 86105 621 4

Compiled by Indexing Specialists (UK) Limited, Hove, East Sussex
Typeset by FiSH Books, London WC1
Printed in Great Britain by Creative Print & Design (Wales), Ebbw Vale

Contents

To the memory of Alan Ross, 1922–2001
Poet, traveller, editor, naval officer in time of war

Englishmen are distinguished by their traditions and ceremonials,
And also by their affection for their colonies and their contempt
for their colonials.
When foreigners ponder world affairs, why sometimes by doubts
they are smitten,
But Englishmen know instinctively that what the world needs most
is whatever is best for Great Britain.
They have a splendid navy and they conscientiously admire it,
And every schoolboy knows that John Paul Jones was
Only an unfair American pirate.

Ogden Nash,
'England Expects', 1936

'Twas Jones, brave Jones, to Battle led
As bold a crew as ever bled
Upon the sky-surrounded main.

Philip Freneau

1

Who was John Paul Jones? An Introduction

The career of John Paul Jones is one of the most distinguished in American history. Nevertheless, during not only his life but also a century and a half after his death, truth in the portrayal of him has been more honoured in the breach than in the observance. The misunderstanding, and in some cases, the deliberate falsification, which began early in his varied fortunes and persist today, apply in some measure to his historical background, and in far greater degree to his personality.

Lincoln Lorenz
John Paul Jones: Fighter for Freedom and Glory, 1943

He knew himself detested, but he knew
The hearts that loath'd him, crouch'd and dreaded too.
Lone, wild and strange, he stood alike exempt
From all affection and from all contempt;
His name could sadden, and his arts surprise;
But they that fear'd him dared not to despise.

Byron
The Corsair, 1814

On the morrow of the War of Independence, the merchants of Boston, New York, Salem and Philadelphia had taken stock of their maritime future. The following years saw their ships reach Europe, the Indian and Pacific oceans and round Cape Horn, their seamen developed under the schooling of Paul Jones, Murray and Bainbridge.

Jean Randier
Men and Ships Around Cape Horn, 1969

1

At the time of writing, November 2001, among American warships moving into the Far East were the *Theodore Roosevelt*, the *Sir Winston Churchill* and *John Paul Jones*. Despite Ogden Nash's jaunty verse, 'England Expects', few English schoolchildren know of John Paul Jones and adults, at best, will only vaguely recall a hick mercenary in either the War of Independence or the American Civil War, and sometimes confuse him with Paul Revere.

'Jones' was not even his baptismal name, but adopted in circumstances decidedly murky. He is associated, probably wrongly, with the Paul Jones dance, with its whiff of sexual piracy. Robert Panquette's operetta, *Suffren* (1890) about a great French admiral, was retitled *Paul Jones* for English-speaking audiences, though HB Farnie's libretto remained unaltered:

> On to Las Palmas o'er the ocean free,
> Set in the sapphire Caribbean Sea,
> Love and Revenge await the Spaniard there,
> Vengeance on Buccaneer and Love to the Fair.

He has been praised as an actor, envied as a lover of a Duchess of Orleans, both roles fictitious, and in Thackeray's *Denis Duval* is mentioned in discussion of some American privateers in which 'the commodore of a wandering piratical expedition was known to be a rebel Scotsman who fought with a halter round his neck to be sure'.

The 1959 Hollywood movie, *John Paul Jones*, misleads. It stars Bette Davis, not as Jones but no less imperiously, as Catherine the Great, and with a love interest about which the scriptwriter knew far more than history has bothered to record. Jones is mentioned in the 1936 film *Mutiny on the Bounty*, though by a habitual liar.

In England he was demonised as 'The devil in a Scots bonnet'. Disraeli remembered nurses hushing children by his name, as, within the last 60 years, did Oxfordshire nurses with that of Oliver Cromwell. Alexander the Great, Saladin, Richard Lionheart, 'Boney' and Winnie with the Long Green Fingers have been likewise used, to enforce discipline. One child who could have been so threatened was Byron.

'Paul Jones', then, is suggestive of banditry and the morals of a tearabout. A Dumfries pamphlet calls him 'a man against Fate...a cantankerous outsider', though conceding, with some generosity, that he was warm-hearted and friendly. SE Morison, rated by AL Rowse as the American counterpart to GM Trevelyan, an honorary admiral, and friend of John Buchan, whom he guided round Jefferson's home, and Civil War battlefields, deplored Jones's 'ungovernable temper...colossal egotism', while adding that, Nelson excepted, none in naval history has accrued so much romance and controversy. The two shared the skills of vanity, jealousy of rivals, and assiduity in exploiting 'influence'. One towering romancer, the elder Dumas, wrote, or at least published, *Le Capitaine Paul*; there is a manifestation of Jones in Fenimore Cooper's novel *The Pilot* (1823), and praise in his *The History of the Navy of the United States* (1839); in Herman Melville's *Israel Potter* (1855) he is midway between hero and rogue, though unmistakably heroic in *Richard Carvel* by the American novelist, 'the other' Winston Churchill.

Remembered in American history and folklore, remembered in Scotland, Paul Jones is usually belittled or ignored by English historians. J Steven Watson's *The Reign of George III*, in 637 pages, grants him one and a quarter lines, and a footnote. Norman Davies's massive history of the British Isles does not mention him. Arthur Herman's *The Scottish Enlightenment* (2002) gives him one paragraph, though a just one.

His ballad reputation soon lapsed: 'The Yankee Man of War' and 'A Song, unto Liberty's Bold Buccaneer' had no place in Edwardian music hall. He was initiated into Freemasonry, perhaps as a precaution following a larceny charge. He had no mystical or theological instincts, though always proclaiming his philanthropy and humanity. 'Honour', a dignified synonym for self-interest, seems his chief concern, and the remark of Sir James Barrie, himself a successful Scot, might be apposite: 'There are few more impressive sights in the world than the sight of a Scotsman on the make.'

He at least chalked up a name, honoured by Congress. The famous French volunteer for the American Revolution, Lafayette, quite possibly sincere, addressed him 'as one who loves you and knows your worth'. Franklin D Roosevelt, when Naval Under-secretary, contemplated writing his biography. London journalists invented tales of him as highwayman and fugitive killer. In Russia, he was libelled as assassin of his nephew. After his armed descent on her Whitehaven mansion, Lady Selkirk, with understandable bias, wrote of:

the great villain, Paul Jones, guilty of many shocking bad things with respect to his treatment of men on board, amounting to their deaths...He killed a man in a sort of duel, but I believe it was understood an unfair stab. [Concluding that Jones] went and offered his services to the Congress, got command of a privateer, took a considerable prize, cheated the Congress of their share of it, and was turned off. He afterwards got command of a privateer, this same *Ranger*, and I think is likely to recover credit with the Congress. He is acknowledged to be very clever but was always very passionate, and of no principles. The attempt to burn Whitehaven, the place he was bred as a boy, represents him in a very bad light.

He is seen in another light by Phillips Russell, in 1927, picturing him in 1768:

Being without employment, John Paul then went on the stage, joining the company of John Moody, playing the island of Jamaica. John Paul's role was that of young Bevil in *The Conscious Lovers*. He was just 21. His training as an actor, though not extensive, no doubt proved valuable in later years. It strengthened his latent histrionic gifts, taught him the use of his body and voice, enabled him to face crowds with equanimity, and gave him that for which he was after-wards to be remembered – 'presence'. In later life his acquaintances used to wonder where this gardener's son acquired his distinct speech and easy self-possession in courts and palaces. His Jamaican stage experience is probably the answer.

It is not. The passage is confident, accepted by one, far better biographer, Lincoln Lorenz, and disproved by SE Morison. Nevertheless, fictions are not invariably lies, and can reveal poetic truths. The military historian, John Keegan, writing of Nelson, suggested that one universally valid explanation for young men wishing to become officers is possession of the theatrical temperament. Alexander, Napoleon, Suvorov, Budenny and Montgomery all had it.

Letters, however bowdlerised or edited, must convey something of his essence, but energetic busybodies enjoy exalting or denigrating the dead. Potemkin, Marie Antoinette, Robespierre, Charlotte Corday, Dickens – long suffered such attentions, as others must have found, albeit briefly.

Jones's writings and sayings include many that sound plausible; others are perhaps apocryphal, and not always very appealing.

Who can surprise well, must conquer.
An Honorable Peace is, and always was, my First Wish.
I can take no delight in the effusion of Human Blood; but if this War
    shall continue, I wish to have the most Active part in it.

I am not Displeased that you can discover a species of Inflexibility in
my Nature. If I cannot rise by Even and Direct Dealing, I will not
rise at all.

I wish to have no connection with any ship that does not go Fast.

This last was a protest when forced to accept command of the slow, French-
built warship *Bonhomme Richard*.

In the endless discharge of proposals, technical advice, remonstrances,
and in love letters, he could be rhetorical, incisive, rude, literary, even
prophetic, almost visionary. Very often bluntly self-seeking, to secure
promotion, or to establish genteel credentials, or as a defence against
slanders and insinuations, themselves sometimes imaginary, they can
appear more idealistic than his nature warranted. He was independent,
alert for slights, a skinful of inner conflicts, eluding absolute verdicts.

Professedly libertarian, he could be fulsome to Catherine the Great, and
to Louis XVI who dubbed him 'Chevalier' but, by ostentatiously using the
title in Republican America, did not endear himself there. A rival, though
incompetent captain, James Nicholson, reported: 'I said many things,
pretty severe, of the Chevalier's private as well as public carrector, too
odious to mention, and yet unnoticed.' This is matched by Admiral Lord
St Vincent, on another sailor; 'Animal courage was the sole merit of Lord
Nelson, his private character most disgraceful.'

As typical of Paul Jones's high-flying sentiments is: 'To you, Madame, I
am Personally Devoted. I would rather have my Head struck off than to see
those broken Asunder which bind me to your service. At the feet of Your
Majesty I swear to be ever faithful to you as well as to the Empire of which
you form the Happiness, the Ornament, the Glory.'

This effusion from an American Republican was addressed to Catherine
the Great, following accusation of his having raped a girl of ten.

History, Tolstoy reflected, would be altogether admirable, if only it were
true. Print can be even less reliable than bardic or tribal tradition, than
urban hearsay and parish-pump gossip. WH Auden mentions 'the hum of
the printing-presse turning forests into lies'. Another poet, Rilke, defined
fame as 'actually the sum of all the misunderstandings that collect around
a new name.' William Pitt's dying words were relayed to a respectful nation
awaiting some uplifting Roman rhetoric; 'My, country, how I leave my
country.' His actual words were: 'I think I could eat one of Bellamy's veal
pies.' Wellington's remark about Waterloo being won on the playing fields

of Eton, which did not then exist, derived from a French mistranslation of: 'I really believe that I owe my spirit of enterprise to the tricks I used to play in the garden.' A Chinese lady of some distinction possessed for Westerners an important-sounding name, which, in her language, was 'My father wanted a boy'. The 'cake' canard against Marie Antoinette can be traced to the Anglo-Norman Archbishop Peckham rebuking the rich and sardonically wondering why the poor did not content themselves with cake. His outcry, 1281, 'The Ignorance of the Priests Casteth the People into the Ditch of Error' long remained topical. The cake libel had also been familiar in eighteenth-century France where, in the previous century, it had been used against the Spanish wife of Louis XIV.

John Paul Jones was remembered by many sayings but, in print, song, and on canvas, his likenesses seldom exactly tally. Morison considered him 'The reverse of an open book.' Warren S Walker (1962) wrote of 'the fabulous Paul Jones... whose feats of daring were so uncannily successful that they seemed to many observers to transcend what was humanly possible'. For another American, William J Norton (1954), he was 'one of the most puzzling of the many fabulous figures of the America revolutionary saga'. Congressman Robert Morris thought him 'a Gentleman of Worth', and Catherine disposed of him as 'wrong-headed, most worthy of acclaim by a mob of detestables'.

Like Churchill, who, in *My Early Life* (1930), summarised courtship and marriage in a sentence, Jones was reticent about his liaisons. Delighting in women, about whom there were countless rumours, he never married.

A Russian proverb is, 'He lies like an eyewitness.' Much here remains ambiguous, untrustworthy, or paradoxical. Triumphant in an extraordinary fight, he yet lost his ship. Subscriber to 'the liberties of America', he distrusted popular opinion. In England, his status is undecided. Kipling referred to 'the notorious Paul Jones, an American pirate'. An Oxford maritime compendium has him as pirate and privateer on the same page. Richard Hough, naval historian, and CE Carrington, authority on the British Empire, name him 'privateer', as does *The New Twentieth Century Encyclopaedia* (1968). As late as July 2002, the noted BBC journalist, John Humphrys, called him 'a pirate'. James Bunting (1973) wrote:

'The last time that Cumberland was to be made the focal point of any hostile action – if you discount the German air-raids during the Second World War – was when John Paul Jones, in command of a privateer during the War of Independence, sailed into Whitehaven and set fire to half a dozen English ships. It was a senseless move, because it availed Jones precisely nothing and he got away only by the skin of his teeth.'

When he arrived, victorious over the British, in neutral Holland, London demanded the surrender of 'a certain Paul Jones, a subject of the King, who, according to the Treaties and the Laws of War, can only be considered a rebel and a pirate'. American opponents – Arthur Lee, Samuel Adams, Alexander Dillon – disdained him as a privateer. Adams, hostile also to Benjamin Franklin, Jones's associate, spitefully wondered in 1781 whether the daring *Bonhomme Richard* expedition, against England, 1779, might not have been 'a Project of the Private-men, so artfully contrived and conducted that they can declare the property to be either public or private as may best suit their interest'. Raymond Postgate, and Cumberland's fine poet, Norman Nicholson, class Jones's *Ranger*, a 'privateer', which Sir Winston Churchill terms Jones himself; Potemkin thought Jones 'a pirate' during the American War, though Simon Sebag-Montefiore, in his remarkable study of the Russian, renders this, more attractively, as 'corsair'.

In truth, from 1775, Paul Jones was a commissioned officer in Washington's 'Continental Navy', and being called 'privateer' always angered him, as an affront to his dignity. Blockaded in Holland by the British in 1779, and urged to escape as a privateer under the French flag, he raged: 'They are not rich enough to buy "the pirate" Paul Jones.' In Paris, he refused privateering offers from Franklin.

Privateersmen he disliked as being difficult or impossible to control, as he knew from experience of those hired to accompany him. Their prime motive was immediate profit, and satisfaction for their ships' owners, whatever their obligations to Congress and the marine office. Jones was less high principled than he liked to boast, but even when jobless and penurious, he rejected such work from the wealthy French administrator and entrepreneur, de Chaumont.

His ability is not disputed. Thomas Carlyle, in his *History of the French Revolution*, saluted him: 'And lo! The desperate valour has suffocated the deliberate, and Paul Jones is now one of the Kings of the Sea!' Admiral Alfred Thayer Mahan, biographer of Nelson (1899), American student of the influences of the sea on world politics, admired his seamanship and acknowledged his influences on American naval development. *The Oxford Companion to American History* (1960) saw him as 'a tactician without peer'. HV Morton (1933) misleads in finding him 'the first accredited American admiral', America then having no such rank, but continues, 'one of the most remarkable and puzzling Scotsmen in history, and one of the most effective rebels who ever opposed British arms'. Morton asks: 'Was he a pirate? I asked a man in Kirkcudbright. "Weel . . . I wouldna say that. He pu the wund up the country sae we that maybe in revenge, posterity has not been verra kind to him."'

Listing his birthday, *The Times*, 6 July 2001, named him 'adventurer'. This encapsulates much of his career, though detractors might observe that the distinction between this and 'mercenary' is thin. Admirers can retort that an adventurer is as valuable as a conformist, and cite Housman's *Epitaph on an Army of Mercenaries*:

> These, in the day when heaven was falling,
> The hour when earth's foundations fled,
> Followed their mercenary calling
> And took their wages and are dead.
>
> Their shoulders held the sky suspended;
> They stood, and earth's foundations stay;
> What God abandoned, these defended,
> And saved the sum of things for pay.

Paul Jones's broad outlines are distinct, the details often smudged. All are at the mercy of hearsay, invention, propaganda. He may have shouted, 'Well done, my brave lads, we've got her now! Throw aboard the grappling irons and stand by for boarding.' Yet one suspects something terser and, until recently, unprintable. His 'Do the best we can with what we have in hand,' is certainly fabricated, though quoted by Admiral King to boost American morale during the Second World War. There are differing accounts of his most famous and verifiable saying: 'Surrender! I have not yet begun to fight,' but this is no great matter. It was quoted by Naval Secretary Knox after Pearl Harbor, to graduating midshipmen, and by AV Alexander, First Lord of the Admiralty (called by Field Marshal Montgomery a mobile whisky and soda), following the Dunkirk retreat, 1940, when broadcasting to the United States and the world Britain's decision not to surrender to the Nazi New Order.

Who then, what then, was John Paul Jones? Stock war hero encased in a trashy Hollywood movie? Flamboyant 'devil in a Scots bonnet' of English hatred? Fastidious officer courted in Virginian drawing-rooms and

Parisian salons? Irresponsible seducer? American patriot? All are disputable, often disputed. Though eulogising America as his favourite country since boyhood, he emigrated there only by accident of circumstance. A wretched biography (1940), may yet be correct in stating that he never belonged to America, and must have regarded that country as alien. President John Adams referred to him as 'this eminent foreigner'. Temperamentally, he needed to satisfy himself and whoever employed him; his finest active service was largely organised by France, but he refused to supplant the American flag with the French. He was loyal to America though, like MacArthur and Patton, to an America very much of his own choosing, and with a future he hoped to help redesign. Only rare Americans – Washington, Jefferson, Franklin, Robert Morris, Richard Dale – escaped his censure or contempt. Like a religious convert, he proclaimed his devotion too stridently, with considerable self-defence. 'I can in no situation, however remote, be Easy, while the Liberties of America seem in danger. '

Genes, environment, intellectual modes, all give clues but do not wholly explain human mystery. Byron, in *The Corsair* (1814), wrote:

> Behold – but who has seen, or e're shall see
> Man as himself – the secret spirit free?

However, it can be safely maintained that Jones was not of the psychological type afflicted by fear of winning. A tennis player, leading 5–0, may yet, in queer paralysis of spirit, convince himself that he has already lost. Paul Jones never had qualms about winning; he was always seeking a distant cup, a grail, almost but not quite unreal, engraved, not with spiritual lustre but with his name, plain and unmistakable. Simultaneously, he may, like William Bligh, have secreted some unimaginative grain of self-destruction in his human relationships. Success confirms the soul and, before the mast, he had no fear of waves and the unknown but, back on shore, could only show dislike of contractors and purveyors, capricious ministers, pettifogging clauses and politicians. He was always 'chippy', with the irritated – and irritating – impatience of talent obstructed by armchair administrators, who were usually corrupt and often amateurish. With Benjamin Franklin, however, man of some genius, he could work well enough. He could mar his fortunes by knowingness and tactlessness, antagonising even his admirers. Something restless and dangerous lurked within him. To again quote *The Corsair*:

There was a laughing Devil in his sneer,
That raised emotions both of rage and fear;
And where his frown of hatred darkly fell,
Hope withering fled, and mercy sighed farewell.

Auden once defined poetry, to the effect that it is a tall story but, if sufficiently tall, it encourages one to go out and find the truth for oneself. It has some usefulness in examining the story of John Paul Jones.

Our 40 gun Frigate from Baltimore came,
Our guns mounted 40, the *Richard* by name,
Went cruising the Channel of Old England land,
With a Noble Commander, Paul Jones was his name,
Hurrah! Our Country for Ever. Hurrah!

Anonymous 18th-century ballad

2

The Boy from Galloway

Much may be made of a Scotchman, if he be caught young.

Samuel Johnson on Lord Mansfield in Boswell's
Life of Samuel Johnson, 1791

Thou lookest wistful over the Solway Brine, by the foot of native Criffel, into blue mountainous Cumberland, into blue Infinitude, environed with thrift, with humble friendliness, thyself, young fool, longing to be aloft from it, or even to be away from it. Yes, beyond that sapphire promontory, which men name St Bees...there is a world. Which world thou too shall taste of.

Thomas Carlyle
The French Revolution, 1837

Sir, it is not so much to be lamented that Old England is lost, as that the Scotch have found it.

Samuel Johnson to Boswell
Life of Samuel Johnson, 1791

A Scot is a man who keeps the Sabbath – and every other doggone thing he can lay his hands on.

Lyndon Johnson
(In Conversation)

Galloway, *Stranger Gaels* (Gaelic foreigners), is shafted deep in history, reaching areas other than those inhabited by Gaels and Picts. By 3,000 BC, it was importing stone axes and, a thousand years later, ornamental bronze Alpine axes. Around 700 BC, immigrants were erecting fortifications, including 'McCulloch's Castle', near Paul Jones's home. Romans based a fleet on the Solway. Welsh, Irish, Scandinavians, Teutons, Normans, Bretons, Flemings added to the native Lowland stock. Eleventh-century Galloway had owed allegiance to Thorfinn the Mighty, of Orkney. Lowland characteristics evolved into the stubborn, courageous, dour, the darkly sensitive.

John Paul Jones, youngest of seven children, two dead in infancy, was born in 1747, following Prince Charles Edward's catastrophe on Culloden Moor. By the Union of Scotland and England from 1707, George II ruled over Great Britain, North America and British India. David Garrick was performing in London, Johnson planning his *Dictionary*, Gray publishing his 'Ode on Eton College', Voltaire produced his detective fable, *Zadig*; Benjamin Franklin, 'Plain Truth'; Gilbert West, 'Observation on the Resurrection', and London first heard heard Handel's oratorio *Judas Maccabaeus*.

Paul Jones began as John Paul, of Kirkbean, of the parish of Arbigland in Kircudbrightshire, that Galloway district famed for horses, sheep, black cattle, tweed and hosiery. The Stewartry Museum, St Mary Street, Kirkcudbright, displays objects illustrating his career. Jones never saw Klrkbean church, built in 1776, after his departure, but it contains his memorial font, presented in 1945 by an American officer to honour, not quite accurately, 'the First Commander of the US Navy'. The font is reputed to be porous, like many stories told of Jones himself. Outside, stands the memorial stone of John Paul, senior, who died 1767, 'Universally esteemed, erected by John Paul, Juneor'. American generosity repaired the cottage overlooking Solway Firth in 1831.

John senior was head gardener to William Craik, MP, of Arbigland, some quarter of a mile away, whose illegitimate son was friendly with George Washington and who helped organise the American Army Medical Service, and corresponded with Benjamin Franklin, whom he met in London. Craik's daughter, Helen, acquainted with Robert Burns, loved her father's groom who was, in fierce Ballad tradition, found dead at a crossroads, reputedly murdered by her brothers.

Daniel Defoe, in his *Tour Through the Whole Island of Great Britain* (1724–6), reported that, though nearby Dumfries was prospering through Scottish Union with England, Kircudbright, in Galloway, was not: markets, harbours and farms were all listless, poverty vitiating initiative and employment. The Pauls were largely sheltered by the father's position, though for boys this was no long-term guarantee.

William Craik was influential in a land which now lacked an independent court and parliament, and where landlord and kirk dispensed patronage and discipline. The grandest landowner was the Earl of Selkirk, across the Solway on St Mary's Isle, a peninsula adjoining Whitehaven, twenty-five miles away. Another magnate was Richard Oswald, tobacco merchant, who assisted negotiations over the Versailles Treaty in 1783, concluding the American War. Further off was the grandest of all, the Duke of Buccleugh, whom JH Plumb reported (1963) as rejoicing in eight country houses (five gigantic), and two London houses (both palaces). From further west came John Witherspoon, signatory to the American Declaration of Independence, later president of what later became Princeton University. One friend both of Craik and Burns was Colonel Arint Schwyler de Peyster, a Dutchman from New York, fluent in six languages and with a Dumfries wife.

To pontificate about John Paul's genes would be inconclusive; more telling is his village background. People worked long, exhausting hours, the Sabbath was abnormally stretched by psalms and sermons. Lives had scant leisure to breed nuance, tolerance and sophistication, or an Enlightenment ethos. Nevertheless, Presbyterian vigilance, at its most extreme akin to the Afghan Taleban Ministry for the Promotion of Virtue and Prevention of Vice, could never wholly exorcise a juicy, almost pagan popular culture, submerged but still pungent. The three kingdoms of George II heard many variants of:

> Blackamoor, Taunymoor, Suck a Bubby
> Your father's a cuckold, your mother told me!

Wrestling frugal livelihoods from soil and water, mines and beasts, Scots imbued qualities also natural to the Anglo-Irish Wellington who, asked to explain his attitude to work, replied that his rule was to do the day's business in the day. Presbyterians identified worldly success with divine approval, failure with likelihood of hell, and were Roman in their contempt for losers. John Paul was to show himself no submissive determinist; divine will, that of a master pilot, might well exist, but complementary to human will. People should rely on themselves, though not overlooking prayer. A John Campbell (see Chapter 3), even Mr Craik's luckless if sinful groom, could aspire to higher reaches; will could control fate.

Freudians need not concern themselves here. John Paul seems – *seems*, *probably*, *allegedly* are frequent in his story – to have been respectful to his father, affectionate to his mother and sisters, in love only with himself, and friendly with William, his elder brother, who emigrated to Virginia. His parents were not nonentities. The head gardener of an estate was respected, and Jean Paul had been Craik's housekeeper and, SE Morison suggests, possibly his mistress. Proximity to great houses certainly affected John, who always disliked squalor and disorder.

His own purposeful outlook and astute generosity are reflected in his meticulous, if unpopular, attention to detail, compulsive also in Nelson and Bonaparte.

Few significant childhood anecdotes survive, even fewer are reliable. He is said to have early imitated sailors, uttering nautical commands and epithets to fellow pupils and even when fancying himself unseen. There are reports that he enjoyed solitude. That he once assaulted the schoolmaster may have metaphorical truth and is not out of character, but is no better substantiated than his love affairs with a Duchess of Orleans, a Russian princess and a daughter of Louis XV. It is safer to assume that the Craik estate offered the prizes to those of more than cabbage-patch vision. The wealthy and their retainers inhabited parks with temples, lakes and naked deities and indulged in extravagant celebrations illuminated by fireworks, these evanescent jewels of night and imagination. Head gardeners could divulge sights of exotic foods, shimmering satins, queer loves and stranger feuds. Visible to all were wigged coachmen, liveried ostlers, chaplains and tutors, all part of the mystery of riches. Riches, though, were always connected with the sea and with coal, tobacco, slaves and timber; with ginger, pepper, raisins, soap and with ships, endlessly vanishing, not always returning, bound for Virginia, Holland, Sweden, France, Italy, Spain, Ireland, and to the Union which provided many new outlets.

John Paul always respected aristocracy, provided it earned its keep, accepting it more readily than stern Republicans found seemly, though only when it suited his interests. His was the craft of the possible. He was ever denouncing courtly timeservers, languid parasites who preferred soft options. He was to find sensible projects constantly obstructed by braided officials sheltered by patronage and graft and, again like Bligh, another great perfectionist, he bristled with social and professional grievances. No more than most Scots did he observe the meek inheriting the earth: resolution and shrewdness sometimes accompanied with a private wink, could gain, if not opulence, at least a respectable reward and minor renown. Independence of spirit and means must be won, then never relinquished. Foreigners noted, often disapprovingly, the independence of British peasantry, and of Scotland, GM Trevelyan, in his *History of England*, 1926, wrote: 'an amazing freedom of speech between classes that were perfectly distinct in a strict social hierarchy, characterised the relations of men who had sat on the same bench at school, and whose forbears had ridden shoulder to shoulder to fray and foray.'

John Paul would always be quick-tempered, racing to smack down insult or threat, sometimes only imagined. Women liked him better than did most men, and he himself appreciated only those who could substantiate their own boasts: sea captains like John Barry, Hector McNeill or Gustavus Conyngham. His frown is easy to imagine, his smile was more varied and questionable, seldom spontaneous or careless, more often sardonic or calculating. As boy and man, he found such caution necessary, though difficult to maintain, granted his explosive temperament, in a society outwardly elegant, but hard, competitive and ruthless. He professed the customary humane sentiments but despised Utopianists, philosophers who could see to the ends of the earth but not to the end of their noses, and who, despite the amplitude of their visions, were often stingy.

A serious boy emerges, tolerated by the Craiks of Arbigland but not one of them. They, like the even grander Selkirks, established the standards and settings he always craved to attain. He was the child debarred from the enchanted garden, the menial wistfully gazing through a window at a forbidden boudoir with a glistening ceiling, perhaps made of spun sugar, beyond all reach.

Nowhere, in the great houses or in the palaces, before the stirrings of the American and French Revolutions, was there any inclination towards social equality: the Duke of Chartres, John Paul's associate, when a boy was forbidden to notice 'such low objects as servants and dogs'. The young John Paul early showed signs of wishing to be more than a servant, certainly more than a dog.

'Solitary trees,' Sir Winston Churchill wrote, 'if they grow at all, grow tall.' Like Nelson, Bligh, Garrick, and Keane, like Don Bradman, also a man of conquest, John Paul grew tall in all but physique. Napoleon was another small man imprisoned in an ambitious self.

Herman Melville's 'Captain Paul', in *Israel Potter*, 1855, has 'a wild, lonely heart, incapable of sympathising with cuddled natures made humdrum by long exemption from pain.' John Paul remained solitary, however often closeted with officers, officials, ministers and ladies he too quickly despised. A figure in love with the future, always impatient, he had small time for self-criticism: no more than Talleyrand, who once fell asleep while reading an anonymous report of his own faults, would he ever have lingered to assess his own shortcomings.

For Scottish youth, the century was propitious. The Act of Union in 1707, following a succession of bad harvests and economic stresses, had made

Great Britain, triumphant in the Seven Years' War, 1756-63, the largest free-trade area in Europe. Scottish and English talents, and English capital, despite nationalist and Jacobite resentments, joined in vitality and enterprise in a century probably the most radiant in Scottish history. Bannockburn could be toasted, Flodden lamented, with equal intensity, but now Scottish industry and agriculture prospered on new technology and, radiating from Edinburgh, Aberdeen and Glasgow, science, the arts and exploration projectst flourished on fresh discoveries and expanding markets. Distance was being overcome; Macadam's roads, Telford's roads and bridges, Brindley's canals, Stephenson's and Trevithick's locomotives, Watt's steam-engine...Scots and English energies were about to transform the world. Less futuristic, though spirited, was WG Grace's grandfather, driving from Bristol to London in a kite-drawn carriage of his own invention.

Edinburgh, 'Athens of the North', was an Enlightenment centre, where scholarship, literature, art, publishing, cultural and debating societies prospered and learned journals multiplied. Ephraim Chambers's *Encyclopaedia* (1728) foreran its mighty French counterpart. Voltaire, in his seldom wholly trustworthy way, declared: 'It is from Scotland that we derive the rule of taste in all the arts, from the epic poem to gardening.' The range of Scottish genius during the century, 1740–1840, is astonisbing. Among many more were: Adam Smith, Allan Ramsay, David Hume, Walter Scott, Tobias Smollet, David Bruce, David Livingstone, James Watt, Henry Raeburn, Charles Cameron, Macaulay, the Adam Brothers, Byron, John Macadam, Robert Burns, Thomas Telford, William Robertson and John Rogerson, the eminent physician, who was summoned to St Petersburg by Catherine the Great.

Of the controversial Union with England, James Thomson of Roxburghshire, much quoted by Paul Jones and rated by the acidulous Pope a great rather than a good poet, wrote in *The Seasons* (1726–30) of the island now advancing from bloody disunity to:

> This deep-laid indissoluable State
> Where wealth and commerce lift the golden head,
> And o'er our labours liberty and law
> Impartial watch, the wonder of the world.

Thomson was one of the new men, looking back, to admire the Scot, William Wallace, yet looking around him and praising the Englishman, premier of Great Britain, William Pitt.

Scottish engineering, architecture, transport innovations, medicine, science, exploration, economics, law... made such an impact on the world that Arthur Herman could title his book *The Scottish Enlightenment; the Scots' Invention of the Modern World* in 2002 and bravely maintain that 'a large part of the world turns out to be Scottish without knowing it'. Scottish genius was prominent in founding the Bank of England, supplying British premiers, exploring Africa, analysing atoms, discovering the causes of malaria, and the formula for penicillin and, through radar, helping to save civilisation.

Education necessarily underwrote this efflorescence. In John Paul's day it was more thorough and widespread than in much of England and most of Europe. Discipline was enforced by Presbyterian rigour, the bladed tongue and cutting tawse, notably against 'cursing, swearing, lying, spreading profanities'. Idleness, insolence, disobedience, were not tolerated, an attitude certainly absorbed and later propagated by John Paul in his relations with crews. Nowhere in Europe or America were schools havens for the faint and the mutinous, or easy refuges for the manic and futuristic. At Harrow in 1771, boys rioted in defence of a master addicted to thrashing them even before a misdemeanour had been committed. An old English countryman reflected that whoever was not thrashed at school was not worth a damn. Adult behaviour, too, beneath the sedate decorum and perfumed salons, was violent: war, duelling, theft, murder and domestic beatings were commonplace. George II himself, in Kensington Gardens, was robbed, though respectfully, of his watch, money and buckles.

Admittedly, Dr Johnson grumbled that Scottish learning was like bread in a besieged town, everyone getting a little, none a full meal. In Scotland in 1594, Napier was famed less for his discovery of logarithms, than for his diatribe against 'the Scarlet Woman'. Nevertheless, small Scotland supported five universities; rich, more populous England only two. Scottish Calvinist and Quaker fervour reached New England, where, by 1770, the literacy rate exceeded England's.

Galloway enjoyed considerable literacy; reading aloud was practised by all classes. As powerful as ballad and legend were the fighting hymns of Kirk and Covenant, where life was a struggle to maintain a foothold on the straight and narrow, to withstand the Devil, and fearlessly assail the unrighteous.

The Kirk had no reputation for genial tolerance and outrageous wit; its ministers were unappreciative of foolery and youthful disrespect. It encouraged thoroughness in instruction, though was cautious of the exceptional pupil. It was harsh though not unrealistic in its estimate of human nature, prone to lechery, covetousness and violence.

John Paul's teacher, Rev James Hogg, an Aberdeen graduate, fostered his literacy, his taste for books and an aptitude for mathematics. Examples of Jones's signature are florid, firm, self-assured, perhaps self-satisfied He early learnt to value knowledge and was to inform the American, Joseph Hewes in 1776: 'A captain of the navy ought to be a man of strong and well-connected sense, with a tolerable Education, a Gentleman as well as a seaman both in Theory and practice – for Want of Learning and Rude Ungentle Manners are by no means the Characteristics of an Officer.' Elsewhere, he mentioned that no man 'is fit to command a Ship of War who is not also capable of communicating his ideas on paper in language that becomes his Rank'.

When a pupil, he may have considered that school routine was at best a strict preparation for the holidays, but he was proficient in mathematics, acquired some useful French, perhaps some Spanish, and gained and retained a fierce self-respect. Moreover, Puritanism had not wholly eliminated the Scottish natural graces explicit in song and dance, in a pagan instinct for colour and passion, nor also the courtesies lately demonstrated by crofters reluctant to accept the advice from the Highland Development Board that they charge money for hospitality.

Years later, Paul Jones was instructing his sister Janet about her children's education:

'We must study the Genius and Inclination of the boys and try to fit them by a suitable Education for the Pursuits we may be able to adopt for their Advantage. When their Education shall be advanced to a Proper Stage...it must then be determined whether it may be more economical and advantageous for them to go to Edinburgh or France to finish their studies. All this is supposing them to have a great natural Genius and Goodness of disposition, for without these they can never become eminent.'

For his niece, he showed conventional restraint in defining her range, recommending Italian music, dancing, dressmaking and, less usual, history. 'Reading Romances only serves to fill young Heads with Ridiculous Visions.' He allows drawing, as genteel and sometimes useful.

He himself, following the mode, would quote Shakespeare, Pope and Addison. He would have known work by the Scottish sailor poet, William Falconer, particularly his *The Shipwreck* of 1762:

> Again she plunges! hark! a second shock
> Bilges the splitting vessel on the rock –
> Down in the vale of death, with dismal cries,
> The fated victims shuddering cast their eyes
> In wild despair; while yet another stroke
> With strong convulsion rends the solid oak:
> Ah Heaven! – behold her crashing ribs divide!
> She loosens, parts, and spreads in ruin o'er the Tide.

He enjoyed quoting Thomson's *The Seasons*, for its identification with natural rhythms, species, the moods of land, sea and sky, with alternate pain and rapture, rough epic and calm philosophy, topography and history. One Falconer verse gets repeated, as in his copious letter to Lady Selkirk and in his address to Louis XVI, of which he was naïvely proud:

> Calm contemplation and poetic ease.
> Let others brave the flood in quest of gain,
> And beat for joyless months the gloomy waves.
> Let such as deem it glory to destroy,
> Rush into blood...

This hitches on to his reiterated desire to retire to some 'little farm', though this sentiment was common to eighteenth-century taste. As Thomson wrote, in the spirit of Rousseau:

> This is the Life which those who fret in Guilt,
> And guilty cities never knew; the Life,
> Led by primeval Ages uncorrupt,
> When angels dwelt and God himself, with Man.

Historians have observed that the classical hero most popular in early America was not Hercules in his pomp, Achilles in his pride, Horatius defiant on his bridge, but Cincinnatus, veteran Roman leader summoned from his farm to yet again defend the Republic then, after victory, seeking no rowdy triumph but quietly returning home. Rather ineptly, Thomson compared him to Thomas More, 'nobly poor'. (The English Lord Chancellor may have been noble but he was never poor.) One Cincinnatus was Paul Jones's future acquaintance, John Adams who, after his presidency, retired to his small farm, saying without fuss that no mausoleums, Statues or monuments would be erected to him.

'Nothing in the language,' Paul Jones wrote, in 1789, 'surpassed Thomson's thoughts and his happy elegance of expression.' The Scottish poet, for all his rhapsodies of England and Great Britain, evoked sights, memories and sensations available to all Scots: sea, mountains, lochs, tarns, storms, stars, moons' birth and death, perils and ease, human encounters fierce, ecstatic, gently loving.

> Your eye excursive roams –
> Wide stretching from the Hall in whose kind haunt
> The hospitable genius lingers still
> To where the broken landscape, by degrees
> Ascending, roughens into rigid hills,
> O'er which the Cambrian mountains, like far clouds,
> That skirt the blue horizon, dusky rise.

For Paul Jones, the hall was that of Lord Selkirk, with whom, snobbishly and untruthfully, he sometimes claimed blood-relationship. Of possible significance was Thomson's publication of *Liberty* (1735–6).

Many of his contemporaries, if able to use a pen, hastened to employ it, in reams of verse sacred and profane, in letters, novels, children's fables, prayers, diaries, journals, pamphlets and anonymous diatribes. A once celebrated clergyman's 'Ode to the Moon' began: 'How brave a prospect is a bright backside.' Jane Austen, at fourteen, was composing *A History of England*, remarking on the way, 'Truth being, I think, very excusable in a historian,' and disposing of Queen Elizabeth as 'that disgrace to humanity, that pest of society'. Wilkes scurrilously libelled George III in the polemical *The North Briton*, edited Catullus, and had his *Essay on Woman* rebuked as 'highly offensive', an understatement.

In America, Benjamin Franklin was a prolific author, under 68 different names, dispensing practical maxims:

> Three may keep a secret, if two of them are dead.
> He that's secure is not safe.
> God helps them that help themselves.
> Early to bed, early to rise, makes a man healthy, wealthy and wise.

The penultimate maxim was particularly applicable to his future colleague, John Paul Jones. Franklin's secretary, Edward Bancroft, excited uproar with an irreligious novel and Tom Paine turned from corset-making to 'writing books with might and main'. Beau Brummell, exemplar of sartorial perfection and frigid hauteur, deigned to write verse, to a butterfly.

> The butterfly was a gentleman,
> Which nobody can refute,
> He left his lady-love at home,
> And roamed in a velvet suit.
>
> I would be a butterfly,
> Born in a bower,
> Christened in a tea-pot,
> And dead in an hour.

In France, Gouverneur Morris fancied that his own verses were poetry, Robespierre wrote youthful love lyrics, his fellow-Jacobin Saint-Just an indecent epic, then explaining that he was young and would later do better. The young Napoleon wrote novellas and verse; his letters fill 64 volumes! and his memoirs were judged by AJP Taylor as dreary as Goebbels's diaries; his sister-in-law, Hortense, wrote stories, verse, songs, a national anthem, and produced Napoleon III, an industrious and wide-ranging author.

Catherine the Great seemed to refrain from writing only in bed, issuing plays, fiction, children's tales, translations, political memoranda, philosophical and educational tracts, instructions on legal reform, satires; and, as co-author, a comic opera, while corresponding mightily with such as Voltaire, Montesquieu and Diderot, and supplying a happy ending to *Timon of Athens*.

Thus, throughout Europe and America, despite censorship, journalism flourished as never before, an outlet for information and scandal.

Paul Jones's letters and reflections themselves fill two substantial volumes and suggest considerable reading, a purposeful attitude to life and a desire for respect for his literary taste. His references to Nature, as affected by Thomson and Falconer, are usually over-literary and stylised when not professionally assessing skies, winds and seas as commodities helping or inconveniencing his navigation and strategy. He never lost a ship while contemplating the beauty of the Pleiades or the wavering lure of the horizon, though he took pleasure in his love poems and descriptions, using an eloquence modish but lifeless: 'The *Ranger* was wafted by the Pinions of the gentlest and more friendly Gales, along the Surface of the Blue profound of Neptune.' And:

> Lo! This Halcyon Season was interrupted:
> 'The gathering Fleets overspread the Sea,'
> and War's alarms began! Nor ceased
> day or night, untill, Aided by mighty
> Boreus, We cast Anchor in this Asylum.
>
> John Paul Jones
> (Private letter)

'Nature,' he was anxious to explain, 'has given me a Heart that is highly susceptible to the "Higher Feelings".' Often his style is inert beside that of Smollett or Fielding, or indeed Captain Marryat; whatever the vigour of the subject, he is usually pedantic, with parvenu pomposity:

'Men of Liberal Minds, who have long been accustomed to command can Ill brook being thus set at Naught by Others not Posted to Claim by the Monopoly of Sense.'

'Night with her Sable Curtains...'

Of his later struggle on the small *Ariel* with an Atlantic tempest, he informed Benjamin Franklin:

'The gentleman Passengers showed a manly spirit and true Greatness of mind, even when Death in all its Pomp stared them in the face.'

Even in a love letter he must still 'Support the Cause of Human Nature'. Having sent some verses to Lafayette, he wrote: 'I am very much concerned and ashamed to understand that my "Numbers" that you received from L'Orient were so ill-composed. It is proof that their Ladyships the Muses, however condescending they may be on the Banks of the Helicon will not dispense their Favours to the Sons of Neptune.'

Other verses he confided to 'the Celebrated Phillis, the African Favourite of the Muse and of Apollo'. She was Phillis Wheatley (1753–84), a slave sold at eight to John Wheatley of Boston, who had her taught English, Latin and Greek; freed her and helped her to visit London where for a while she was a fashionable novelty, visited by the American agent, Benjamin Franklin, and publishing *Poems on Various Subjects, Religious and Moral* in 1773.

On the French king, from whom Paul Jones sought subsidies, he inflicted an ode:

> Protector of Fair Freedom's Rights,
> Louis, thy Virtues suit a God.
> The good man in thy Praise delights,
> And Tyrants tremble at thy Nod.

He could, with equal composure, with a single alteration, have dispatched this to Washington, Catherine, the Akond of Swat or Frederick the Great, but not perhaps to George III, the Sultan or the Pope.

To Lady Selkirk, depicting his tussle with HMS *Drake*, he strains artifice too earnestly: 'The awful Pomp and dreadful Carnage of a Sea Engagement, both affording ample subject for the Pencil, as well as Melancholy Reflection for the Contemplative Mind. Humanity starts back from such scenes of Horror and cannot but execrate the Vile Promoters of this detested War.' He adds lines presumably his own:

> For They, t'wo THEY, unsheath'd the ruthless blade,
> And Heav'n shall ask the Havoc it has made.

Of his prose memorial to Louis XVI, Lincoln Lorenz judges that 'he laboured over the style with the care of the artist; the completed manuscript was simple and terse, poised and impassioned.'

When Paul Jones was not using his eloquence like a bespoke toga, this assessment was true of his professional writings, despite their running complaints and protests. Emphatic and practical, they may be tribute to the rule of Rev Hogg, and to agreement with Johnson, that the only end of writing is to instruct – a rebuff to most novels and almost all poetry. His opinions of ships and officers have Johnsonian tartness: 'I have determined that if I subscribe to Nonsense, it should be Nonsense of my own, not that of others.'

For his own advantage, he could warm, writing to Robert Morris: 'I will return thanks to the Select Committee, but what form of thanks shall I render to you? Words are wanting here! I am utterly at a Loss, nor know where or how to begin. The Obligations I owe you are so many, so Important and were so Unexpected that I must be Ungrateful indeed if I did not feel more than I can express.'

Walter Scott's 'Nanty Ewart' in *Redgauntlet* is assumed to partly originate in John Paul Jones. 'What is called a smart little man,' and: 'It was plain, Ewart, though a good seaman, had not been bred upon that element. He was a reasonably good scholar, and seemed fond of showing it, by recurring to the subject of Sallust and Juvenal; while on the other hand, Sea-phrases seldom chequered his conversation.'

Scottish schools and homes were unfavourable to waste and slick repartee. The Kirk, although in gradual decline in the age of Encyclopaedias and the

Royal Society, elegant scepticism and researches in natural sciences, was still potent. A minister is depicted by Scott: 'A true chip of the old Presbyterian block, walked his parish like a captain on the quarter-deck... off went the Laird's hat to the Minister, as fast as the poor man's bonnet.' When revolution tormented America and ravaged France, William Cobbett ascribed the comparative docility of the Scottish poor to the influence of the minister on Poor Law Relief. Also, surely, to blood-drenched memories of Culloden and its aftermath.

Marx called religion the heart of a heartless world. Kirkbean, John Paul's home village, as not heartless but he would have regularly heard denunciations of vice, exhortations to work hard and to practise thrift, accompanied by repentance stools and dramatic pulpit rhetoric, the theatre that buttresses authority. In war, he himself would take caustic delight in a theatrical gesture and the dapper externals of uniforms, decorations and official insignia. He was more Long John Silver, alternately ruthless and ingratiating, than sobersides Captain Smollett, though he would have been glad of him as a first mate. Ben Gunn would never have passed muster and, in Benjamin Franklin, was sensible, high-minded Dr Livesey.

Puritanism presupposes conflict between the Christian knight, Death and the Devil, no quarter allowed. Niceties of theology and error fostered incessant debate and special pleading, helpful for lawyers, of whom Scotland had ample share. School demanded concentration on scripture, grammar, mathematics, perhaps some Latin and classical history, and love of music, itself carrying dangers of profanity, sexual licence and satire. The week ended with the boredom, fear and emotional excitements of the Sabbath. The Calvinist, Isaac Watts (1674–1748), benefactor of American education, fed many cheerless, if sometimes bracing, hymns into young imaginations.

> There is a Dreadful Hell,
> And Everlasting Pains,
> There Sinners must with Devils dwell
> In Darkness and in Chains.

This pall, as much English as Scottish, was not wholly dispersed by rationalism and revolution. In Cumberland, across the Solway, Norman Nicholson (1914–87) recalled his Protestant childhood: 'I had been led to believe that Catholics went about in continual fear that the priest would turn them into nanny-goats if they missed Mass.'

The Kirk emphasised the Old Testament more vehemently than the New, its ruffianly and unscrupulous heroes the expression of another tough minority, then outnumbered in hostile territory, defending stolen acres with divine sanction, scared of outlawed gods but secretly, sometimes brazenly, lusting after them. Imagination could be twisted or stimulated by apprehensions of a God of pains and penalties, countenancing war and genocide with the instincts of a provincial sergeant. The Sermon on the Mount would have made small impact at Bannockburn or Flodden Field or Culloden Moor and, sighting enemy masts, Paul Jones rushed, not to prayer, but to his guns. In Valentine Blacker's 'Trust in God, my boys, and keep your powder dry', he might have amended *and* for *but*.

He might also have queried Hume's conviction that a religious man must be a scoundrel, but his private beliefs are disclosed only in a patter of biblical phrases and moral maxims in the Benjamin Franklin manner. 'Tell it not in Gath,' he admonished the Paris Commissioners in 1778, over a disputed expense account. Throughout, in kirk tradition, he disbelieved that a question might have more than one side. True, over Lieutenant Simpson, who betrayed him on *Ranger*, when his feelings cooled, he lapsed into judicial sententiousness: 'Every lesser virtue will pass away, but Charity comes from heaven and is immortal,' but few people were less prone to upsurges of forgiveness. He cherished grudges as he might godchildren, or like a bandit enjoying his pistol.

Despite his father's flowerbeds and the beauties evoked by Thomson and Falconer, John Paul's imagination was at the mercy, not only of these black chantings and tyrannical threats, but of the prevailing drift of Scottish folklore and historical images, with their indisputable evidence of Johnson's dictum, that man is no more naturally good than is a wolf. As a healthy antidote to psalms and dire sexual warnings were tavern choruses, robust and disrespectful, thumping military marches; schoolyard obscenities; farmyard wit and street rhymes, easily overheard. Isaac Watts might not have endorsed a lampoon on George II's wife:

> Here, wrapped in forty-thousand towels,
> The only proof that Caroline had bowels.

The anti-Jacobite Terror still festered. All knew that 'Butcher' Cumberland, victor of Culloden, prospered mightily down south. Ruined Highlanders were being recruited for English regiments and finding slave conditions that incited four mutinies between 1778 and 1789: crushed by gibbet, lash and the musket, the victims were sometimes chosen merely by lot.

Galloway had long memories of Border raids, cattle-reeving, clan and baronial feuds. At least one English castle still remained as a symbol of repression and, at Dumfries, stood the Repentance Tower raised against English invasion. The region had bred such giants as St Ninian, William Wallace, and Robert Bruce, who at Dumfries had slain the Red Comyn. Children knew of Queen Mary Stuart fleeing for safety in England and meeting her doom, spending her last wretched hours in Scotland at Dundrennan. The English had beheaded her grandson, Charles I, and overthrown her great-grandson, James II. The Lowlands were also the terrain of another native strain, that of the pitiless Solemn League and the Covenant, pledged to resist Charles I and his bishops, with Leslie's troops bawling 'Jesus and no quarter' as they killed men, women and children at Phillphaugh in 1645. Leslie himself, victorious over Montrose, being then roundly defeated by the Englishman, Cromwell, in 1651. More stories could bewitch children with their savagery: Lord Kenmare leading criminals and renegades under his 'brandy-bottle' flag, to rape and plunder; Archbishop Sharp's murder in 1679; two Wigtown Covenanters being pegged to Leith Sands in 1685, and left to drown; Catholic Highlanders stabbing and torturing Covenanters; the Levellers' Revolt in 1724, which TC Smout calls the first instance of class war in Scotland, with thousands up in the hills denounced for 'incest, crime, godless pleasures'. And Scott, in 1800, reported that the Border still remained full of forgers, smugglers and other malefactors.

Always, John Paul was goaded by loathing of England. 'To be captured, armed against her, upon her Assumed empire of the Ocean, was an Intolerable Crime. Fear alone prevented England during this War giving the World for the second time the unhappy Spectacle of the Horrors which desolated Scotland in 1745.'

Many Scots would also have known of the English in Ireland: penal laws, navigation and land acts, evictions, confiscations and discriminatory taxes. Scottish history was incomplete without bloodshed. Following Duncan and Macbeth many Scots rulers and nobles perished violently. One Scot, to whom the English were to compare John Paul Jones, was the weak, drunken sailor, William Kidd (1645–1701), a privateer. Dispatched against pirates, and accused of joining them, he was hanged at Wapping Steps for murdering his gunner, his defence allegedly being weakened by the governor of Boston suppressing vital evidence. His fate would be remembered by Paul Jones, in later and critical circumstances.

A dark wind blows through the northern ballads, across their hills, lochs, tarns, moors and shores stricken with blood, with their stark simplicities of love and pathos, death and wild beauty, immoderate cravings and vengeful hatreds, under the harsh sky of a world pared to essentials.

> O mak my bed, Lady Maither, he says,
> O mak it braid and deep,
> And lay Margret close at my back,
> And sounder I will sleep.
>
> Lord William was dead lang ere midnight,
> Lady Margret lang ere day,
> And all true lovers that go thegither,
> May they have mair luck than they.

For many, perhaps most children, poetry is more convincing than prose, enfolding the extraordinary, startling and bizarre, with the exact and familiar details of nature, of quarrels and twilight, and the the antics of grown-ups, Auden's 'enormous comics'. Literacy could bowdlerise, but not extinguish, a bracing literature of robber-lords, cattle-rievers (rustlers), outlaws, handsome seducers, gypsy lovers, and of such fateful escapades as the drowning of Sir Patrick Spens, victim of a feckless king. Northern folk heroes, the outlaw Murray, Johnny Faa, the Percy and the Douglas raging at Otterbourne, had American avatars in Pretty Boy Floyd, the James brothers, the fighters at the *OK Corral*, and the young cowboy carried dead on the streets of Laredo.

The naked emotions of the ballads and the ploughmen's tales, and the visionary intensity of the Hebrew prophets and psalmists, can still give children entry to a world of infinite possibilities, of ambush and triumph, strange deaths and cravings, never-never woods and beasts, multiple passions for revenge, darkness, dawn and the unknown.

> The're bodyes bathed in purple blude
> They bore with them away
> They kist them deid a thousand times
> Ere they were clad in clay.

HG Wells once defined education as the building up of the imagination.

The likes of John Paul had imaginations unsentimental, quick, often harsh, fitfully sensitive, pausing in the field, by the loch, on the mountain, to listen to what Ezra Pound called the voice of the nightingale too far off to be heard. In imagination was always a further region, imprecise but glowing, beyond morals and sermons, toil, lessons, the law, and within the astounding territories of sleep. For thousands of European non-conformists – the rebellious, the ambitious, the downtrodden, the lost – that region could be beckoning as El Dorado, the Golden Man, possibly an illusion, a deception, a trap. In Scotland, these aspirations were as potent as anywhere else.

3

Preparations

How holy men look when they are seasick.

Samuel Butler

To sail is an occupation at once repulsive and attractive... a beckoning from powers outside mankind.

Hilaire Belloc.
The Cruise of the Nona, 1925

O I had dreamed a wearie dream
Beyond the Isle of Skye:
I dreamed a dead man won a fight,
And I dreamed that man was I.

Anon

'I had been fond of a Navy from my boyish days up,' Paul Jones recalled from his days by the Solway, itself now blue as a jay's wing, now dark as a Newcastle collier, now grey as mist rolling in from the Irish Sea. Far out plunged schooners, sloops and merchantmen from great Whitehaven. Sky was filled with glories or dimmed with forebodings, moon sent messages of tide and weather, stars were no classical roll-call but a nautical almanac. Sailors were the space invaders of a now vanished age and obsolete language. How many readers can identify royals, top gallants, main shrouds, halyard, mizzen, capstan, poop, jibbing; or distinguish between cutter, brig, sloop, frigate and clipper? Romance is glorification of distance, and the obscenities and knockabout angers, the tarry breeches, hairy bellies and stinking armpits were the realities behind the polished, trimly furbished ships in Dutch and English paintings, blown across the heaving waters out of spume and haze. Actuality prompted Johnson to exclaim that when men

29

come to like a sea life, they are not fit to live on land. Paul Jones had objectives on both land and sea, but they were the well-built house and the captain's bridge, not a labourer's hovel or the bleary fo'castle.

Before the accelerations brought by technology, swifter transport and rapid information, children changed little. Like the sailors, they were foul-mouthed, raucous, superstitious, affectionate and bullying, fascinated by sexual mystery, capable of being unexpectedly ambushed by glimpses or intimations of beauty and wonder, quickly revoked. Soon they must be at work, facing the wide world, the other side of the hill, the demand of roads and waves. With little time to dawdle or dream, a John Paul might yet have agreed with another child, who mused, 'Everyone is special, especially me.' Later, he could also have respected Rabbi Hillel, contemporary of Jesus, whose famous remark was never flaunted in the kirk: 'If I am not myself, who will be?'

Near Kirkbean is Carse Bay, with its caves – Paul Jones's Cave is still shown – and beaches where smugglers are said to have landed, thriving on the new opportunities offered by the Union. John Paul could have relished caves, as, Angus Wilson thought, Kipling did, on the Devon Coast in 1879. Rocks, trees, hillside vistas, steep cliffs, all these could stimulate exploration, adventurous daydreams and smuggling. Traditions that John Paul Jones himself engaged in smuggling between Solway and the Isle of Man are unsubstantiated, though would not have been foreign to his nature. Smuggling was regarded more as a chancy game than a vicious crime, and had been commonplace since the thirteenth century, with vessels frequently built with false compartments, like some of those he captured off the West Indies when commanding *Alfred* during the American Revolution. The eighteenth century was the peak of smuggling, all classes participating:

> Brandy for the Parson,
> 'Baccy for the Clerk;
> Laces for a lady, letters for a spy,
> And watch the wall, my darling, while the Gentlemen go by.
>
> Rudyard Kipling,
> 'A Smuggler's Song',
> *Puck of Pook's Hill*, 1906

Lord Chancellor Macclesfield, later impeached for selling legal appointments, when treasurer of the navy, employed an Admiralty barge to fool the revenue officers and carry his champagne and burgundy. Even the upright James Cook is tentatively accused of smuggling. Arson, gang warfare, protection rackets, kidnapping and murder were part of the game.

The Scots were a fringe people, but they knew of larger games in the greater world, where Frederick the Great of Prussia, Louis XV of France, Catherine II of Russia, collected anecdotes like income. The gardener's son would have heard of chances more promising than petty deceit and theft. From Kirkbean itself had come John Campbell, the minister's son, who had sailed on *Centurion* with Anson on his stupendous world voyage (1741–4) netting £250,000 worth of Spanish loot, borne in 32 wagons. Scots could do well abroad. Anson gained the governorship of Newfoundland; Patrick Gordon and John Perry had been indispensable to the semi-mythical Peter the Great; Lord Marischal and the Keith brothers were serving Frederick in Prussia. A privateer captain, Woodes Rogers, amassed £148,000 in prize money, published his adventures and became governor of the Bahamas. A Scots pirate, Bart Roberts, was as famous as Admiral Robert Duncan for supposedly sinking 4,000 ships. Lionel Wafer was buccaneer, surgeon, author, and an instigator of the disastrous Darien Scheme under his compatriot, William Paterson. This, a colonial financial project, ruined 2,000 Scots, 1698–1700, but Paterson later helped found the Bank of England. James Gregory pioneered the reflecting telescope; James Bruce, exploring Africa, reached Ethiopia and charted the source of the Blue Nile. James McCluer was surveying Asian waters, Murdoch Mackenzie established himself as a hydrographical expert, Admiral Sir Charles Watson profiting with Clive and the East India Company. Fashionable in St Petersburg were the Scottish physicians, Guthrie, Mouncey and Rogerson, Mouncey introducing rhubarb to Scotland as a medicine. Catherine, on the Adam brothers' recommendation, was employing Charles Cameron for her neoclassical palaces, with 60 Scottish bricklayers, masons, plasterers. Nearer home, Robert Burns (1759–96), encouraged by his autodidactic father and the village schoolmaster, John Murdoch, was to write *Selkirk Grace* at the Selkirk Arms, Kirkcudbright.

John Paul had no ambition to be a bricklayer, mason or plasterer, but he had to decide his course. He was twelve, too late for the Jacobite campaign. He could not linger in daydreams. Children matured early, were usually forced to. Hume was at university at eleven and Nelson was a midshipman at fourteen, an age when Collingwood and Richard Dale were at sea. A boy of ten sailed on Nelson's *Victory*, 22 boys were on *Bonhomme Richard* and, in early teens, the future Admiral Lord Calder had earned his share,

£13,000, of a Spanish capture, though he was subsequently court-martialled for bad judgement when facing French and Spanish fleets off Cape Finisterre.

John Paul, unconcerned with new agrarian engineering, manufacturing or religious developments, fancied his literary qualities, but these were not those of a Burns, and even Burns had gone hungry, once considering departure to Jamaica. Neither had John Paul any desire to follow his brother William, now a tailor in Fredericksburg, Virginia. He lacked the means to purchase an army commission, even if helped by Mr Craik, and was disinclined to foot-slog in the Seven Years' War. Soldiers, Wellington's 'scum of the earth', were everywhere despised and impoverished; looting was a hanging offence, though this, as the Americans were to know, could be disregarded. The navy had more respect, more admirals than generals sat in the Lords. Prize-taking was encouraged, all benefiting according to rank, though, with victory over France assured by Hawke's great victory at Quiberon Bay in 1759, prospects must decline. Merchantment often paid better, promotion was more by merit than social influence, and a captain could buy and sell cargoes on his own account, as 'supercargo', sharing profits with the owners.

England, most powerful trading nation in the world, was a young Scot's most obvious chance but, with Scotland as its junior partner, despite the Union, and with Scottish emotions still divided, he had no inner allegiance to the Germanic king in London. For many Scots, the 1707 Union had been a betrayal, contrived without popular mandate by cabals of grandees, City interests, fortune hunters and intriguers. The City had refused to succour Scots financially stranded by the Darien speculations which, like the court, it had initially supported. He had no interest in sport, would visit England only on business, and invitations from the Selkirks were unlikely. To John Paul, English institutions, traditions and eccentricities were alien or mad. Brummell, asked his favourite lake, ringing the bell for his valet to answer the question. 'Windermere, sir.' Charles Kingsley, presenting a set of his sermons to Mr Ackland, aged two. Longleat newspapers ironed before reading. Lady Desmond, reported by the *Chronicle of the Times*, dying at 140, from falling from an apple tree. Nor would he have admired the barely finite gradations of the English social system which could catalogue a person as lower-upper middle class and which for many Scots was, like law and theology, a mechanism to mystify the 'lower classes' and keep them in their proper place, the lowest. The wit of Sydney Smith, which convulsed London salons, would not have convulsed John Paul Jones.

Furthermore, to seek employment would be hazardous in the south, where, in bland disregard or ignorance of Scottish cultural efflorescence, Scotland was considered an unnecessary and barbarous northern adjunct swarming with brutes with incomprehensible brogues. A region of skirted ghosts, warlocks, bandits, in the shadow of Macbeth, with its own stories freakish or weird: James IV paid courtiers to allow him to extract their teeth; Glamis Castle concealed a live monstrosity; James Starkie of Cameron hanged a dog, *on the Sabbath*; rats on the dining table obeyed orders from the Dowager Countess of Eglington, and at Glenluce, a monkey forged the abbot's signature. Sawney Bean allegedly ate trespassers on his Highland fastness, Lord Drumlanrig roasted his spit-boy alive; the vaults of Castle Urquhart concealed not only treasure but Black Death; Templars haunted Roslyn, where the chapel contained the Grail.

Scots, like Africans, were envied or feared for their alarming sexual potency, and were regarded as possessing habits almost as disreputable as those of the Irish, though they were considered less devious than the Welsh. For the English, all these minorities were forms of impertinence, and targets for immoderate prejudice. 'The moment the very name of Ireland is mentioned,' Sydney Smith observed, 'the English seem to bid adieu to common feeling, common prudence and common sense, and to act with the barbarity of tyrants and the fatuity of idiots.'

Pepys had chiefly abhorred Scots. 'So universal and rooted a nastiness hangs about the person of a Scot (man or woman) that renders the finest show they can make, nauseous even among those of the finest quality.' Boswell, in the famous anecdote, on first meeting Johnson, admitted coming from Scotland, but this he could not help. 'That, sir, is what a great many of your countrymen cannot help', was the riposte.

Lord Bute, George III's mentor, was unpopular not only for incompetence and for not being Lord Chatham, but for being Scottish. The vitriolic political journalist, Junius, designated Scots as 'cowardly, hypocritical, uncouth, and unpleasant'. Such feelings were no more dissolved by an Act of Union than people were made to cherish virtue and abhor superstition by decrees of the French Revolutionary Assembly. Or proscription by the Committee of Public Safety. Sydney Smith himself gibed that a surgical miracle was required to get a joke well into a Scots-man's understanding; 'Their only idea of wit is laughing immoderately at stated intervals.' Byron, though a Gordon, dismissed Scotland as a land of meanness, sophistry and lust, while Lord Melbourne refused a Scottish peer the Order of the Thistle, on grounds that he might eat it. William Paul reported similar prejudices in Virginia. Arthur Lee, future enemy of Paul Jones, particularly disliked Scots.

Scots were also feared. All England remembered Charles Edward's Highlanders reaching Derby in the 1745, making for London where, rumour insisted, they were eager to massacre and sack.

All this, but, in the perverse recesses of mind, one can crave admiration, even love, from those one resents. Paul Jones was to write: 'The English Nation may hate me, *but I will force them to respect me too.*'

He remained a Scot in all but his temperate drinking habits, a truculent Lowlander, but with some charm lurking beneath a cool surface, alert for condescension, canny but not mean. Out in the world, however, having to transform handicaps of birth and physique, nationality was less relevant, Scotland merging into Great Britain. In 1779, he wrote: 'I was indeed born in Britain, but I do not inherit the degenerate spirit of that Fallen nation, which I at once lament and despise. They are Strangers to the Inward Approbation that greatly Animates and Rewards the man who draws his sword only in support of the Dignity and Freedom.' Concluding, 'America has been the country of my Fond Election ever since the Age of thirteen when I first saw it.'

Each age mints its peculiar clichés and slogans, not least our own. Only the most vigorous eighteenth-century writers avoided the repetition of Dignity, Freedom, Polite, Honour and Liberty, though it is possible that Jones and his contemporaries possessed a vocabulary and knowledge of poetry scarcely inferior to our own.

In 1761, aged thirteen, John Paul crossed to Whitehaven, a town secure from attack since Viking times, with an Atlantic fleet of some 200, many of which were to be lost to American privateers. He was soon apprenticed to John Younger, one of 41 local merchant shipowners, and whose Queen Street house still survives.

The future, now in his own grasp, would not be easy. He would never be the ornamental neuter who becomes the rich man's runner-boy, widow's pet or royal favourite. He did, however, possess self-esteem, a quality appreciated by Flaubert who declared that, with cheek, a man can get on in the world. Once he wrote to the American politician and administrator, John Hewes, 'I may be wrong, but . . .' This being only a familiar preliminary to asserting the opposite. About a ship, a seaman, a bargain, he never believed himself wrong, though elsewhere he could lead himself into mistakes, some of them disastrous. He was capable of affecting drawing-room modesty.

After his finest hour, off Flamborough Head in 1779, he replied to Thomas Scott, an English well-wisher, 'Whatever the People of Britain may think of me, I must console myself with the Hope that the rest of the World will do justice to my Character and remember it with Affection when I am no more.' In some moods he seems at one with Shakespeare's crippled and cruel Richard III; 'There is no creature loves me,' in others 'Richard loves Richard; that is, I am I.' F. Scott Fitzgerald once wrote: 'Show me a hero, and I'll show you a tragedy.'

John Paul Jones is remembered as a hero, but never one space-sick with gambler's recklessness or craziness, and was spendthrift only with references to his qualifications, his prudence, experience, professional capability and insight. All were kirk ingredients, common enough in Scotland, together with a temper always dangerous to himself and to others, though handy in an age when mugging or death could be met on any street or alley, on the royal highway, under a bridge or arch; when accidents were plentiful, fraud and injustice were rampant, and many scented fools sat in office. When necessary, he would risk his life in battle, shirking no opportunity for personal leadership, and, less often, act upon hot-blooded impulse or anger, once, in 1783, rescuing a Pennsylvanian citizen from robbers, the latter making the mistake of threatening him with violence. But 'Delia', one of his vaguely glimpsed mistresses, spoke truth: 'You were not born to live in obscurity', and while confessing herself really to be 'only too happy with a cabin and my lover', soon realised that his ardour had prudent limitations, and that intimacy, with some frequency, was rocked by his evil temper.

His prudence was never pious attitudinising; waste not, want not was an established rural practice, and always a useful precaution against accusations of extravagant expenses and all the traps of officialdom, careless or malign. He became a methodical hoarder of accounts, instructions, demands, testimonials, together with copies of his replies. Thus when Commodore Hopkins accused him in 1777 of thefts from a prize ship, he promptly countered with his agent's receipts. Carefully filed letters and written evidence were essential in dealings with Congress's departments, French and Russian bureaucrats and ministers, all the exquisite chicanery, courteous double-dealing, unobtrusive mischief that accompanies administration, yesterday and today. His Highness Prince Potemkin, Serenissimus in all his glitter, the most extraordinary grandee in Europe, was once forced to admit error when the Scots employee, during a dispute about battle tactics, unexpectedly thrust at him his flag captain's signed witness and support.

For the moment, though, a raw youth from nowhere was about to dare the unknown. Tracing the motives of adventurers, JRL Anderson in 1970 cited the qualities of Ulysses: courage, selfishness, practical abilities, physical strength, powerful imagination, self-discipline, self-sufficiency, leadership, cunning, unscrupulousness and strong sexual attraction. The test would be, how many of these were lodged, or could be simulated in little John Paul. The weakest would be 'self-discipline', his capacity to keep ill-temper securely leashed, and perhaps 'leadership'. That he would transform setbacks to assets, not flinch from attack, learn from and master the sea, was less in doubt.

One adventurer who would pass the test was fictional – Byron's Conrad, hero-villain of *The Corsair*, who at times displayed the traits of Paul Jones, in an odyssey of piracy, adventure, killings and passion, of capture and escape, trickery and tragic love, traits that were hinged on a personality sketched in black, direct lines dominating a fiery Mediterranean.*

> That Man of Loneliness and mystery,
> Scarce seen to smile, and seldom heard to sigh.

---

*There is a longer description of Conrad in Appendix 1 on p. 245.

4

The Sea

No man will be a sailor who has contrivance enough to get himself into jail; for being in a ship is being in a jail, with the chance of being drowned. A man in a jail has more room, better food, and commonly better company.

Samuel Johnson in Boswell's
Life of Johnson, 1791

> Landsmen, they have money for to lend,
> But what a sailor gets, he will always spend.
> He runs like a madman when he gets on shore
> Drinking all night and home with his whore.

Anon

Landlubbers, doubtless in envy, grinned at jokes of the sailor's wife in every port, listened to yarns of Old Jack Jervis, Black Dick Howe, Old Grog Vernon, FoulWeather Jack Byron; got sodden in the Admiral Benbow, the Rodney or the Nelson Arms. Henry Newbolt's poem, *Admirals All* is not quite forgotten:

> 'Effingham, Grenville, Raleigh, Drake,
> Here's to the bold and free,
> Benbow, Collingwood, Byron, Blake,
> Hail to the Kings of the Sea!'

This remains more evocative than *Air Hostesses All, Taxpayers All*.

For two centuries, such songs as 'Sweet Polly Oliver' and 'Our Captain cried All Hands', stoical, foul, packed with cheerful innuendo, puns and double-meanings, were whistled and danced in tap rooms, bar parlours, gin palaces and low theatres.

'So nimble was this pretty girl, she did her duty well,
Only mark what follows, the song it soon will tell,
By eating the Captain's biscuits her colour did destroy,
And the waist did swell of Pretty Nell, the Female Cabin Boy.'

Sea-lore infiltrated popular speech: *son of a gun*, from illicit birth under the cannon; 'Begotten in the Galley and born under a Gun, every hour a yarn, every tooth a marline spike, every finger a fish-hook, and his blood right good Stockholm Tar', has Falstaffian vigour: *swing a cat* recalls the bloody cat-o-nine-tails; *show a leg*, men sleeping on board, often with women and, at morning shake-up, identified by the bosun by their legs; *mainstay, sail close to the wind, go by the board, taken on board, above board, true colours, cut of his jib, take the wind out of his sails* – all these phrases come from ships' lore – the sea flows through them.

Maritime qualities, despite mishaps in prison or brothel, molly-house or grog-shop and gutter, were, especially in peacetime, more generally respected than were the soldiery. Save in crisis, soldiers were largely regarded as instruments of repression and as thieving scoundrels and seducers. Jolly Jack Tars had some popularity, derived from ignorance and the romance and mystery of the sea, and from famous stories. John Hawkins's injunction, 'Love one another, preserve your victuals, beware of fire and keep good company,' if scarcely obeyed to the letter, had popular appeal.

A certain chivalry could exist between those endangered by elements worse even than warfare. Drake hated Spain, but a Spanish admiral acknowledged his humanity to prisoners. Captured by Paul Jones in 1779 the Englishman Pearson had little to complain of in his treatment, though complain he did; he himself was praised by Jones for his courage in what a historian calls 'that strange moonlit mirage off Flamborough'. Zealous in caring for his English captives in Holland, Jones was outraged in Russia when his Greek associate, Pandiotti Alexiano, burnt 3,000 Turkish galley slaves in 1788. On *Ranger*, Paul Jones abducted two Irish fishermen, ordered them to serve as pilots, saw their boat sink, but having captured *Drake*, released them with money and a fresh boat, receiving their cheers as they sailed back into Belfast. On his early command on *Providence*, he was ordered by Congress to be 'careful of your sloop thereby recommending the American Naval Service to all who engage in it, and we also recommend Humane kind treatment of your prisoners.'

Few generals received such orders. Sailors, though, saw themselves as Masefield's 'barbarous maltreated men'. Daniel Defoe, who saw many men,

many conditions, called sailors 'Les Enfants Perdue... the Forlorn Hope of
the World'. Men of valour and pathos, often diseased and impoverished,
some remained defiant, others surrendered to drink, crime, or suicide
Churchill, a navy-lover, was yet sardonic: 'The naval tradition! Beating,
brandy, buggery!' Admiral Vernon (1684–1757), sailors' 'outspoken friend',
deplored the fleet's being 'defrauded by injustice, manned by violence,
maintained by cruelty'. Loyalty, or sullen subservience, was granted or
denied less to sovereign or Admiralty than to commanders of exceptional
benevolence, viciousness or personal peculiarities.

Recruitment, like prize fighting and pimping, thrived on poverty. A Mr
Younger, with full purse, could readily collect crews but, for the king,
merciless press gangs scoured streets, taverns, asylums and brothels, to
drag men out to serve at sea. When Basil Williams describes them (1965),
he quotes the young James Watt, future engineering genius, working in
London for eight shillings a week, and scarcely daring to stir out of doors
'for fear of being seized for a man o' war or for service in America'. John
Newton (1725–1807) Parson, author of the hymn 'Amazing Grace!', was
early press ganged, 'walking through the streets, guarded like a felon', and
plotting to murder the captain. Before ordination, he himself commanded
both a warship and a slaver.

Crews were perforce polyglot. Among Nelson's 800 men on *Victory* were
80 foreigners, including French and Americans. On *Bonhomme Richard*,
Paul Jones had to control eleven nationalities, some of which were barely
classifiable, a situation more suggestive of a fairground than a warship. At
Waterloo, the Duke's troops were some one-third British.

Crews so miscellaneous were generally, but not invariably, ill-educated
and remained superstitious. A priest stepping on board denoted bad
luck; a carved naked figurehead might placate an agitated sea but a live
female could be blamed for misfortune. All must respect the albatross,
bearer of souls of the dead. In the next century, when Brunel's *Great
Eastern*, the largest ship in the world, was constructed with a double
bottom, a riveter got trapped between the two layers, and for years
sailors claimed to have heard him knocking for release. An old whaler
reminisced, 'I've a natural fondness for ghosts, I was raised with one,
and feel as if they were my best friends.'

The men most hated stinginess and unfairness. Some captains cheated
them over food and clothing, for extra profit. Jones was considerate in this
and, after the war, spared himself little in attempts to secure his crew's
overdue wages. 'I made it my first case to show the Brave Instruments of my

Success, are as dear to me as my own.' Doubtless overdone, but with a core of truth.

Radicalism and subversion, crystallising in Paine's widely distributed *Rights of Man* (1791–2), long simmered, but were slow to flare up, on those primitively equipped ships where danger was always close and discipline was vital. A show of hands would not avert fire, shipwreck, smallpox, typhoon, though before challenging the powerful British warship, *Drake*, Jones had to ellicit just this ('The officers and men of the *Ranger* characteristically chose to argue instead of to obey.'). Despite his professions of Liberty, he would not have applauded an incident in Belgium, however, when Biron, commanding a French Revolutionary force, gave orders to charge, which were cancelled by majority vote. Fox and Byron might have smiled, not Paul Jones.

Punishments – running the gauntlet, hanging, keelhauling, flogging round the fleet, to the tune of 'The Rogue's March' – were legalised torture. On Spanish ships, striking a captain entailed the culprit being fixed to the mast by a dagger. A royal jolly (marine), William Godfrey, was sentenced to 500 lashes for stealing wine; another, William East, 150 for smuggling in a woman. On French slavers, black men could be disciplined by one of their number being hacked to death, the rest then being forced to grasp pieces of his flesh. On *John*, John Paul personally flogged his carpenter Mungo Maxwell, almost to death; before *Bonhomme Richard* sailed, after a fracas between French and American volunteers, British ex-prisoners, now recruits, plotted to abduct him to England. Discovering this, he sentenced their leader to 250 lashes.

Officers were not immune. For cruelty, Captain Hughes was murdered in 1789, the crew then surrendering to Spain. Admiral John Byng was court-martialled, then shot in 1757 for failing to break the French blockade of Minorca during the Seven Years' War, George II vehemently insisting on the death sentence. 'Pour encourager les autres,' Voltaire quipped. The case was never wholly forgotten. In a private letter, 1957, John Masefield wrote:

'It is easy to be wise and cocksure 200 years after the events that I hesitate to write yet; I do not know enough, but I do know that skunks in power make him a scapegoat and murdered him for their own dirty skunkery and its results. It is a terrible tale; and it is terrible to find, *in this century*, members of the guilty families writing deliberately, lying books to clear their dirty forbears, who did not shrink from falsehood, forgery, theft and inconceivable baseness to hide their guilt – and make Byng die for it.'

Daily routines were perilous. Masts and rigging could make a shuddering ordeal, with ascents under a gnawing wind on a wild sea, bleeding hands fumbling with frozen ropes, screaming gales tearing at the sails.

Desertions to privateers were common in the early American navy, which was allowed to retain only one-third of its spoils, its rivals doing far better. Paul Jones eventually, and successfully, argued for a more equitable division. Captains Jones, Barry, Biddle, McNeill, Conyngham, Manley, were all afflicted by wartime desertions.

No revolution exorcises for very long the treacheries and corruption that ensured its own success. Even Washington uncovered plots to replace him among his own officers. Some American commanders disputed more energetically with each other than against Britain. Led by officers, *Ranger*'s crew conspired to abandon Jones to the British at Whitehaven. In his second American command, he was deserted by Captain Hackett, of *Providence*, flinching from November seas.

If much of Jones's life was a search for someone to blame, to find someone was never difficult. He was morosely sarcastic against 'Some Respectable Gentlemen who accepted the appointment of Captain and Lieutenant of a provincial Vessel for the Protection of the River, after our Fleet had sailed from it; and on board of which they had refused to Embark, though, I Pretend not to know their reason.'

His rages could swiftly dissipate his charm. Unlike Byron's Conrad, he could not exact instant obedience by a glance or silent threat. Among his sailors, unlike Nelson, he was not loveable, though generally admired and occasionally idolised. Pierre Landais, an outrageously unconvincing witness, was complaining to Benjamin Franklin in 1780 of 'the ignorance and misbehaviour and mischievousness of a man who would freely sacrifice the reputation of the officers and men of a whole fleet to establish himself'.

Men of any rank, on renowned ships, could be thieves, rapists, spies, illiterate philosophers, killers, minor poets or capable dancers. One Congressman reported the first naval recruits for the revolution limited to 'tinkers, shoemakers and jockeys'. George Washington, not given to rhetorical exaggeration, attested: 'The plague, trouble and vexation I have had with the crews of all the armed vessels is inexpressible. I do believe that there is not on earth a more disorderly set.' He was mistaken. The Spanish could be hooligans; great French admirals – Suffren, de Grasse – had daring plans aborted by negligence, disobedience and incompetence. When in Russia, in 1788, Paul Jones found his crews 'conscripted serfs who knew nothing of the sea ... and Foreign Adventurers who were no less Ignorant of their calling than unprincipled in their quest for Gain.'

The system, or lack of it, discouraged general initiative and enthusiasm. Deceit was as common as greed and apathy. To raise a force in France in order to raid Britain, Paul Jones had to imply his intention to do the reverse, to return to America. Lieutenant Fanning, on *Bonhomme Richard*, often vindictive about his captain, is plausible about the Scot whose 'smoothness of tongue and flattery to seamen when he wanted them, was persuasive. In this he excelled every other man I was ever acquainted with.'

Hands would, justly, accuse Jones of inducing or forcing them to sign misleading agreements, though this would have been from despair rather than natural dishonesty.

All nations found war prisoners ready to escape jail by volunteering to serve against their own country, a dangerous practice endangering commanders less patient even than Jones. One Irishman played traitor at Whitehaven, others deserted off Ireland. Few could have felt unalloyed loyalty to America with its doubtful future and internal divisions. Nothing more shows John Paul Jones's naval skills than his outmanoeuvring newer, faster British warships with the resources he was forced to handle. On *Ariel* in 1781, having saved ship, supplies and dispatches from HMS *Triumph*, he had then to save himself from mutiny by English volunteers. The fledgling American navy could rely on no traditional respect for officers, and in Russia, before he arrived to command *Vladimir*, Paul Jones realised that Alexiano was inciting its men against him.

Of his best ship, *Bonhomme Richard*, Paul Jones wrote that its company 'were so ungovernable that I found the sole Expedient by which I could control them was to divide them into two Parties and to place one Knave under the eye and guard of Another.'

He almost had to prattle when appealing for volunteers on *Ranger*, 'for men determined to go with me Anywhere and Everywhere in Pursuit of Honor, and who, having the Happiness to bear commissions under the Flag of Freedom, are Far Too Proud to consider as Servants by the Year or merely as Sons of Interest.'

Sadly, pursuit of honour was at best spasmodic, sons of interest were plentiful, and Paul Jones's mastery of ships and elements were superior to his mastery of men. He appreciated what Victorians would call team spirit only if the team accepted his leadership without dispute.

Patriotism was an unreliable eighteenth-century foible and was usually applied by one political party to distinguish itself from unworthy or disloyal opponents. The Seven Years' War provoked resounding songs of victory, glory and deprecation of foreigners, which may have fostered or expressed some wider loyalties, even national cohesion. Earlier, Thomas Arne's 'Rule Britannia' was known by 1740, and 'God Save the King' responded to the 1745 Jacobite crisis. Allegiances, however, had seldom been absolute save to local lords and bishops. English guns had been supplied for the Armada, James I and his ministers accepted 'pensions' from Spain, whose ambassador, Gondomar, 'the Devil in a dung-cart', helped destroy the English hero, Raleigh. To escape Parliamentary restrictions, Charles II accepted French subsidies. Arrears of service pay had been a prime grievance even in Cromwell's New Model Army, and Pepys's sailors likewise protested, many joining Dutch ships fighting the English. Unpaid wages were a subsidiary element in the Nore mutinies and of an American revolt against the generous-minded Lambert Wickes.

Paul Jones had to inform Potemkin: 'I can assure you in advance that the brave officers and crews I have the Honor to command will do their Duty courageously, despite not having been rewarded at all for their very important services already rendered to the Empire…It was upon the Sacred Promise I gave them to demand Justice for them upon Your Highness that they have consented to conceal Grievances and keep Silent.'

Lafayette, who paid 80,000 livres for his military commission, had personally to finance his fellow-volunteers in America. Paul Jones, like all others, paid, equipped and fed his men, trusting to government reimbursement, alarming Franklin, and outraging Arthur Lee and Sam Adams. 'It ought not,' Jones expostulated, 'be expected of me to be always ready and able to pay the Demands that every Officer in the Service may think to saddle me with.' Payment for his 1778–9 adventure, which was delayed until 1781, this including personal dues owing since 1775. His brave victors over *Serapis* in 1779, many wounded and ill, were left in Holland for months, penniless save for what he could provide. Despite drastic changes of mood, he remained loyal to the flag, but on conditions very much his own. In France too, Beaumarchais, with more ideals and less greed than is usually alleged, found the Crown niggardly, tardy and dishonest in settling debts.

Perhaps the majority of sailors died destitute. And not to be overlooked, on docksides the world over, hovered skinny-eyed women, waiting to rob them of their pitiful savings.

The words 'Privateer', 'Buccaneer' and 'Pirate' can be confusing. The first was a merchantman licensed to attack an official enemy. English ships confronting the Armada had many privateers: Drake and Hawkins energetically privateered against Spain, the queen herself sometimes, though unobtrusively, investing. Alexander Selkirk, 'Robinson Crusoe', privateered with William Dampier, whose *New Voyage Round the World* (1697) would have been known to Paul Jones. American syndicates and individuals – Washington, Robert Morris, Esek Hopkins – had privateering interests. Two privateers ventured out with Jones in 1778 but, preferring private to public enterprise, soon deserted.

With America hugely outnumbered at sea, Congress had to engage privateers, from many hundreds. These did most of the fighting, under such capable men as John Manley, Joshua Barney, Gustavus Conyngham, who interchanged with the 'Continental Navy' as required, under both hats capturing some 60 British ships. Tom Paine, who was to sit in the French Revolutionary Assembly and help draft the 1793 Constitution (exceptionally democratic though ineffective), who barely escaped the guillotine, almost obligatory to the job, at 16 had fled his apprenticeship. He hoped to enlist on *Terrible*, a privateer commanded by the suitably named Captain Death. His father frustrated this, but during the Seven Years' War he did succeed in joining another privateer, *The King of Prussia*, serving a year. He could not have learnt much, maintaining in *Common Sense* (1776) that the American war effort did not need to be discouraged by lack of professional sailors. Such theorists always angered Paul Jones and, for himself, privateering was unlikely to provide either social esteem or naval status. The term smacked of 'trade' and lacked the coarse glamour even of 'sea-dogs'.

He might also have paused over another of Paine's confident assertions: 'The terrible privateer, Captain Death, stood the hottest engagements of any ship in the last war, yet had not twenty sailors on board, though her complement was upward of two hundred. A few able and social sailors will soon instruct a sufficient number of active land-men in the common work of a ship.' But this was foreign to Jones's own experience.

'Buccaneers', also licensed, or claiming to be, were distinct from pirates in that they were not legally entitled to attack their own nationals. Lord Chatham's grandfather, 'Diamond' Pitt, had buccaneered as had Sir Henry Morgan, adventurer pirate and deputy governor of Jamaica (1674–83).

'Pirates' were lawless freebooters, the loose cannons hated by all save romantic novelists. The most powerfully organised were the North African 'barbary pirates' who, between the thirteenth and early nineteenth centuries, preyed on all western shipping as far as the Channel and Irish Sea, making an occasional landing, and briefly capturing Lundy Island during Charles II's reign.

Naval enterprise of whatever colouring was linked with trade and investments which required protection, foreign bases, exploration and reliable maps. Admiral Lord Howe, a leading British commander in the American War, spoke in terms constantly employed by Paul Jones himself: 'I have observed throughout life that the test of a man's Honour is money, and the test of his Courage is Responsibility.'

Paul Jones never demurred at wealth but detested it being squandered on rotten supplies, slush money, gifts to officials, ornaments or acquisitive women. Few men were equipped to wholly withstand temptation. No American officer, however upright, could overlook Admiral Keppel's prodigious £25,000 for capturing Havana in 1762. In a memorandum, Paul Jones declared: 'When Gain is the ruling principle of Officers in an Infant navy, it is no Wonder that they do not Cultivate by their Recepts nor enforce by their Example the principles of *Dutiful Subordination, Cheerful Unrepining, Obedience* in those who are under their command nor is it strange that this Principle should weaken the Sacred Bond of Order and Discipline, and introduce the mistaken or baneful Idea of Licentiousness and Free Agency under the specious name of Liberty.' Worthy, indisputable and exasperating.

His cruises had strategic and propagandist objectives lost upon subordinates who were avid only for plunder. After 1777, his officers were mostly provided by Ray de Chaumont, French privy councillor, contractor, speculator and secret agent, with privateering interests and often negotiating between Jones and the marine minister, the assiduous and resourceful de Sartine who almost bankrupted the French Treasury in efforts to outmaster the British at sea.

Jones's association with Chaumont, his paymaster, helped to give him false notoriety as a privateer. In 1779, a document was forced on him that delineated his financial obligations to Chaumont's personal agents, obligations considered by these men as more important than any necessity to fight the British. For Chaumont, not unreasonably, Paul Jones's blazing victory over *Serapis* in 1779 was insignificant beside failure to capture the opulent Baltic fleet the British ship was protecting. Chaumont's tortuous, often ambiguous, legalisms, directives and perhaps deliberate indiscretions were often conducted for political, financial and diplomatic ends unknown to Jones, vitiating much of the power of surprise by which, with such puny resources, he prepared to distract tremendous Britain, Great Britain.

On board, the menace of fire or disease, punishment or shipwreck, forbade prolonged listlessness and introspection, as the young Nelson discovered on *Dolphin*, a sympathetic captain rousing him from dejection. 'Well, then,' he decided, 'I will be a hero and, confiding in Providence, I will brave every danger.'

Paul Jones, no man's fool, feared neither waves nor fire, but failure. Failure meant literal ruin for all but the well endowed with riches and influence. Dorothy and William Wordsworth met an aged man, beggared after 50 years at sea. A Scot, John Adair, lost his savings through publishing, at his own expense, an important maritime survey, dying in poverty in 1772, while a compatriot, William Symington, steamship pioneer, was to die in distress in 1831. Paul Jones was no Peer Gynt, seeking gold in order to become emperor, but he wished to be acceptable to such as Mr Craik, Lord Selkirk, Washington and Jefferson, to astonish old friends and enemies in Galloway.

Inevitably, his brusque ascent affronted others. James Nicholson, crony of the inescapable Arthur Lee and Samuel Adams, the senior and least worthy of the Republic's original captains, never ceased libelling Jones. This was not entirely due to the newcomer's abrasiveness. Even Nelson underwent professional jealousies and the purloining by rivals of credits belonging to himself. The sensitive, very private and public-spirited George Washington was unforgiving to those he considered disloyal to him.

No more than in France could American captains freely select their officers. In Providence, Rhode Island, Commodore Hopkins vetoed most of Jones's personal selections, and in Russia, using his less inflated prose, Jones described Alexiano as 'Ignorant of seamanship as of military affairs, who, under an Exterior and Manners of the most Gross, concealed infinite Cunning... enriching himself by piracy.' This could seldom have provided an effective testimonial.

Relatives and political busybodies insisted on the inclusion on *Ranger* of the insolent and treacherous Lieutenant Thomas Simpson. *Bonhomme Richard* was almost fatally endangered in mid-battle by Pierre Landais, the Chaumont protégé and one of the Lee-Adams faction, a fact which saved him from the court-martial demanded by Jones and their other target, Benjamin Franklin, in 1788. Of Landais, Paul Jones informed Sartine: 'That hare-brained man has been employed in marring every Idea of mine that was ever calculated to promote the Common Cause.'

Like other naval individualists – Nelson, Cochrane, Fisher – Paul Jones, in all his projects, was ambitious but methodical; he resented interference and suspected other people as guilty until proved innocent. Temperamentally more akin to Charles Gordon than to Admiral St Vincent or Dwight Eisenhower, he was barely capable of delegating authority though, excepting Richard Dale, he was ill served by senior officers, or he was ordered to command in harness with the grotesquely incompatible. To Empress Catherine he remonstrated in 1788: 'A Conjoined Command is hurtful and often Fatal in Military Operations. There is no Military Man who is so entirely Master of his Passions as to keep free of Jealousy and its Consequences.'

The ultimate intention or meaning of many great teachings of the pretechnological past can be obscured by ignorance of the tone of voice or facial expression behind them. There are many more ways of uttering 'Love your Enemies' than of 'To be or not to be.' Paul Jones's tone in naval matters is always recognisable: hard, slightly querulous, convinced, well informed, assertive, with impatience and indignation not very successfully concealed.

Like Fred Astaire, he preferred performing alone. In Paris, in 1780, he was ceremonially hailed by the president of the Nine Sisters Masonic Lodge: 'You were simultaneously Pilot, Gunner, and Seaman, without for one instant ceasing to be Captain.' Jones might privately have added a few more roles, but this was one of those rare occasions when he might conceivably have acknowledged that he was allowed his due.

Even at the age of twelve John Paul could have anticipated much of what awaited him. Those tossing ships, sails brimming with wind, almost alive with thrilling purpose, with symmetries of hull and canvas tilting against cloud and sea, were beautiful in the paintings of Van der Velde and in Thomson's verse but were vile at close quarters and, on broadsheet, in fashionable caricature or cheapjack illustration, are depicted with a ruthlessness that still troubles. Jungle faces, leering or vicious, as if jutting from heads pig-tailed, scarred and brutally naked, are glimpsed through foetid air, the exhalation of the cramped, the rancid, the worst. Men suffered abnormal sexual rhythms, bullying, the depredations of gambling and thieving, cruel, sometimes fatal, practical jokes, much hatred and despair disguised by rowdy shanties and neat deck dances. Pierre Landais's *Alliance* was rank with dirt, vermin and sickness. Jean Randier wrote of ships struggling round the fearful Cape Horn:

> The sanitary facilities were in the bow. One had to descend to the heads, a platform with gratings suspended between the rails; there one had to crouch down, hanging on a rope's end or stanchion, soaked

to the skin and swept with spray, and perhaps racked with fever or dysentery... Inside the sea-chests and in the timbers, hordes of yellow and black beetle, cockroaches and rats scuttled, swarmed and crawled in the unending damp.

According to Lorenz, Paul Jones's Russian vessels:

...were, if possible, less reliable than the men. Their serviceability appears to be inversely proportioned to the huge sums expended upon them because of corruption and inefficiency. The ships were of such timber as to rot within six years. For defence, many of the frigates could not be expected to sustain the first broadside: for offense, there was in some instances such difference between the bore of the cannon and the size of the shot that a rude device of covering the latter with pitch to equalise them was so likely to result in an explosion as to strike fear into the heart of the boldest gunner.

Bonhomme Richard, 'the slow and literally rotten ship, the cast-off cannon and desperate crew', was a converted merchantman on which Paul Jones had to grapple with the Bay of Biscay, the Irish Sea, seeking fights, enter the storm-racked north, pass Cape Wrath, pass the Orkneys, and encounter the heavier and better-armed *Serapis* in 1779.

On his first American cruise under staid, unenterprising Hopkins, Jones saw smallpox ravage those already blotched and limp from malnutrition, frostbite or gangrene. The admiral, 60 officers, 4,000 ratings had died of Yellow Jack, at Porto Bello in 1726. From 198, only 21 survived from *Falmouth*'s voyage to South America, 1705–7. On Anson's great global feat, 145 returned out of 2,000, with only four dead from fighting. If conditions were perilous, remedies could be worse. On *Bonhomme Richard*, Lieutenant Fanning considered Dr Lawrence Brooke more a butcher than a surgeon. Naval doctors were frequently too old, sick, or seeking refuge from disgrace on shore.

Joseph Conrad's insistence on fidelity, integrity and fortitude, was necessarily a reaction from an earlier, laxer, more haphazard age in which officers could be both heroes and manic criminals. Many thought this of John Paul Jones, finding him vain, arrogant and quarrelsome. After the raid on England, Lieutenant Henry Lunt wrote to him: 'Sir, you have treated me with disrespect all the last Cruze, which makes my Life very unhappy when I think of it, and that almost all the time. I have said, and say it still,

I would sooner go in a Warlike Ship with Capt. Jones than any man, ever I saw, if I could be treated with respect. But I have Never Been, which makes me very uneasy and discontent.'

This sounds both authentic and telling. Yet here Jones must have used 'smoothness', for Lunt remained with him until the end of his American command.

Russian disrespect for eyewitness must be remembered. Contrasting Lunt's testimony is that of Colonel Wiebert, French marine commander on *Bonhomme Richard*, alongside Lunt:

'Commodore Paul Jones, far from commanding with haughtiness and brutality, as certain persons have tried to circulate, was always thought very strict and sharp in the service, was affable, genteel and very indulgent, not only towards his officers, but likewise towards sentries and soldiers, whom he ever treated with humanity.'

It can with some certainty be admitted that Jones lacked imaginative sympathy with those without proved ability; that his abiding weakness was in diplomacy, with fatigue and poor health added. The sea, with its moods and hazards, he could master, understanding its nature, but like another superb seaman, William Bligh of the *Bounty*, he could show bad judgement of men and situations. In a rare effort of reconciliation with Landais in 1779, he risked his most famous enterprise. He accepted praise, kindness, blame and indifference, at face value, with insufficient allowance for the secretive, the concealed order, the unconscious. Voltaire and Talleyrand both believed that men were given speech in order to conceal their thoughts. Jones could be too frequently ambushed by the whims of that human nature he so pompously extolled, in the tone of youth and the Enlightenment. He saw society simply as a ship risking perilous waters and requiring a capable hand on the wheel. This was plausible, but begged more subtle questions. His psychological vulnerability, his straightforwardness, would test him throughout: so his prospects at the age of twelve were problematical: his temperament, as much as his skills, would decide. Fate was a matter not only of inheritance and circumstance, but of choice.

In one conviction, he was wholly correct. Men in general respect leadership, if performed at personal risk and some showmanship. Commanders divide between those who order 'Go on', and those who cry 'Come on'. Like Prince Rupert, like TE Lawrence, like Saint-Just and Suvorov, he was decidedly among the latter. Like Wellington, who hanged the unruly, he could be unpopular with those who nevertheless trusted him in crisis, though the Duke had many outside critics, Byron deploring him as a 'bloody booby who breaks heads', and Jones was notorious for many imaginary crimes. Disliked as an exacting little Scot, he had the erratic temper of the courageous, gifted Captain Norris, who struck a flag-officer dead on his own quarter-deck. He also had a tongue to match, once dismissing a Paris-loving Captain Thompson as 'My sister officer'. He would have understood, without wishing to recruit, Mr Stan Rivkin, New York extradition agent, who declared in 1978, 'My business philosophy is simple: do unto others before they do unto you.'

Why were mutinies, hysteria and suicide not more common? Probably because of strong instincts to survive at whatever cost, the giant theme of history. Grumbling, fantasies, song, gossip, jokes and unlikely hopes, gave strength to the day and parts of the night. Sometimes, too, a respect for the job. 'Crew' meant not a homogenous entity but groupings as pronounced as that within a great house, a St James's club, a thieves' kitchen. Rank was moulded not only by birth and influence, but by occupation. A ship's complement could embrace carpenters, riggers, netters, gunners, cooks, clerks, smiths, painters, corkers, draughtsmen, cartographers, botanists, servants, a chaplain, sometimes musicians and passengers, all conscious of the dignity and rights of their calling, and apt to condescend to the sailors in the fo'c'sle, and with their distinct jargon and rituals. A captain needed manifold resources to unify such an assembly. Humour was useful, almost essential, to withstand, then manipulate, dumb insolence, sea lawyers' retorts, grievances and rebelliousness.

Service humour is crude, obscene, but observant and, in the popular usage, philosophical, like that of the Great War Tommy complaining of the bread ration: 'Blimey! I thort it was 'oly Communion!' Pursers were held to be in direct descent from Judas Iscariot. Ancient tales and jests were polished almost new: Long Ben kidnapping the Great Mogul's daughter; Dampier's sailors threatening to kill Captain Swan; Humphrey Gilbert before drowning in the stern of the sinking *Squirrel*, calling out: 'We are as near to heaven by sea as by land'; the *Terrible*, haven for curious names, sailing from Wapping with 200 men, returning with 16, among them Mr Ghost, Mr Spirit and Mr Bosom Butcher.

In spaces simultaneously narrow and universal, nauseating and wind-blown, imagination was unlicensed, and inevitably much focused on officers, vital hinges of the routine, whose characteristics, appearance and prejudices were natural targets for hate and affection, legend, caricature and wonder. All knew the ludicrous tale of Mary, Lucy and Jane, no-good London girls who pursued to Jamaica the future 'Nimble Lord Nelson, the pride of the Fleet'. The three lived with him until his recall to England, when he shot them all, to avoid domestic squabbles on arrival home. Their crosses allegedly survived for a while at Port Royal, near the Nelson tablet: *You Who Tread His Footsteps. Remember His Glory.*

The great admiral is still remembered, though not always for his glory. Lawrence Durrell ends his 'A Ballad for the Good Lord Nelson' (1943),

> 'Now stiff on a pillar with a phallic air
> Nelson stylites in Trafalgar Square
> Reminds the British what once they were
> Aboard the Victory, Victory O.
>
> If they'd treat their women in the Nelson way
> There'd be fewer frigid husbands everv day
> And many more heroes in the Bay of Biscay
> Aboard the Victory, Victory O.

Of the many actions, in another vein, ascribed to John Paul Jones, one sounds authentic. A Scottish baronet, scared of Jones's approach in 1779, dispatched his yacht to beg powder from a ship anchored nearby, flying British ensigns, with British uniforms visible. This was actually Jones's *Bonhomme Richard* preparing assault on a Scottish town. Courteously invited aboard, the suppliant was allowed a keg by the smiling captain who, in return, requested the services of one of the yacht's crew, to act as his pilot. This man, performing well, announced that the 'terrible pirate', Paul Jones, deserved hanging. Jones, at his most pleasant, agreed, before revealing his identity, then reassuring the terrified pilot.

Such a tale annoyed politicians and the pompous but amused the populace for whom, despite rowdy chauvinism, mavericks with a sports-man's panache – highwaymen, murderers, colourful generals and courtesans generous with public winks and greetings – were more acclaimed than the miserly and respectable.

The warfare of Rodney, Nelson and Jones was not yet depersonalised by technology: personal antics and idiosyncracies were cherished, then converted to legend and folktale. Kirkbean would have remembered John Smollett, Scottish secret agent, who, primed by Elizabeth's rather sinister master intelligence chief, Francis Walsingham, bluffed his way into the Spanish galleon, *San Juan de Sicilio*, which had fled the Armada defeat in 1588 and lay wrecked in Tobermory Bay. Discovering the gunpowder stores, he carefully strung out a fuse, lit it, and silently, unobtrusively departed. The explosion blew the ship up, all hands perishing.

In Paul Jones's day, naval reforms had begun. A Scot, James Baird, shocked by Anson's casualties, in 1753 announced the vitamin properties of fresh fruit against scurvy, though his discoveries, save by such a captain as Cook, were long vitiated by official apathy. Eventually they were adopted by his disciples, Lind and Blane, and supported by the newer school of admirals – Rodney, Boscawen, Hood, Lord St Vincent (Jervis). Paul Jones freely adopted novel health measures and, with avuncular resignation, Franklin complained of 'his great quantity of medicines'.

Jones lacked the anthropological curiosity of Cook but, like him, and like Mountbatten, he knew the all-importance of good health, while always remaining the paternalist, granting, providing, but seldom sharing. He was devoid of the bluff good nature of another New Man, Adam Duncan, who more conformed to the jovial pub sign of an admiral. Duncan (1731–1804), victorious over the Dutch, once quelled a mutinous crew and evoked roars of merriment by dangling a ringleader over the side with one hand. 'My lads, look at this fellow! He dares deprive me of my Command!' Lord Richard Howe, victor over the French on 'The Glorious First of June', revered by the fleet, he declared the Nore mutineers 'the most suspicious yet generous minds I have ever encountered.' Old St Vincent swore, with whatever truth, that he had never forsaken any who had served under him. Nicholas Biddle, one of the few British officers to join the Americans, was a famous humanitarian. Nelson, in Robert Graves's poem, '1805', plays leapfrog with his men, and an admiral complains; 'He made the whole Fleet love him, damn his eyes.'

No stories survive of Paul Jones leapfrogging with anyone. Expert navigator, adroit tactician, indomitable fighter, he shied from familiarity. Having earned rank rather than inheriting it, he was over-anxious to preserve his 'honour'. Potemkin objected that he was no comrade-in-arms. He was, however, another kind of New Man, strenuously pleading urgency for changes, foremost in lengthy demands for a professional naval corps with methodical training, to replace nepotism and haphazardry. His proposals for an American counterpart to the Royal Naval College, Dartmouth, eventually materialised in the founding of the Naval Academy at Annapolis in 1845.

In England, James Hannaway (1712–86), the first Londoner to sport an umbrella, created the Marine Society, to train destitute boys, 'stout and well-made, and to have no disorder upon them further than the itch'.

*

Despite his convictions of superiority, childhood had left Paul Jones always anxious to learn from books and live examples. Like Peter the Great, Carnot, Wellington and Montgomery, he never sacrificed the immediate and achievable for a grand chimera. Like Bonaparte, he would never overlook details, however unglamorous: the bolt on a gun carriage, a rope's knot, a rusted nail. This was a characteristic that could burden a good story but was much appreciated by the money-conscious John Adams and Benjamin Franklin, and proved supreme during storm and battle. The thoroughness of Jones – his inspections and consequent demands irritated the officials, contractors, agents and suppliers, to whom his inflexibility was intolerable. However, with British financial support abandoned and the French Crown insolvent, the moral positions were less one-sided than he claimed.

Whatever his followers might have preferred, he was not a buccaneer, a money-lender or a social benefactor, but a man strictly on the job, demanding capability, in the spirit of GK Chesterton's 'We may fling ourselves into a hammock in a fit of divine carelessness but we are glad that the maker did not make the hammock in a fit of divine carelessness.

Melville's Captain Paul had 'genius to plan the aggregate'. A new ship made John Paul Jones eager to strip her down, rerig, refit, even redesign, causing delays and grievances, intensifying his expense accounts though, despite Sam Adams's accusations, his personal percentages were small. He never, however, slackened his absolute determination not to sink into the slime in which thousands fell daily. Thus he would lose no ship through negligence or lack of foresight. Again like Bonaparte, he was adept at fire power, personally training gunners who made famous *Alfred*, *Ranger*, *Bonhomme Richard*, and momentarily made Great Britain panic. Whatever the crew's wishes, he sought chances to fully employ their strengths. Racing to overtake a competitor to be first to inform France of Burgoyne's defeat at Saratoga, he crossed the Atlantic in all possible speed, 'especially at night'.

The naval Great Powers – Britain, France, Holland, Spain – were conservative but their cartographers, astronomers, botanists and illustrators had all been charting seas and skies hitherto unknown, discovering and cataloguing new species. Paul Jones noted all developments of professional interest, harassing his superiors with fresh demands and suggestions, so that Congress might have authorised his departure to France, with considerable relief to escape his nagging.

Developments were various. A Franco–Spanish attack on Gibraltar had used floating batteries, though the presence in high command of the

Dutchman, Prince de Nassau-Siegen, an international adventurer, was sufficient to ensure failure. The British were experimenting with techniques to soften iron and copper, rendering guns less liable to explode. Paul Jones's Russian guns were, at their best unrivalled in naval technology. They were designed by the Englishman, Samuel Bentham, who, with Marc Brunel, father of Isambard, also inaugurated mass production of naval pulley blocks. Yet even Nelson was curiously indifferent to an inventor's new gun-sight, currently on offer.

Everywhere Jones found officers disinclined to employ new French signals, and the codes of his own device. In the pre-electronic dispensations, signals were crucial, the English Admiral Graves, partly due to misunderstood signals, losing the Capes of Chesapeake, crucial in the American War. Only the Frenchman, Captain Cottineau, attended to Jones's signals from *Bonhomme Richard*.

He knew, however, that a ship's morale depended no more on gadgetry than Rev Hogg's school was governed by furniture. Off Flamborough Head, *Alliance*, under Landais, and *Serapis*, under Pearson, were better appointed than *Bonhomme Richard*, but the first was disgraced by its captain and the second defeated. However illiberal, the commander's will must prevail. Lafayette knew this while leading his troops in America, but, commanding in Paris, during fateful 1792, he shrank from vital decisions, failing the monarchy, failing the moderates, failing himself. Very different was the little German who became Catherine the Great of Russia, after conniving at her husband's deposition and murder. Louis XVI had too little resolution. Frederick the Great, perhaps, too much. By personal determination, Washington saved the American Revolution. Of Waterloo, Wellington remarked, in effect, that it was a damned good thing that he had been present.

Paul Jones, almost always isolated, in pride or obsession or frustration, always desired to be first, whether in command, in prowess or in rank. He also enjoyed the glamour of office, but could be shrewd, recognising that the 'silence, reserve and a forbidding air', acceptable, it seemed to the French, would antagonise Americans. 'It is bad policy,' he wrote, as always in professional memoranda without resort to Juvenal and Sallust, 'in Superiors to behave towards their Inferiors as tho' they were a Lower Species; such conduct will damp the Spirits of any Man.' This he himself did not obey to the letter. With men he lacked the sort of charm defined by Camus as the knack of getting the answer 'yes', without having to ask anv definite question. However well intentioned and percipient, he could never contrive to imitate Nelson and Duncan, in their flair for winning over 'inferiors', though Franklin, a dubious authority on daily life in a navy, did praise Jones's sweetness and purity of language. This would not have been confirmed by Mungo Maxwell or Lieutenant Lunt.

In compensation for natural dourness and sardonic humour, Jones, like royalty and most leaders, appreciated the value of externals: of plumes, stars, braid, medals, salutes, trumpets, titles, standards, in inspiring, manipulating and sustaining subordinates. They assisted the make-believe that underpins society. French and Russian revolutionaries attempted to abolish them, but quickly restored them. For an operatic, largely illiterate epoch, dazzling insignia were as necessary as they were delightful, as had been the pennants and armorial emblems of medieval knights. Hungry for recognition, Jones craved the cocked hat as much as the full purse, the respectable address and sham-classical metaphor. Nelson too loved personal theatre, not only to quicken morale but for self-satisfaction, and this, what John Keegan called posturing and childlike pleasure in baubles and fancy dress, cost him his life at Trafalgar.

Paul Jones was gratified by the official censure of Landais for his scandalous behaviour in battle, and the decision, one more testimonial, that 'Captain Jones hath made the Flag of America respectable among the Flags of Other Nations'. Fact and symbol in one sentence. His attention was seldom diverted from the progress of others. When Prince de Nassau-Siegen, whom he considered had twice, by incompetence, deprived him of complete victory over the Turks, was promoted above himself, Paul Jones refused to acknowledge the Dutchman's seniority, at whatever risk of offending the all-powerful, cyclopean Potemkin. 'The First Duty of a man is to respect his own Honour.'

In an effort for promotion, praise or sheer vanity, he sent George Washington replicas of his Russian insignia: 'Loving Glory, I am perhaps too attached to Honors, though Personal Interest is an Idol to which I have never Bowed the Knee.'

His letters, like all those of his time, were subject to editing by the respectable and prudish, and only show him at his best when discussing matters purely professional.

The infant American navy was so small that it could not be taken seriously, though he was soon, and regularly, pleading for office, advertising his merits with a persistence that must have irked whoever received it. 'Rank, which opens the way to Glory, is too near the heart of every Officer of true military Feeling to be given up in favor of any other man who has not by the Achievement of some Brilliant action or by known and superior Abilities merited such preference,' he wrote in one of his incessant memoranda to the naval authorities.

He never ceased to hanker after 'some brilliant action'. Today he would not have been grateful to be listed as working class, proletarian or socially mobile. He was himself, and demanded just rewards for being so. An outsider, in the mould of James Wolfe, Cochrane, Ulysses Grant and George Patton, he had no loyalty to his origins. As himself, he desired respect. Thus he absorbed himself in designing a coat of arms, incorporating the bearings of some English Pauls, possibly related, with those of Welsh Pauls, of no relationship whatsoever. He never quite relinquished nonsensical claims to a Selkirk connection. Coats of arms, for him, were badges as significant as medals, stripes and ceremonial swords, all were rungs of self-fulfilment. Within his libertarian expressions, professional self-promotion and self-belief was considerable snobbishness. An actor-manager himself, he disliked incorrectness, insubordination or hogging the limelight in others, and would have glared at TE Lawrence who, as a guest on a warship, teased the officers by continually referring to the bridge as 'the verandah'.

Like Garibaldi, Montgomery, and the French flying ace of the First World War, the Marquis de Rose, Paul Jones liked to wear unorthodox uniform, a characteristic generally unpopular in the mess, less so in the ranks. John Adams, inspecting *Bonhomme Richard* at L'Orient, assessed its captain, John Paul Jones, as 'the most ambitious and intriguing officer in the American Navy. Jones has Art and Secrecy, and Aspires very high. You see the Character of the Man in his uniform, and that of his officers and Marines – variant from the Uniforms established by Congress. Golden button-holes for himself – two Epaulettes – Marines in red and white instead of green. Eccentricities and Irregularities are to be expected of him – they are in his Character, they are visible in his Eyes. His voice is soft and still and small, his eye has keenness and wildness and softness in it.'

Very likely. One can imagine Franklin and Sartine paling at the expense accounts, scarcely appeased by softness of voice, by keenness of eye. Meanwhile, he is not Paul Jones, merely John Paul, barely thirteen, inconspicuous, at everyone's beck and call, on his first ship, untried and thus a stranger even to himself.

5

Early Adventures

I had hove him down by the Mangroves brown,
Where the mid-reef sucks and draws,
Moored by the heel to his own keel to wait for the
Land-crab's claws.
His lazar within and lime without; ye can
Nose him far enew,
For he carries the taint of a musty ship – the reek
Of a slaver's dhow.

Rudyard Kipling
The Rhyme of the Three Captains, 1890

There's sand-bagging and throat-slitting,
And quiet graves by the sea-shore,
Stabbing, of course, and rum-hitting,
Dirt, and drink, and stink, and crime.
        In Spanish port,
        Fever port,
        Port of Holy Peter.

John Masefield
Port of Holy Peter, Ballads and Poems, 1910

The parent sun himself,
Seems o'er this world of slaves to tyrannize,
And with oppressive ray the roseate bloom
Of beauty blasting, gives the gloomy hue
And feature gross – or, worse, to ruthless deeds,
Mad jealousy, blind rage, and fell revenge,
Their fervid spirit fires. Love dwells not there.

James Thomson,
The Seasons, 1730

Beware and take care of the Bight of Benin,
There's one comes out for forty go in.

Anon

Madame, shall I tie your garter,
Shall I tie it 'bove your knee?
If I should be a little bolder,
Would you think it rude of me?
No Sir, No Sir, No Sir, No.

Anon

In 1761, John Paul was a reefer, a sea apprentice, still continuing his education in the merchant brig *Friendship*, 148 tons, captained by Richard Bennison, owned by Younger, sailing to the Caribbean and Virginia. In Virginia he could visit his brother, William and his distant cousin and patron, William Jones, who, according to a nineteenth-century journalist, J Robison of Kirkcudbright, tried to persuade John to cancel his indentures and accept his help for a career on land. Fanning, Jones's loyal lieutenant, later mentions his 'somewhat rounded shoulders...the appearance of great application to study, which he was fond of.' He would also have studied the niceties of 'supercargo' jointly managed by employers and captains, to enrich both.

The Seven Years' War ended in 1763, with all the rewards and dislocations inherent in victory. John Younger's business failed and, at seventeen, with a number of unexceptional voyages behind him, John Paul, no longer an apprentice, transferred to another seafaring interest, slavery, becoming third mate on the packet, *King George*, a Whitehaven slaver, with a share in the profits, then, in 1776, joining the brig, *Two Friends*, on the Guinea–Jamaica run. Slaves were selling at an average of £35 each, and profits could be enormous. One Liverpool merchant, in 1804, was to make £25,000 on a single voyage, over a million in present terms. A young man's share in such an enterprise would help him escape the sea for ever.

Slavery had a role in British economy as large as, and sometimes overtaking, that of cotton, cloth, sugar, tobacco, rum, sea coal, land, and the growing insurance and banking interests. The aristocracy, the squirearchy and the City; patrician ease, gentlemanly restraint and clerical comforts, were all partly or wholly endowed by slavery. The new great houses, with their strict Attic lines, pillars gleaming above lawns and fashionable bay windows, their Augustan busts glimmering in libraries, reminders of

Cicero, Plato, Demosthenes; the classical urns brimming with overseas flowers, the chaste or heroic statues, all were financed by slavery. The Adam table and trim spinet, satinwood marquetry and friezes with hints of Corinth, Spoleto, Tivoli or even the Minoan, the lavishly stacked and galleried sideboards with turned legs and brass handles, the intricate carpets from France and Asia, the glowing curtains, the Bartolozzi, Dunkarton, Zoffany and Reynolds paintings…all these, too, relied on slavery, the stinking underside of the perfumed, bewigged Age of Reason, the Age of Elegance.

A London manifesto in 1749 praised the trade as 'justly esteemed, an inexhaustible Fund of Wealth and naval Power to this Nation'. British slave interests competed with French, Danish, Dutch, Spanish, Portuguese, all colluding with African rulers and Arab middlemen, selling black captives to Western Indian sugar planters, American cotton and tobacco growers, and to such gentlemen as Washington and Jefferson on their estates. In Cuba or the Philippines, Cartagena or Mexico, blacks, poor whites and captured rebels were only hunks of live flesh, commodities, lumped together, as they were by British contractors, with wigs, eiderdowns, wax, honey and straw.

Nearer home, in 1800, Sir Walter Scott saw Scottish salters and miners wearing iron collars stamped with their masters' names, and noted that they were denied rights of combining, protesting or departing, by legislation dating from 1606, an Act of 1701 excluding them from Habeas Corpus. Scott wrote in an appendix to *Redgauntlet*, 'so low was the reputation of the serfs that, in parts of Fife, the rest of the population would not allow them to be buried in consecrated ground.' Vagrants could be forced into the pits, without redress.

History is a record of mixed motives. During the American War, British promises to free the Southern slaves were partly humanitarian, but also a means of weakening the rebels, by recruiting energetic blacks. On one occasion, the British were accused of releasing several hundred blacks, rife with smallpox, loose among the colonials. The embryo American navy, in its shortages, permitted entry to slaves, with a very ambiguous status. Millionaire Liverpool and Bristol, and some Breton ports, grew to prosperity on the slave trade. Bishops defended slavery in the Lords, royalty invested in slave-marketing syndicates; Catherine the Great was having slaves purchased in London in 1769. The Society for the Propagation of the Gospel in Foreign Parts owned slaves in Barbados, and could refuse them Christianity, fearing its social messages. Gladstone's father was reputed to have benefited from 3,183 slaves.

Slavery was accepted as a natural phenomenon, like gender, height and temperament. It was vouched for by Aristotle, who believed some peoples were designed as slaves by nature; it was sanctioned by the Bible. Serfdom had been an accepted part of medieval England. In 1772, slavery had been, rather uneasily, declared illegal in England, though not the overseas slave trade. Nelson, though far from inhuman, was no abolitionist; Burns, poet of the common man, had considered slaving a possible career: the Rev John Newton, author of 'How Sweet the Name of Jesus Sounds' and of 'Glorious Things of Thee Are Spoken', had captained a slaver. Boswell argued that abolition would 'shut the Gates of Mercy on Mankind' by depriving blacks of the true religion. He was opposed not only by Horace Walpole but by Dr Johnson himself, who demanded: 'How is it that we hear the loudest yelps for liberty amongst the drivers of negroes?'

John Paul would not have risked demotion or dismissal on behalf of slaves, whatever his support for liberty and philanthropy, though eventually, for whatever reason, he denounced the trade as 'abominable'. From school, on ships and in business offices, his estimate of almost all his fellow humans was pessimistic. He does not seem to have possessed generalised racial prejudice; on *Ranger* he carried two ex-slaves, Cato Carlile and Scipo Africanus, treating them as he did all others, sternly, but preferring to avoid injustice, and he seems to have favoured Britain, a black servant on *Alfred*. Despite their denigration by Washington and Jefferson, he praised the poems of Phillis Wheatley.

Benjamin Franklin incurred some unpopularity by campaigning against slavery and, almost alone of the Founding Fathers, freed his own slaves. He rejected his own son for refusing to support the French Revolution, as an effort for freedom. Washington hoped for eventual abolition but recoiled from the difficulties of initiating it. Empress Catherine wrote that slavery injured the state by sapping initiative, industry, art and science, weakening prosperity and honour, but her thesis remained academic, and her own slaves were never freed. The French Revolutionaries, in their first headlong rush towards universal brotherhood and equality, hastened to legislate against colonial slavery, but were affronted when San Domingans, thrilled by the Declaration of the Rights of Man, massacred their white masters, thus delaying full French abolition until 1848.

John Paul, for once, followed the majority: respect for 'natives' was very limited, despite the testimonies of James Cook. Rev Charles Kingsley, whose 'water babies' were impeccably white, and who was so angered by cruelty to 'climbing boys', nevertheless despised the Irish as 'white chimpanzees' and blacks as 'ant-eating apes', though his biographer, Susan Chitty, relates him enjoying a long friendship with a wasp he had saved from drowning. David Hume thought that, historically, civilisation was exclusively white and Locke ignored slavery. Presbyterianism believed blacks were tainted by some aboriginal enormity, crudely expressed in the Old Testament by Ham, who was cursed by his father for having mocked him while naked and drunk: 'slave of slaves shall he be to his brothers.' In a further tradition, respected throughout the west, Ham was changed to black for bad behaviour to his father, Noah.

Thus an ambitious seafarer might be undisturbed by slave trading, though Trevelyan does add: 'The English seamen, as among themselves, had a spirit of freedom. They always regarded with horror the use of galley-slaves by the French and Spaniards. This was not the English idea of the way in which a ship should be manned.'

John Paul swiftly rose to be first mate, then captain, but he could not have been wholly content. He had always been fastidious, and West Africa was far from Mr Craik's gardens and Mrs Paul's neat ways. Nor was the Caribbean a tourist haven. Prospects could have been discouraging. He endured several 'very severe fevers', and could have soon realised that Gold Coast white mortality was so steep that even governors were denied pensions, their tenure being so brief. Blacks and whites accused each other of cannibalism. The notorious British drunkenness was one refuge from disease and melancholy. Harlotry he might have sought, like Nelson at Leghorn, but the perils were often fatal.

These voyages were no Victorian adventure yarns. Harbours were dense, not with crises of right and wrong, but with a slow, creeping evil, insidious as cancer, a degeneration sunk to extremes, with the stench of physical and spiritual rot. Pellucid waters and clear sands deceived. Jungles menaced with the flitting and half-seen, throbbed with cryptic drums; settlements were rank with the callousness of traders, official indifference and the listlessness of naked captives growing mindless through terror of the lash and the unknown. A slaver's imagination soon dwindled to the immediate and profitable. Youngsters sailed from narrow homes, over dangerous seas, into badlands of the venomous, the malarial, the grinning and toxic. Under a plague wind were muttered incantations and spells: the witchdoctor danced in his dusty circle, from grass and hut were chilling rustles. If the universe had purpose, it was diabolical, jeering: more likely it merely drifted, through pain, towards nothing.

Slave ships were hellish, soused with vinegar, holds crammed with bodies, the lamps barely visible in the grossly thickened air. When nerving themselves to descend, officers were never unarmed. Aloft, slaves were ordered to sing and dance, their movements believed effective against malaria and bloody flux. The sick and surly were tossed overboard, methodically listed as 'lost', for the insurance.

By 1768, John Paul had had enough. Already he had considerable funds banked in London and Tobago. His exact motives are imprecise though an excess of sentimentality is improbable: more likely they were to do with his intermittent ill-health and a desire to escape contagion. A few years later he would declare himself, with a straight face, 'A Fighter for Christian Freedom...struggling for so long and so desperately for the cause of Human Liberty in General and the Rights of Man at large', claims that signally ignored his five years trading in Black Ivory, save that he did once profess disgust as the exploitation of 'colour and misfortune'.

Present-day Europe, in which Nazi and Communist slavery recently prevailed on a scale so massive that it would have stupefied Jones and Lafayette, Franklin and Jefferson, would nevertheless condemn Jones as a sanctimonious hypocrite, though such hypocrisy remains rife among politicians and advertisers. The sanctimonious, of course, though repellent, can also be comic, as Dickens illustrated so well, and hypocrisy can at least exact outward conformity to humane standards, whatever the private disposition. Sincerity, in its turn, can be destructive and merciless. Few can doubt that many intolerant Scottish Covenanters, and English vandalising Puritans, were sincere, if self-deceiving.

Paul Jones could also have heard that businessmen were starting to question the economic value of slavery, though perhaps more important for him was an appreciation that active 'blackbirding', though legal, was no universally recognised passport for a gardener's son into great houses, no guarantee of intimacy with such as the Selkirks however much such families, like Jane Austen's Sir Thomas Bertram, might discreetly benefit from it. His family attributed his withdrawal to reasons of humanitarianism, but without evidence. His letters give no very persuasive answer and, whatever the truth, he took passage home on a small brigantine, *John*, owned by Currie and Beck of Kirkcudbright. Luck was with him: in mid-ocean, captain and mate died of disease and the officers unanimously elected John Paul to command. He managed so well that he retained it for the next two trips, still with share of profits.

By now the future commodore is discernible, still an undersized youth; yet ruling those larger and older than himself. In himself, and doubtless from watching Rev Hogg, Mr Craik, his father, he apprehended the rules of authority, though rules differed between decks. For ill-disposed crews largely indifferent to nationality, custom or civil usages, there was no place for urbanity, literary allusions, the deft manipulation of a lorgnette or snuffbox. Deceit, cruelty, rough humour and racy expletives were more relevant, and a trained eye. Ivak, the Cossack, recalled that in Russia 'he examined us as if he wanted to pierce through our character'. As always, Phillips Russell is wordy, and factually unconvincing, though here, wlth a very blurred tinge of imaginative insight, he presents Jones rather differently than did John Adams and Franklin: 'A Courtier of the Waves, bearing himself with irrefragable aplomb, and speaking in a resonant baritone a language to remind them faintly of something read in leather-bound classics.'

For Jones's motley illiterates, the sight of leather-bound classics would rather have reminded them of the advantages either of the pawnshop or of a blazing fire on a wintry night. In crisis, Paul Jones kept his nerve but little aplomb, that inbred, imperturbably coolness of Burgoyne and Wellington, though the latter's temper could be uncertain. Nor is he, in this respect, wholly comparable to Chinese Gordon, cigar in mouth, cane in hand, biblical quotations on his lips, nonchalantly leading the attack. Paul Jones ignored the cigar, even as a theoretical prop and, though addicted to quotations, preferred a pistol to a cane.

His genteel pretensions would not have impressed people of similar origins, but his own qualities usually carried the day, hinged on one vital fixture, his self-respect. Like Robespierre, another small, tidy man, he guarded his dignity, his honour like a virgin her modesty. Unlike Drake, rough but easy with subordinates, the reverse with nobility, Jones, though relishing applause, an arrant individualist, was at one with Coriolanus in disdaining to seek it from below. Here was weakness, potentially fatal. Such a man finds subservience, even normal assent, a painful effort and, in authority, has to glance behind his back, against treachery, sometimes even to ascertain whether his orders have been obeyed. He is thus liable to sly ridicule, even open revolt, from the equivalents of Wellington's 'vagabond soldiers', 'scum of the earth'. Even more than the Duke's, Jones's temper was often at flash-point. Both men, however, from social stations so different, possessed exceptional gristle, moral and physical fortitude, though whatever reputation Jones may have acquired as 'a Courtier of the Waves', was about to be abruptly dispersed.

*

By 1770, John Paul was 23. His career threatened stagnation, showing reliability in routine commerce and Atlantic hazards but with no outsize opportunities offered. He had a satisfactory bank account, some shipping investments, and sometimes journeyed to London on business, supposedly lodging in Poland Street, a brothel centre appropriate for his robust appetites. In London, he was the sharp, solvent Scot, a man of affairs with respectable references, but he desired more. The gentry might mock his affectations, the spurious Selkirk connection, but this would not deter him. Everywhere, life was short, conditions unwholesome, chances insufficient, but a few surely waiting to be grabbed. They could be won, not through passivity, but only by action, sometimes violent action.

Opportunity was unexpectedly provided, but in the manner of classical fate, familiar to those versed in *Macbeth*. Not for nothing does *precarious* derive from *preces*, meaning prayer. Prayers get answered but it is dangerous to expect too precisely whatever one has prayed for. John Paul desired fame; his desire was fulfilled overnight, though promising not ascent but perhaps a literal long-drop.

After quitting *John* for *The Two Friends*, in what he called 'a stupid affair in Tobago', in a madhouse rage he thrashed the Scots carpenter, Mungo Maxwell, for clumsy work and unacceptable attitudes: 'I found it necessary to subdue him with a belaying pin [cudgel].' He was over-zealous with the cudgel and, reaching Tobago, Maxwell sued him for assault in the Court of Vice-Admiralty, but lost. The court judged his injuries insignificant, his previous conduct blameworthy, and it vindicated Captain Paul. Maxwell recovered sufficiently to transfer to the *Barcelona* packet, on which, however, he soon died 'of a fever and lowness of spirit'. Prolonged post-mortems were unusual in such circumstances but the Maxwell family lived at Clonyards, near Kirkbean and, when Paul Jones arrived home, they had him arrested for murder.

Briefly locked in Kirkcudbright Tollbooth, grievous for his self-esteem, another instance of worldly injustice, he was then allowed bail, to collect affidavits and references. In court he was indignant and self-righteous, as uncompromising as any sea lawyer. He had no doubts, his innate being revolted at any dispute to an officer's authority, Maxwell had left in excellent health, merely unfit for employment or duties whatsoever on account of his rebellious disposition. A *Barcelona* sailor, James Eastman, in an affidavit sent to Mansion House, London, testified that Maxwell had never complained of Captain Paul or expressed any ill-will. Character witnesses were innumerable, surely the jury would see the absurdity of the prosecution? In this, John Paul would have contradicted Dr Johnson that, were a man to enter your room with a cudgel, you would doubtless feel compassion, but you would knock him down first and feel compassion afterwards. At no time would John Paul have felt the compassion.

He was again acquitted, but the mishap entailed serious consequences. He had outraged the Maxwells and much local feeling, lost the regard of the Craiks of Arbigland and all hopes of social acceptance from the Selkirks, though these had, at best, been absurd. Thereafter, in England, he would always be taunted as a murderer, and in Scotland his name would be equivocal. While on bail, he had successfully petitioned the Kirkcudbright Freemasons for entry into the lodge of St Bernard, though, in one account, under the name of 'Paul Jones'. He last visited Scotland in 1771; Mr Craik objected though later admitted that he was satisfied of Paul's innocence.

Retaining command of *Two Friends*, he behaved not only as wholly guiltless but as one abominably treated by Maxwell and his defenders. In London, in 1772, he wrote to his mother and sisters: 'I have had but poor health during the voyage; and my success in it, not having equalled my first sanguine Expectations, has added very much to the asperity of my misfortunes, and I am well assured was the cause of my Loss of Health.'*

Currie and Beck, like Younger, then failed, momentarily leaving John Paul unemployed, but he was swiftly engaged to command a trader plying between the Isle of Man and Solway, a stopgap appointment but giving him experience of the tides and currents that were useful in grimmer times. Detractors claimed that his trading ventures included smuggling – possible but unproved. From this, he recovered status by accepting the position of captain and part-owner of a substantial London merchantman, *Betsey*.

All appeared well. At 26, he was well known in London, in Jamaica, Barbados and Tobago, and was even sufficiently affluent to consider at least on paper and in polite talk, retirement to that 'small farm' as gentleman landowner and, like brother William, possibly in Virginia, caution advising him against a hasty return to Scotland, within reach of the Maxwells.

The first voyage was lucrative and uneventful; the second saw the greatest misfortune of his life. Whatever his real desires, they were again, and more dramatically, dismantled. Short of ready money to secure a homeward cargo, reluctant to borrow from his employer and partner, Archie Stuart, at Tobago he risked informing his crew, not as proposal but

*The complete letter appears on p. 246.

fact, that he would pay them their wages, now due, only on arrival home. This he told an angry gathering on board ship. The crew included a number of Tobagans, black and white, all discontented, many drunk. They preferred to cheerfully squander their wages at once. His offer of extra clothing appeased none, only further infuriated them. Tumult led to what Paul called 'a great hulking brute of a man' with an iron bar shouting, 'the Grossest Abuse that vulgarism could dictate'. This paragon chased his diminutive captain into his cabin, dignity and philanthropy foresworn. Eventually, with the men still raging, Paul emerged, with sword drawn for self-protection, to be greeted with 'Horrid Imprecations...language and Attitudes too indecent to be mentioned'. A violent altercation, then assault, forced him towards an open hatch; outraged, self-control gone, he struck out at 'the Ringleader', fatally stabbing him.

The uproar subsided, but was renewed on shore, where he surrendered to the magistrates though his self-righteousness was unavailing. The victim was a Tobagan, who was popular, or was claimed to be, and his supporters were in no mood for reasoned appraisals or judicious evidence. They wanted more blood. Nor was the white man placatory or pleading. John Paul seldom felt the compassion recommended by Johnson. Once again, his legitimate authority had been challenged and minor rights and wrongs were irrelevant. He had always held the maxim, though unprepossessing to today's values and certainly not gratifying to the maddened Tobagans, that 'true as may be the Political Principles for which we are now Fighting, the ships themselves must be ruled under a system of Absolute Despotism.'

In Common and in Maritime Law, his case may have been sound. Before the killing, the men had already plundered the ship's stores of drink and clothing, and self-defence during riot would probably have been accepted by a London jury. In this instance, however, objectivity was in abeyance. Tobago crowds were instinctive, *Betsey*'s mate was disaffected, the other officers conveniently ill or missing. It was John Paul's second scandal here, though he more cursed his misfortune than regretted his loss of self-control. Now he was an alien on an explosive island, awaiting a doubtful court surrounded by hostile crowds. In so inauspicious a crisis, Archie Stuart could have advanced money but not guaranteed safety. A thought of Captain Kidd drying out on Wapping gallows was unavoidable. All Britain knew of Half-hanged Smith, sailor and thief. Hanged at Tyburn, 1705, he dangled fifteen minutes before a royal reprieve arrived. Cut down, he recovered, the *Newgate Calendar* subsequently reporting:

'When he was turned off, he, for some time, was sensible of very great pain occasioned by the weight of his body, and felt his spirits in a strange commotion, violently pressing upwards; that having forced their way to his head, he, as it were, saw a great blaze or glaring light, which seemed to go out at his eyes with a flash, and then he lost all sense of pain. That after he was cut down, and began to come to himself, the blood and spirits forcing themselves into their former channels put him, by a sort of pricking or shooting, to such intolerable pain, that he could have wished those hanged who had cut him down.'

A reality haunting any of the unprivileged above the age of eight. The gibbet was omnipresent, looming above hill and common, lurking in dreams, standing in bleak menace at crossroads, outside a jail, or at the doorway of a felon's victim. With his literary tastes, John Paul would have known the gist, even perhaps the text, of *Macbeth*: 'To Horse: and let us not be dainty of leave taking.'

John Paul was not dainty. Few ambitious men will risk what they know is latent within them. 'It was the advice of my Friends...that I should retire Incognito to the Continent of America and remain there, until an Admiralty Commission should arrive in the Island, and then return.' How ardently he wished for that commission is only surmisible. Hastily relinquishing his affairs in Tobago and London to such agents as Thomas McCall, Robert Young and James Ferguson, who stole his money and besmirched his name, he rode desperately across Tobago with £50 in his pocket, finally gaining sea passage to his brother's town, Fredericksburg in Virginia.

The next months are obscure. He lived with his brother's family for a while, without interest in the tailoring craft, and now called himself Jones. The name was probably adopted from Captain Jones of *Falmouth*, a ship on which he had served, replacing him when he died of fever and signing all papers 'Jones'. Such a name, lacking singularity, was virtually, safely, anonymous. One remembers another great adventurer Prince Louis Napoleon, in London exile, adventuring after ladies varied but handsome, using the unadventurous name of 'Captain Jones', and the sinister, gentlemanly Mr Jones in Joseph Conrad's novel, *Victory*, a name certainly not his own.

The Tobago killing was never quite exorcised, though its warning was explicit. Resolutely independent, seldom free with confidences, John Paul Jones seems to have mentioned it to Benjamin Franklin, Robert Morris and Joseph Hewes, but no further. A few women may have wondered. An early biographer, Edward Hamilton of Aberdeen, ignoring the matter, considered that 'Jones' was adopted to protect the Paul family from associations with treason, and to protect Paul himself if captured in war. A journalist, J Robison, like Hamilton writing after Jones's death, connects it with his brother's patron, the wealthy planter, William Jones, once of Kirkcudbright.

William Paul died in 1774. This entailed some family work for Jones, which was scarcely burdensome, perhaps helped by William Jones. More important, benefiting from his brother's solid, if unglamorous, repute, he had already made contacts in higher social strata, some of them Masonic, and in particular with two prominent Virginians, Robert Morris and Joseph Hewes, and Dr Read, nephew-in-law to none other than Benjamin Franklin, renowned on both sides of the Atlantic and still American Agent in London, currently protesting against the Stamp Act being levied on the colonists. Little is very reliable about the next two years. Jones may possibly have appeared in theatricals: he may, as he told Lady Selkirk, have considered himself retired from the sea, for 'calm contemplation and poetic ease', perhaps as gentleman farmer. Whatever his occupation, he made no very obvious success of it, and war was certainly a chance to escape stagnation and doubtless dwindling resources.

Robert Morris, from Pennsylvania, one of the wealthiest Americans, was to be Jones's most constant supporter in Congress, as he acknowledged: 'You are indeed the Angel of my Happiness.' As Treasury chief, Morris, adroit though risky in his policies, was to be the financial impresario of the Revolution, taxing, borrowing, cajoling, using personal savings and, as much as Washington's resolution and military acumen, and Rochambeau's and Lafayette's gallantry, ensuring Cornwallis's defeat at Yorktown. Morris was foremost in establishing the Bank of North America in 1781 though, like many economists, he ultimately fell short of financial expertise and, as though in a moral tale gone askew, he found himself in a debtors' jail. Frank C Bowen (1925), an American historian, judged him as did Paul Jones: 'A big good-hearted man, direct and forceful in conversation . . . a hard worker, with a quick sympathetic warmth of manner, he was just the sort of man to appreciate Paul Jones and win his confidence.'

Furthermore, in Philadelphia in 1775, Jones gained approval of perhaps the most renowned of the Founding Fathers, Thomas Jefferson, third president, who already, like Franklin, was known to the European intelligentsia, as a linguist, classicist, student of history, natural science, law, mathematics and agriculture.

*

The Houdon bust of John Paul Jones, commissioned by the Paris Freemasons in 1780, was analysed by Lincoln Lorenz as displaying 'contracted and protuberant brows, revealing the energy and concentration of his thought reinforced by feeling; the slightly lidded and averted eyes confessing his secret pondering and aspiration, his circumspect searchings and his canniness.' Granted this, he had now to effect transformation from the errant ex-slaver to Captain JP Jones. Secluded in Virginian decorum, he was at safe distance from the shanty-town howls and bloody Tobagan fisticuffs, the nauseating hell-ships of the Atlantic Middle Passage, from Poland Street madams and Galloway resentments.

This new atmosphere developed his social skills that would one day soften the rough Prince Suvorov, hero of Russian wars, impress Abigail Adams and the Duke of Chartres, and even contrive not to offend Tom Paine. Paine was already outspoken, publishing his inflammatory *Common Sense* in 1776, and demanding a free American republic.

Concealing his cantankerous side, Jones was what was once called 'a ladies man', and imagined by Herman Melville in *Israel Potter* with 'a light and dandified air, switching his gold-headed cane, and throwing a passing arm round all the petty chambermaids, kissing them resoundingly, as if saluting a frigate.'

Women were necessary, though more as offshore support than as full consorts. Bad temper is an uncertain support in marriage and he generally appears rather coldly controlling his sexual manoeuvres, as if making love in silence, avoiding commitment like a stage lover with an eye on the trap door. Evidence is less than many biographers have summarised and indeed exhibited, but there does seem within him some awareness of the old Spanish proverb, 'Love is a furnace, but it don't cook the stew.' On occasions, as with Madame de Chaumont and the Duchess of Chartres, his gallantry may have been more directed at the husbands' influence than at the wives' attractions. His writings show that some phrases and verses were sent to more than one woman, like those of many young men, and tend towards conventional coyness, with his allusions to 'Fair Daughter of Liberty', 'Our Agreeable Widow', 'My Little Affair of the Heart at Providence', 'Miss Wendell and the Other Agreeable Ladies of Portsmouth', and 'the Fair Miss XXX'.

An early affair, often mentioned but barely known, was with the Virginian, Dorothea Dandridge, who afterwards married Patrick Henry, a politician and vehement opponent of the Stamp Act, who was remembered for his outcry, 'Give me Liberty, or Give me Death.' Patrick Henry was twice

Governor of Virginia, though quarrelling with Washington and Jefferson. Jones's active relations with Dorothea were brief, and like many of his subsequent liaisons owe more to surmise than to real evidence. Mlle Dumas, at the Hague, received his love verses but was scarcely more than a schoolgirl. In Paris was 'the Fair Delia', Countess de Murray de Nicolson, and 'Madame T', variously identified as Aimée de Telison, romantic star of the 1959 movie, and as a Thérésa Townsend. There was also a Countess de Lowendahl; all of these women were jumbled together in popular report. Styling himself 'a Gentleman of Rank', he looked for rank in others, though these names, whatever their owners' worth, do not suggest grandeur of lineage.

Often successful with women, he failed with the very highest, and could suffer reverses elsewhere. During the war, he wrote to the intellectual Madame d'Ormoy: 'I am extremely sorry that the young English Lady you mention should have imbibed the National Hatred against me. I have had proofs that many of the First and Fairest of that Nation are my friends. Indeed, I cannot imagine why any Fair Lady should be my enemy, since upon the large scale of Universal Philanthropy, I feel, acknowledge and bend before the Sovereign Power of Beauty.'

This could easily explain the lady's aversion, though some pathos and simplicity lurk beneath the affectation, the vanity, the complaints and the humourless verbiage. It is permissible to suppose that his women were more for use than for companionship, few arousing his respect or even interest. 'Delia' appears too facile a conquest, Dumas too young, 'Madame T' too impecunious, Lowendahl too scheming, with some inference of dishonesty. By nature he was wary, untrusting and self-centred. His humour was usually at others' expense, conforming to Hobbes's definition of laughter, as sudden glory at the sight of an inferior. An enduring human relationship with John Paul Jones – witty, affectionate sparring; emotional generosity; shared interests; prolonged conversations and mutual, expanding delight – was possible but improbable. His copious writings show little delight in anyone, and imply desires not for full partnership but for admiration, submission, physical refreshment, on terms scarcely negotiable.

In letters, his sincerity is unascertainable, with sentiments expressed in the stock cant expected at sedate Virginian gatherings where ladies were intrigued by the small, neat, hazel-eyed newcomer, with reddish hair and easy tongue; virile and somewhat mysterious. 'You have never told me of your circumstances', in a private letter Delia wrote to him later, apparently not in reproach but in admiring wonder. Men might find such paucity of circumstances slightly suspicious – distorted reports from Tobago might have reached Fredericksburg, balancing the down-market respectability of brother William of the different surname. However, he was ready to please and, anxious for a place in this New World sanctuary, could afford no enemies of either sex. Worldly wise, rather than wise unto salvation, he recognised the deference due to propertied nonentities. The impulse to criticise all but himself must be restrained, false modesty be practised, though without cringing or mincing.

Successive comments from diverse quarters are often helpful but none is definite. To many courteous and amiable Virginians, he was the tailor's brother, social upstart with dubious name, captain without a ship, making his way with purposeful flatteries, borrowed phrases and hints of a more alarming personality unlikely to be very long satisfied with provincial salons and local gossip. If Virginia had much to solace the bruised sea captain, it lacked the majesty of Selkirk's great house and the cruder amenities of Poland Street.

Whatever their essence, people tend to shift their outward personality according to immediate requirements – Tom Paine was visited by a courteous gentleman with considerable range of reading, and a taste for political philosophy and objective discussion, whom he later discovered was M Sanson, the Paris executioner – and Paul Jones's parlour self was signally at odds with the scowling seaman who had drawn blood from Maxwell and sworded 'the Ringleader'. Abigail Adams, the shrewd, intelligent and literary First Lady of the United States, 1797–1801, who was never given to the sham, the fulsome or the imprecise, wrote from Paris a few years later:

Chevalier Jones you have heard much of; he is a most uncommon character. From the intrepid character he justly supported in the American Navy, I expected to have seen a rough, stout, war-like Roman – instead of that I should think of wrapping him in cotton wool and putting him in my pocket than sending him to contend with cannon-balls. He is small of stature, well-proportioned, soft in his speech, easy in his address, polite in his manners, vastly civil, understands all the etiquette of a lady's toilette as perfectly as he does the masts, sails and rigging of his ship. Under all this appearance of softness, he is bold and enterprising, ambitious and active. He has been here often, and dined with us several times; he is said to be a man of gallantry and a favorite among the French ladies, whom he is frequently commending for the neatness of their persons, their easy

manners, and their tastes in dress. He knows how often the ladies use
the baths, what color best suits a lady's complexion, what cosmetics
more most favorable to the skin. We do not often see the warrior and
the abigail thus united.

If five people describe the same person, the same event, in identical
terms, while none is lying, only one may be telling the truth. To Baron von
Grimm, assiduous and wily correspondent with Catherine the Great, Paul
Jones was 'A Man of the World, of great intelligence and sweetness'.
Commending him to Catherine and Potemkin, Lord Wemys wrote that he
was 'A brave and great sailor...agreeable...full of all sorts of attainments'.
An Englishman in the Hague in 1779, observed of the victor over *Serapis*:
'He is a very different man from what he is generally represented...good
sense, a genteel address, and a very good, though small person.' In his last
years, he was acquainted with the famous French painter, Vigée Le Brun,
who said, 'I have never met a man more modest; it was impossible to get
him to mention his great deeds; but anything else he would talk about, with
great wit and without affectation.'

Examples of his wit are rare but, when he so desired, he undeniably had
the wit to please.

These citations would have astonished Rev Hogg, Congress's Marine
Committee and his own officers who would have heard, not his wit, but his
pugnacious and adaptable wits, his professional versatility, his raw temper
and immoderate demands, though his letters stress his 'moderation' and
'prudence'. At bottom, these qualities may well have been authentic,
though bad temper and exasperating problems were apt to disrupt them.

Social respectability, nevertheless, can irk coarse-grained, outsize
personalities. Fox, Danton, Mirabeau, Potemkin; it would have gratified
George III but not his sons, 'Prinny' and Clarence, to whom an empty wine
glass was personal insult.

Like Walt Whitman, like many others, 'Captain Jones' contained
multitudes, but his more alarming or pernicious selves were concealed as he
trod the social round, itself pleasant, if unexacting, and unlikely to be
prolonged. He does seem to have studied navigation manuals and naval
tactics. In 1609, a poet had nominated Virginia as 'Earth's only Paradise',
and though slaves were now digging America's first coal mines, Whitman
was to praise Virginia's breadth of scenery, prodigal forests, 'most luscious
skies, rich and elatic nights and prodigal sun'. Good, but not quite good
enough. Dalliance with Miss Dandridge might have passed the time but he

needed to quicken and intensify time. His powers remained insufficiently used. Though later admitted, along with Lafayette, to the prestigious Order of Cincinnatus, open only to the Valiant, he is not easily imagined as squandering his life savouring quiet New England afternoons of tea, mild dancing and the play of fans. In 1775, he resembled an author, talented, youngish but not youthful, eager for publication, unconcerned with the morals of publishers and readers, but to whom readership, press cuttings and royalties mean much. He made, however, an influential contact, Joseph Hewes, substantial merchant, future Congressman, signatee of the Declaration of Independence and who was to recommend Jones's first official appointment.

Had Paul Jones been hanged in 1775, he would have been briefly remembered as a competent though quarrelsome skipper, ingratiating seducer, popular guest, but as no smouldering Byronic corsair. Some would have detected traces of stubborn pride that would bear him into the future, with what Herman Melville described as 'a look as a parading Sioux, demanding hostage to his gee-gaws'.

With his relations and new acquaintances he would inevitably have discussed the worsening political situation, primarily over 'British tyranny', London's taxation policies, states' rights, and party rivalries and disputes about allegiance to the Mother Country. Britain, now flushed with conquests in three continents, but mindful of the future, was provoking American discontent in demonstrations and protests against exacting or arrogant state governors, and demands for new colonial contributions for defence from revived and vengeful France and Spain. France was particularly feared, with its large population in Canada and hopes of eventual reconquests. For Americans, the British acquisition of French Canada and the capture of Quebec actually removed all necessity for defence taxes and, indeed, had fortified their own self-assurance. Incipient nationalism enflamed desires to revolt against thoughtless or haughty British officialdom and grandee representatives, against indeed the ignorant, over-casual Westminster legislators who, regarding colonists as mere digits, too easily reckoned that 7,000 miscellaneous troops, backed by the world's largest navy, could enforce colonial reform. This included opposition to white Americans' plans for free access to tribal lands, for expropriation and exploitation, though regarded by many, in Britain and America alike, as common theft.

For the majority, little was clear cut, loyalties were divided and divisive. Deep-seated memories and resentments survived among thousands of descendants of those who had already fought and destroyed one English king, and who had emigrated from fear or hatred of others. In contrast, the Crown retained some mystique, appealing to emotions less obviously defined than those of Puritanism and Non-Conformism, but still obstinate and at times reckless.

This said, America was not being trundled towards open rebellion by Republican fanatics and irresponsible libertarians. Tom Paine, 'who did by his *Common Sense* pamphlet free America', was fiery with his pen but no buccaneering man of action. The Founding Fathers were legalistic in tastes, culture and political training; fearing mobs and demagogues; disposed to debate and seek legal precedents; evoke 'Natural Rights' and quote Locke, rather than harangue, issue rallying calls or swing the tocsin. George Washington's language, when he presented Lafayette with a copy of the New Federal Constitution was not that of Marat or Danton. 'If it be good, it will work its way. If bad, it will recoil on the framers.' While disputes and tempers became inflamed, he avoided rhetorical blather: 'At a time when our lordly masters in Great Britain will be satisfied with nothing less than the deprivation of American freedom, it seems highly necessary that something should be done.'

When first hoisted by John Paul Jones, on *Alfred*, on 3 September 1775, the Grand Union Flag still contained the Union Jack with States' stripes added. This suggested lingering hopes of King George, not felt by Jones himself as, always alert for personal showmanship, he proclaimed, at his most parsonical:

> I have not Drawn my Sword in our Glorious Cause, for hire, but in support of the Dignity of Human Nature, and in Obedience to the Genuine and Divine feelings of Philanthropy! l hoisted with my own hands the Flag of Freedom in the Delaware, and I have attended it ever since with Veneration on the Ocean. I claimed and obtained its first salute from that of France before our Independence was otherwise announced in that Kingdom; and no man can wish more ardently to support its Rising glory than Myself.'

This was to be acknowledged by the inscription beneath Jones's statue in Potomac Park, Washington: 'In Life, he Honored the Flag, in Death the Flag shall honor him.' It is sometimes suggested that his first flag included Virginian emblems, such as a pine tree defended by a rattlesnake.

When resuming service, Jones regarded the flag as his personal crest. Failure of an American privateer to salute *Ariel*'s colours, by then the Stars and Stripes, enraged him like a slap in the face, and he wrote to the miscreant captain:

'I cannot answer your Letter more Particularly as there are several Words in it that I do not understand, and cannot find in the Dictionary. I will lay your letter to me before the Board of Admiralty with a Complaint against You for having Dared to Insult the Flag and Sovereignty of the United States.' He conceded, probably not quite wholeheartedly: 'It is not me you have offended, You have offended the United States of America.'

Unlike Paine, he needed not to change the world but to grab proper place in whatever lay before him. Without rejecting outright the egalitarianism of Paine and Burns, both, like himself, humbly born, he would have appointed neither first mate. He was a status hound, who knew he had been born socially inferior to Mr Craik, even Commodore Hopkins, so must surpass them. To his crews, ill-rewarded or never rewarded, he was severely paternalistic, strenuously besieging the Marine Committee or Sartine on their behalf. His assertion of support for 'The Dignity of Human Nature through every stage of the American Revolution', seeking 'Only the Esteem of the Good and the Virtuous' was surely more practical than emotional.

When war with Britain began, he was unemployed, with funds frozen or embezzled in London and Tobago. Around him, loyalties were necessarily confused. Most colonists were of British stock; the Crown had been scarcely questioned for a century, though many had fled Britain to escape royal and ecclesiastical interference. Gouverneur Morris's mother was loyalist, his brother fought for the king, he himself opted for Independence, and, when an American representative in Paris, had sympathies with the early French Revolution, seeing France and America setting moral and political examples to the world, sympathies which were withdrawn by the Terror. Franklin's brother, governor of New Jersey, was ejected for loyalty to George III.

Paul Jones had less choice than he admitted. He was very hostile to Britain, where he was still an indicted criminal. Colonial violence against British troops that April entailed immediate naval embargo on American trade, and wrecked any chance of clearing either his name or his London bank accounts. Thus, when Commodore Esek Hopkins proclaimed his need of officers for an independent American navy, Jones saw the luminous opportunity to break from the long Virginian afternoon. He could have sought a privateer, but privateers had frail allegiances, were barely controllable, and were dedicated mostly to private gain. He at once realised the colonists' need for a national fleet responsible not to commercial houses but, as in Europe, to a professional admiralty, publicly funded. His own advantage would come from centres of political power, not with capricious employers liable to financial collapse or waywardness, like John Younger and Currie and Beck.

Without delay, he responded to Hopkins's call, adopting new expectations, chances for action under a new flag, together with considerable reference to 'the Sacred Cause of Human Dignity', though, once engaged, enjoying the game for much of its own sake, and always strictly professional in his participation. Few rebel colonists were wholly altruistic – Franklin, Samuel Adams, Robert Morris – all had personal interests to consider, and most wagers in 1775 must have been on the United Kingdom of Great Britain, under its renowned aristocratic generals and famous admirals, swiftly regaining control.

While applying to Hopkins, Paul Jones was now known to Morris and Hewes, both installed on the first Marine Committee. Furthermore, he was known to Jefferson, soon to be among those drafting the Declaration of Independence. Confident that his experience entitled him to a command, he was ready, not to be grateful for tips but to accept rewards, navigational, financial, even sartorial.

Before the Navy List was announced, the colonists were reading George Washington's proclamation, its opening touched with dramatic irony, to be noticed by America's enemies: 'The time is near at hand which must probably determine whether Americans are to be Free Men or Slaves.'

It continued: 'The fate of unborn millions will depend under God, on the Courage and Conduct of this Army – our cruel and unrelenting Enemy leaves us no choice but a brave resistance or the most abject submission...We have therefore to Conquer or Die...and if we now shamefully fail, we shall become infamous to the whole world.'

6

International Currents

In democracies, almosl all is managed by the drones...leaders distribute rich men's money to the populace...teachers fear and flatter their pupils...anarchy penetrates to the home.

Plato,
The Republic

The Guardian Prince of Albion burns in his nightly tent,
Sullen fires across the Atlantic glow to America's shore,
Piercing the souls of warlike men who rise in silent might,
Washington, Franklin, Paine and Warren...

William Blake,
A Prophecy, 1793

Savages would blush at the unmanly Violation and Rapacity that has marked the tracks of British Tyranny in America.

John Paul Jones

Churchill called the Seven Years' War (elsewhere referred to as the Third Silesian War), the First World War. It was fought in Europe by Frederick the Great of Prussia, heavily subsidised by Britain, against Austria, France, Russia, Sweden, Saxony and Spain; and by Britain mostly in India and Canada against France. Even by eighteenth-century standards, official excuses were grossly hypocritical and yielded exorbitant profits for Britain. In 1763, the Peace of Paris formalised British conquests of French Canada and India and her gain of small but vital Mediterranean bases, the Empire thereby attaining a magnitude surpassed only by Rome and China. This provoked much debate at Westminster, many economists, idealists and quiet gentlemen being inimical to empires and suspicious of their motives.

Arguably, the British Empire was more humane than the empires of Assyria, Carthage and Aztec Mexico; more progressive than the Egyptians; more enduring and as cultured as those of Babylon, Persia and Moghul India; less bigoted and more financially sophisticated than the Spanish and Portuguese. France was now chastened, Spain and Holland, though still powerful, had passed their meridian. London had replaced Antwerp as the world's foremost financial centre, and some of the vigour with which seventeenth-century Holland had withstood the magnificent Louis XIV, won an immense maritime trade in spices, luxuries, rare woods and exotic plants, together with an artistic display at which connoisseurs still wonder, was ebbing. Some complex self-doubts may have assisted this, an unease which would one day afflict Britain, but not the Britain of George III and the Regent of Wellington, Pitt the Younger, Canning, Peel and the young Disraeli.

Unlike the Roman Senate and the Cromwellian Republic, Georgian Westminster was not subservient to any successful general. Since the Lord Protector's unpopular major-generals (whose impact has been exaggerated), only Marlborough – and his wife – and Wellington had political significance, and the latter's sense of public duty and constitutional decorum astonish and abash his present-day parliamentary successors.

With Calcutta established by 1690, the British East India Company was on course of becoming a Great Power in its own right. Although the advantages to India were not yet seen to be very pronounced, the abolition of private wars and banditry, the partial introduction of British Common Law and the encouragement of Indian culture, financial reforms and, for a while, amicable racial and social relationships, were to win defenders. More immediately, a Bengali word infiltrated the English language: *loot*. For Britain, Indian possessions were incalculable, even if the ruling caste was in no haste to share them with the mass of the population save as employers and patrons. The American philosophic historian, Brooks Adams, one of that esteemed family and power-group which produced two of the first six presidents, wrote: 'Possibly since the world began, no investment has ever yielded the profit reaped from the Indian plunder, because for nearly fifty years, Great Britain stood without a competitor.' Franklin, typically, reflected that no nation is ever ruined by trade.

Britain won acclaim for more than brute conquests. The Enlightenment revered Cromwell, conceived as a liberator, together with British Parliament, law and religious tolerance. Newton had altered the perspectives of the universe. The liberalism of Locke and Hume was unencumbered by superstition. British technology would overcome time and space, alter landscapes, tame seas. Sir Walter Scott's historical stories changed the European mind.

The London political scene, however, was not, in 1775, at its best. Since Egbert, all English monarchs, save Edward V, had distinct personalities, even George I, though an unpleasant one. Of George III's household, Thackeray submitted in 1860 that the household was the model of an English gentleman's. 'It was easy; it was kindly; it was charitable; it was orderly; it must have been stupid to a degree which I shudder now to contemplate.' America's last king, George III, was one of those summarised by Johnson as having but one idea in his head, and that a wrong one. At this instant, the one royal idea was America.

Wretchedly trained, jealous of his royal prerogatives, bone-headed, George III was to be a target for EC Bentley's clerihew:

> George the third
> Ought never to have occurred.
> One can only wonder
> At so grotesque a blunder.

Abused in Britain and America for stupidity and insensitivity, he was entering a period of personal failure and considerable unpopularity, a butt for Rowlandson's and Gillray's cartoons, and for Wilkes, who savaged him in the polemical *North Briton*. Nicknamed, 'Old Nobbs', 'Farmer George', as 'Robinson', he wrote dull articles for an agricultural journal, was known to love apple dumplings and, in his plain but forthright way, to deprecate Shakespeare. 'Poor stuff,' he assured Fanny Burney, 'but we're not allowed to say so.' At times, his talk seemed orchestrated by 'What!' several times repeated. His defects were remembered longer than his gifts, which ensured the nucleus of the British Library, his founding of the Royal Academy – J Steven Watson, historian of his reign, thought him more concerned with art patronage than any monarch since 1688, though competition was surely meagre – he bought Canalettos, Raphael drawings, a Vermeer; he founded an agricultural college, is famed for his patronage of Capability Brown, the Adam brothers, of William Herschel, great discoverer of Uranus and his courtesy to Johnson. His kindness is amply testified. Walter Scott told of an old, obdurate Scots Jacobite, so loyal to the exiled dynasty that he would tolerate no mention of the Hanoverian usurpers: George sent him congratulations on holding to his principles, thoughtfully written not as King of Great Britain but as Elector of Hanover.

He possessed some presence and, had he ever deigned to visit America, might have delayed the crisis. Despite political bigotry and personal ambition, he eventually acquired more magnanimity, jolted by periodic mental instability.

Notwithstanding all this, in 1775, the king and his premier, Lord Bute, were ignorant of their Empire and, when they thought of Americans at all, imagined them as loyal, docile and homogenous; at first signs of unrest, they expected no long and bitter resistance. George later explained: 'We meant well to America, just to punish them with a few bloody noses, and then to make laws for the happiness of both countries.' Folly mixed with wishful thinking.

Parliament was oligarchic, brisk with classical quotation, languid in legislation, cheerfully corrupt. Merchants with Caribbean and African interests would buy seats in order to oppose the abolition of slavery: nabobs from India, aristocrats and provincial gentry, all controlled seats and bribed voters, from interest, family loyalty or, in exquisite self-deception, from conviction that they owed it to society. Pitt, Lord Chatham, the Great Commoner, castigated by the king as 'that great Trumpet of Sedition', was in physical decline. The Whigs, sympathetic to America, were seldom in office, and their most engaging member, Charles James Fox, showed no outstanding ministerial ability when occasionally invited to display it. Fox at no time confirmed Carlyle's belief that the Englishman's greatest talent is for silence, though his great speech of 1807 guaranteed the abolition of the slave trade. The Tory, North, of whom a Johnson could have said only that he filled a chair, was no war leader, in glum contrast to Chatham. His colleagues were social assets, without political insight. Lord George Germain, minister of war, hastened the Saratoga débâcle when, over-anxious to reach the grouse moor, he signed vital instructions to General Lord Howe, though forgetting to dispatch them to another commander. Able enough in Parliament, though shy, he fancied he could supervise the American war from his office and, though hero of a celebrated duel, his prestige had lost lustre from his dismissal from the army for disobedience during the battle of Minden.

Hanoverian government was never a helter-skelter stampede towards Utopia. Some years later, Sir Henry Taylor, for thirteen years, by repute never entered his colonial office. At no time was Dickens's satirical Boodle, Coodle, Doodle theory of government, with its attendant Circumlocution Office a novelist's fantasy. George Lefevre in *The French Revolution 1793–99* (1967) gives a snippet of the gentlemanly Cabinets, which lost America, withstood the French Revolution and defeated Napoleon:

'Windham would have agreed to participate in the government. Pitt was willing to include him, but Dundas, who was head of the Home Office, Minister of War, Secretary of Ireland, and Treasurer of the Navy, obstinately refused to reduce his extravagant pluralism. Dundas, however, merely held the title of Minister of War. Knowing nothing about the army, he turned it over to Yonge, First Secretary of the War Office, who was not a member of the Cabinet.'

London streets applauded the pantomime of Fox and Lord Richmond drunkenly leading an exuberant crowd 'to break ministers' windows, sack the Admiralty, chase Lord Sandwich down Whitehall in a nightgown'. The acidulous political commentator, Junius, wondered:

> Was ever a Nation so governed before,
> By a Jockey and Gambler, a Pimp and a Whore?

JH Plumb (see Bibliography) considered that the party system and serious political debate were invigorated only by the American war.

The role of ideology in that war, as in the Crusades, the British Empire, Marxist purges and general history, is always disputable, and indeed unsettled. Christian Venice had prospered by selling fellow-Christians to Muslim slave markets, Muslims behaving likewise. Seventeenth-century Anglo-Dutch wars were between fellow-Protestants. Catholic France could ally itself with Muslim Turks and Protestant Swedes against Catholic Austria, abolitionists' zeal to destroy the slave trade had not always the purest motives, some wishing to weaken rivals and augment British sea power through 'right of search'. Magna Carta, cherished by British and American Whigs, had been signed only on behalf of 'free men', that is, the propertied. Eighteenth-century slogans, Liberty, Freedom, Justice, the People, were flourished incautiously; John Paul Jones's 'Fight for Liberty', being akin to Robespierre's 'The French People decree the Liberties of the World', exciting rhetoric. 'Liberty' could mean self-defence or, like 'liberation', an excuse for territorial and economic plunder. Perhaps Mussolini, for once, was free of ideological cant: 'Fascism is Mussolini-ism.'

Widespread British sympathy with the Americans could transcend whatever party beliefs existed, the Tory Burke joining with Fox in assailing North, with much City support. The ailing Chatham virtually killed himself with impassioned appeals for restraint. These too were not wholly altruistic. Though trade returns from America were insignificant compared to India, he maintained that New England was 'the Fountain of our Wealth' and, to save its capture by France, he advocated granting all the colonists' demands save total independence. He was certain that the empire won by the Seven Years' War was mortally endangered.

In all classes were those who felt that the English art of compromise, inherited from pre-conquest Saxon and Danish rule, was being abandoned, Common Law itself at risk from an irresponsible Crown, an uninformed Cabinet and a grasping Treasury. Of the Stamp Act tumult, Chatham applauded American resistance: 'Three millions of people, so dead to all the feelings of Liberty as voluntarily to submit to be slaves, would have been fit instruments to make slaves of the rest.'

Burke, who was to denounce the French Revolution and British injustices in India, insisted that government policy would incite American sedition. David Hume enthused over the Declaration of Independence in 1776: 'I am an American in my principles, and wish we would let them alone to govern or misgovern themselves as they think proper.'

During the war, Whigs would correspond with Benjamin Franklin in Paris: Admiral Keppel and others, though willing to defend Britain against the French, refused to serve against the colonists. Replying to John Paul Jones in 1788, Lord Selkirk admitted of the king's ministers: 'I have generally disapproved of most of their measures, and in particular of almost all their whole conduct in the unhappy and ill-judged circumstances. '

Wilkes had been discussing British and colonial political reform with American politicians and gleefully applauded Paine's rhetoric in *Common Sense*:

'Freedom has been hunted round the globe, Asia, Africa, have long expelled her, Europe regards her like a stranger and England hath given her warning to depart . . . We have it in our power to begin the World over again. A situation similar to the present hath not happened since the days of Noah until now.'

The Quaker Tall hat was adopted to display support for the rebels, though not by the old Tory, Johnson: 'I am willing to love all mankind, except an American.' He was at odds with most prominent British intellectuals and artists, including Joseph Priestley, Adam Smith, together with John Wesley, Sheridan and Southey.

No more than Roman Britain had America been allowed a trained native army. On land, civilian rough-heads, yokel loudmouths and chattering lawyers, must have beggarly chances against seasoned redcoats and their aristocratic generals; on sea, no chances at all. American ports and commerce would be defenceless without help from Britain's defeated enemies, France and Spain, and perhaps Holland. The French, however, were unpopular in America, with its memories of the recent 'French and Indian War' in Canada. Also, 'Indian' tribes and southern blacks largely judged the British the less predatory and despotic. 'Native Americans', too often dismissed by London and by white colonists as 'the savages', fought on both sides at Saratoga. The British sought black support earlier than their opponents.

Black slaves could in fact benefit from the British, some 30,000 eventually being helped to flee victorious America, together with white loyalists, to Canada, Europe, and to Sierre Leone, established for blacks by City financial and philanthropic groups, Evangelicals and abolitionists between 1788 and 1791.

London was to be dismayed by the extent of French aid to the rebels, and realised that French volunteers were evading the blockade. Foreign volunteers, however, had seldom won wars, and the perils of an anti-British European coalition were shrugged off, in the spirit of the Victorian Lord Salisbury, who grandly declared that 'England does not seek alliances, she grants them.'

Such insouciance was fatal. Loyalist support, though considerable, was overestimated. British troops included Hessians, Brunswickers, Canadians, nondescrlpts and 'savages', few very enthusiastic. Administration was slack, supplies uncertain and liable to capture by French warships, American privateers and such official commanders as Paul Jones. There was considerable negligence at home. Decades later, British quartermasters in the Crimea were displeased by receiving large quantities of military boots, for the left foot only.

There was small comprehension and less concern about how best to fight English-speaking communities in vast and unfamiliar terrain, itself further complicated by the presence of ancient and baffling tribes. The king was remote and would never condescend to join them, information scanty and often bewildering. The troops grappled with sickness, marshes, rivers, forests, infrequent pay and unfamiliar food, and might hear discouraging reports, extravagantly enlarged, of Fox slamming insults at Lord North: 'A blundering Pilot who has brought the Nation into its present difficulties.' North, however, remained in charge of a Cabinet, which, with no coherent policy, possessed only 'Folly and Madness', The soldiers were too frequently in arrears of pay: Wellington himself, years later in the Peninsular, had to rely for urgent funds not on the Treasury but on Nathan Rothschild.

In the American War, no army possessed the efficiency, and discipline, even the exceptional inner convictions of Cromwell's New Model Army over a century previously. The German hirelings were hated by the colonists and disliked by their British associates. Ill discipline, which so plagued John Paul Jones, infected all nations until drastic measures were inflicted on all ranks, generals and admirals alike, by the French Revolutionary 'Agents on Mission', early commissars. George III, during the American Revolution, complained that 'lack of skill and energy in the navy, and lack of unity at home,' betrayed the British war effort. Ordinary Americans, fighting for Liberty, did not overlook their own liberties, though, back in 1759, Washington had reminded Virginian officers: 'Discipline is the soul of an army. It makes small numbers formidable, giving success to the weak and esteem to all.' He was to have many occasions on which to repeat this.

The British rank and file performed better then might have been expected, though leaving hatreds in America that, a century later, had never been wholly extinguished. There were weaknesses on top. General Viscount William Howe, like his brother, Admiral Earl Richard Howe, was able and industrious; Lord Burgoyne was an Enlightenment ornament, scarcely dedicated to war and administration; he was urbane, coolly courageous, literary and artistic, witty, author of several amusing comedies, confident of his own abilities and pleasantly disparaging those of others, in defeat preserving the dignified unconcern with which he would have accepted victory. Lord Cornwallis, though conscientious, failed to overcome logistic and strategic difficulties, while receiving insufficient assistance from London, which only too late understood the overall political significance of what had seemed merely disagreeable unrest.

The British navy could muster over 180 warships, but these were widely dispersed, having to cover the Mediterranean, the Indian Ocean, the Pacific and the Atlantic. It was nevertheless rightly feared by Jefferson, Morris and by Paul Jones. Nelson was still in the wings but Rodney, almost as great, held British mastery in Atlantic battles save for a few, though crucial, months when he was ill and absent, and the fleet, opposed by de Grasse, failed to relieve Burgoyne at Saratoga. To maintain the blockade intact against the French required not exceptional tactics but exceptional numbers, perforce lacking. Rodney, like Nelson, disliked at the Admiralty, was popular with his men and finally routed de Grasse in 1782.

His naval masters, though singular, were not of the finest qualities. The Earl of Sandwich was competent but not outstanding, as engaging and dissolute as his fellow gambler, Fox. He is remembered, not for administrative genius, but for devising the sandwich, to relieve himself of leaving his official desk to dine, and for giving his name to some Pacific islands. Sailors chiefly knew him as 'Jemmy Twitcher', the only First Lord actually known to have installed a resident mistress in the Admiralty. Under such as him, the navy, despite its valour, retained conditions that led inexorably to the Nore Mutinies in 1797.

Paul Jones was realistic about the general naval situation at the start of the war, informing the Marine Committee: 'We cannot yet fight their Navy, as their Numbers and Force are far Superior to ours. Therefore it seems to be our most Natural Province to surprise their Defenceless Places and thereby Divert their Attention and draw it from our Coasts.' This, he never ceased to insist, and, given sufficient ships, would have backed himself even against Rodney, but the shortage was never surmounted.

Nor was the inadequate organisation he so deplored. Pepys, long before, had remonstrated against inexperienced 'gentlemen captains', promoted through court influence at the expense of professional but socially inferior 'tarpaulin captains', like John Campbell, William Bligh and Cloudesley Shovel. The luckless Byng had once used 'influence' to evade an inconvenient assignment. Paul Jones's French associate, Chartres, royal duke, though devoid of naval talent, was intriguing to succeed his father-in-law as Grand Admiral.

Despite the clamour in 1775, British 'colonial tyranny' was not by Russian, Spanish or Portuguese standards very oppressive, save in finance and defence. A growing and prosperous American population was far freer than much of the British poor, though irked by the commercial restrictions. An early assignment of Nelson's was to help enforce one-sided navigation laws, benefiting the City of London interests.

Arguably, poor psychology rather than oppressive legislation, absentee landlordism and monopolies lost Britain its American colonies. Laxity, arrogance and disdainfulness were at least as significant as misapplied brawn, ignorant administration and Generals' failing co-operation.

British oligarchs and moneybaggers, despite virulent accusations from Paine and Fox, the protests of Franklin and Washington, did not regard Americans as slaves, but as second-class clients and social inferiors. They found threats to back politics by armed force easier than moral and legalistic discussion, like those teachers whose first move against pupils difficult but reachable was to reach for the cane. 'Every Man in England,' Franklin moaned, 'seems to consider himself as a piece of a sovereign over America; seems to jostle himself onto the throne with the King, and talks of "our subjects in the Colonies".'

Tolerant, slightly amused and a trifle bored, English gentlemen saw colonials as awkward squads not far from those of Falstaff and Bottom the Weaver. Milords and dandies could snigger at visions of Jefferson swigging with his muddy feet on the table, Washington blowing his nose on the tablecloth – Washington, from one of the oldest Northamptonshire families and whose ancestor, Walter de Wessyton, had fought in the battle of Lewis in 1264. At St Sepulchre's in Northampton, a brass depicting a handshake adorns the sixteenth-century tomb of another ancestor, Lawrence Washington, mayor. Though he had led British forces against the French in Canada, George was refused a regular commission, perhaps from misplaced snobbery, and it rankled. Jefferson, with multifarious cultural interests; John Adams, industrious and scholarly; Robert Morris, of a clan owning vast Hudson estates; Benjamin Franklin, of international scientific and literary renown – such men and their wives were not scrounging desperadoes or tyro Jacobins. Abigail Adams, in civility, intelligence and poise, could have matched any Lady Holland or Lady Mornington, outmatched the patient, dutiful and unexceptional Queen Charlotte and, more emphatically, the genial though pretentious Lady Hamilton.

Snobbery and prejudice were not exclusive to the mother country. Nathaniel Hawthorne was to declare the United States fit for many purposes but not for living in.

Also dangerous for Britain were Scots and Irish, reaching America and indisposed to cease brooding over old wrongs and injustices, an attitude amply reciprocated. JH Plumb mentions that, for the landed British ascendancy, 'the Americans were linked with the Irish, a difficult and disagreeable people, best kept under'.

King and Cabinet, with a woeful knowledge of history and no sense of it, misread the colonists' demands, condemning as a rebellious novelty what had long been English convictions. 'No Taxation without Representation' harked back to beyond the relevant Civil War and was traceable to the thirteenth-century Edward I: 'What touches alle sholde be approved by alle.' Americans were tenacious of English Common Law, with nearly a thousand years behind it. Jefferson was to insist that his University of Virginia should study Anglo-Saxon laws and administration, alongside Hume and Locke.

British arrogance was not dissolved by defeats at Saratoga and Yorktown. British memsahibs would send Indians scuttling away in alarm, British sahibs, impeccably honest, would debar Indians from 'the club'. The Duke of Windsor, wartime governor of the Bahamas, informed Lord

Mountbatten, the last viceroy, friend of Gandhi and the Nehrus, that successful colonial administration depended upon coloured peoples being forbidden to use the front door of Government House.

In 1775, therefore, despite British weaknesses, the rebels had to improvise some central administration, while prime loyalty was almost always given to the individual states. Many recognised, however reluctantly, that Congress would be more interfering, even more authoritarian, than Westminster. A number still felt Britain their safeguard against Europe, Mexico, Canadian French and Spain.

Furthermore, nowhere were people entirely rational. There are always those who rally to the flag, the cause, even against their own interests – His Majesty, the Old Country, the Oath, or be passionate against them, at whatever risk. Few Americans actually wished for war, fewer still wished to fight without pay. Washington's leadership was periodically endangered by faction, intrigue, personal rivalries, although, as Major-General JFC Fuller wrote in 1954, 'It was the unswerving determination of Washington, which, alone, at times, kept the rebellion alive.' An American engineer, viewing the early political situation, admitted: 'There is a hundred times more enthusiasm for this revolution in any café in Paris than there is in all the United States together.' Robert Morris testified: 'In the Eastern States they are so intent upon Privateering that they mind little else. '

Another member of the New Marine committee, William Whipple, had to add: 'Those who actually engage in it [privateering] soon lose every idea of Right and Wrong, and for want of an opportunity of gratifying their insatiable Avarice with the properties of the Enemies of their Country, will, without the least Compunction, seize that of their friends.'

As controller of imports, then Superintendent of Supplies, Morris himself, as was customary everywhere throughout the century, profited not only from privateering investments but from war supplies he obtained from overseas agents, themselves no utopianists or fanatics for liberty. The best known was Pierre Augustin Caron de Beaumarchais, author of *The Barber of Seville* (1775) and *The Marriage of Figaro* (1784) (to his astonishment the latter was believed to have helped instigate the French Revolution). Congress officials, like the scheming entrepreneur Colonel Langdon, needed the multiple hands of an Indian god to discriminate between public and personal dues.

There was no rush, patriotic or political, to join Congress's Continental Navy, and almost all active seamen were being recruited by businessmen for themselves. Moreover, many officers were loyalists, and had transferred their ships to Canada, Jamaica or Britain itself. Paul Jones testified in 1776: 'It is to the last degree Distressing, to contemplate the State and Establishment of our Navy.' On *Providence*, a few months later, he told Hewes:

'It appears that the Seamen, almost to a man, had entered the Army before the Fleet was put on foot, and I am well informed that there are four or five thousand seamen now in the Land Service.'

A number of these were to mutiny in the field, at New Jersey in 1781, incensed by unpaid wages.

'We had no system for the Government of our Navy,' Jones recalled in 1787. The American Revolution began and ended with only a token fleet. 'Was it a proof of madness,' he asked Morris in 1782, 'in the first Corps of Sea Officers, to have at so critical a period, launched out on the Ocean with only two armed merchantmen ships and one armed Sloop, to make war against such a Power as Great Britain?'

He was immediately aggrieved by Committee officials and their selection of officers: as a matter of course, influence predominated over character and experience. His early commander, Captain Saltonstall, whom he thoroughly despised, was brother-inlaw to the powerful politician, Silas Deane. Lincoln Lorenz delineates 'the Family Compact' of the four Lee brothers, each with a seat in Congress, and variously holding four ministries, the French Commercial Agency, and a London aldermanship under Wilkes, with whom Arthur Lee was close. Arthur Lee was aggressive, disliked and, in Paris, from malice more than public concern, successfully intrigued for the removal of Silas Deane, fellow commissioner with himself and Franklin. Lee was hostile to Paul Jones, as was Samuel Adams. Cousin to John Adams, Samuel had been an incompetent tax collector, then a radical politician and propagandist, a leading organiser of the anti-British Boston Tea Party, and whose radicalism much alarmed George III.

The Continental Navy's first Commodore, the ageing Esek Hopkins, was brother of Stephen Hopkins, chairman of the Marine Committee, which Esek himself rated: 'Ignorant lawyers' clerks and a pack of damned fools'. Of Esek Hopkins, Paul Jones wrote: 'The Navy would be better without a head, than a bad one', leaving no difficulty about implying where to seek a good one. John Manley, whom he respected, secured his own promotion, and most subsequent demands, by threat of resignation. James Nicholson, always Jones's enemy, was appointed senior captain by blatant political jobbery. A twentieth-century British First Lord, the reforming Admiral John Fisher, was to breezily remark that the secret of success was favouritism.

Congress, established in Philadelphia, was a nest of state factions and personal rivalries, Alexandre Gerard, the first French representative, reporting in 1776:

'Personal disinterest and financial probity fail to honour the American Republic with their presence... selfish and calculating spirit is widespread in this Land... mercantile cupidity forms, perhaps, one of the distinctive traits of the Americans, especially of the Northern People, and it will undoubtedly exercise an important influence upon the future Destiny of the Republic.'

George Washington would have contradicted none of this. In 1796, long victorious, he was still deploring 'the baneful effects of the Spirit of the Party'. Faction hampered his presidency as it had his generalship, and as it did the presidency of his successor, John Adams, even from his own Cabinet. Between 1792 and 1794 the Jacobin committee in Paris, far removed from American democracy, outlawed all spirit of party save their own, though most members lost their heads in the process. Bonaparte, too, had no patience with faction, saw no necessity for party, in an Empire designed for efficiency, French hegemony and glory, itself defined by Louis Blanc, nineteenth-century revolutionary, as the sum of the dead.

Everywhere, politics, finance, commerce, diplomacy and 'honour', were inextricably entwined, as Paul Jones painfully realised in dealings with Langdon and Deane, Sartine and Chaumont, and with the entourage of Serenissimus, Alexander Potemkin, Prince of the Tauride, and his sovereign lady. Muddle and graft encouraged his rudeness, invective, anger and accusations. During the first months of war, there were sparkling opportunities within reach but likely to be denied him, the talented newcomer, while the third-rate prospered through family money and social connections, all the recognisably British heritage. In wearisome self-approval, he saw others, under Hopkins and Saltonstall, fighting more to enrich themselves than to damage the oppressor. He would have castigated Chesterton's aphorism that, if a job is worth doing, it's worth doing badly. He was almost always unappeased, even when, in peace, Jefferson belauded 'the Disinterested Spirit, the Devotion to the service of America' of this nagging, ungracious little man.

On 7 June 1776, at Philadelphia, Richard Henry Lee, of the Family Compact, seconded by John Adams, amid vehement dispute, muted hesitations, fears of defeat and of British vengeance, introduced a resolution, that 'These United colonies are, and of right are to be free and independent states; that they are absolved from all allegiance to the British Crown, and that all political connection between them and the State of Great Britain is, and ought to be, totally dissolved.'

Meanwhile, the New Republic urgently needed diplomatic recognition, arms, and, if possible, fighting allies. Silas Deane was dispatched to Paris to join Franklin and Arthur Lee in efforts to regularise French aid and induce France to enter the war. Sharp-witted, no idealist, Lee could see France as financially unstable, divided socially and politically, with the rich nobles and ecclesiastics cherishing with elegant detachment their own almost total exemption from the taxation that could save them. As in America, taxation, the distribution of other people's money, was a supreme issue with governments, theorists and rogues.

The French king, Louis XVI, was intelligent, tolerant, conscientious and with instinct for reform. He was popular, though temperamentally too sluggish to lead an attack on political, economic and administrative anachronisms shackling a nation so recently mauled by Great Britain. He was incapable of those vulgar, spectacular, resonant gestures by which crowds are galvanised. When a mob invaded his palace, he was offered the red cap of liberty, and graciously, stoically, donned it, but he should have already seized it, like Napoleon at his coronation, crowning himself, forestalling the Pope. He can be imagined as always fumbling for a tiny, jewelled key but, bound by some absurd etiquette, not first removing his tight, scented gloves. He had some wit, telling, if not subtle. Irritated by constant praise of Benjamin Franklin and the Franklin medallion with its inscription eulogising the American's experiments with electricity – *He tore down the lightning from heaven and the sceptres from the tyrants* – Louis had it reproduced at the bottom of a chamber pot and sent to one of Franklin's female devotees.

French ministers were understandably cautious of the American Revolution. Toppling a throne, even a British one, endangered all monarchy and perhaps property. Furthermore, Britain, though Protestant, notoriously stupid, sottish, overblown with beef and ale, had a perplexing knack of winning wars. The Treasury feared the expense of intervention, though a noisy war party sought revenge for loss of French India and Canada. Young males hankered to display valour, their elders sniffed the profits of arms sales, shipbuilding and victories. Cafés throbbed with youthful lawyers and journalists, revering Cromwell, instructed by Locke, Montesquieu, Voltaire,

Condorcet, enthralled by Rousseau, while too often misunderstanding all of them. Incorrigibly optimistic, they insisted on the goodness of humanity if left untainted by corrupt institutions, the superstitions of throne and altar. They revered Nature as a benevolent creative power, polluted by greedy men. Their vision was more reckless and ill-researched than that of the Encyclopaedists, who regarded Nature as a field for objective study, of impersonal climate, soil, plants, animals and human fluids.

Those radicals resembled the English gardener, described by JB Priestley as speaking of Nature as if he were a member of the small committee that had appointed her. The text of one young lawyer from Arras, inflexible in his dedication to justice, humanity and public spirit, would soon be penetrating the stale, perfumed atmosphere of Versailles; Maximilien Robespierre had begun his short, equivocal career, declaring, more than once: 'It is the most sacred duty of a people whose rights have been violated, to rebel.' On his way to supreme power, or what many, at home and abroad, assumed was supreme power, he extended his rhetoric: 'The Constituent assembly has in its hands the destiny of France and the Universe.' More soberly, Talleyrand murmured that anything exaggerated is witless.

Hitherto, colonial arms and militia had been supervised and restricted by Britain, and the Revolution had left the Republic confused and indigent, with few means of defence and less of attack. Arthur Lee had to liaise urgently with Beaumarchais in purchasing, mostly on credit and on exorbitant terms, thousands of muskets, small arms, cannon, grenades and tools which, with France still officially neutral, had to be sent through a fake business house, Hortales et Cie. In terms of statistics, supplies were ample, though Franklin was soon deploring them as mostly second-hand cast offs, and French volunteers, as adventurers or idealistic partisans, a herd of seducers and ruined swindlers, 'fitted to infect us with their own corruption'.

This was unjust to one young Frenchman, 'hero of two continents', entering the American Revolution like a roll of drums: Marie Joseph Paul Yves Roch Gilbert Motier, Marquis de Lafayette (1757–1834), departing despite court opposition. No royal favourite, 'pale, lanky, red-haired, with a pointed nose and receding forehead, he looked less like an officer than a wading bird,' Motier, according to Vincent Cronin, 1974. Nevertheless, he was soon respected by Washington as brave and trustworthy, though when returning to a France disorganised and threatened, and granted onerous and vital responsibilities, he appeared politically uncertain, morally weak, craving popularity from those he over-valued.

Marriages of convenience, domestic or political, are seldom whole-hearted. Though appreciating the gallantry of Lafayette and Rochambeau, and the impact of 6,000 French volunteers, John Adams was suspicious of France's ulterior designs, and indeed in the forthcoming Franco–American Treaty of Amity and Friendship – such documents are plagued by the habit of using more words than necessary – Versailles shrewdly inserted a clause providing against the colonists making a separate peace. Congress took its own precautions: British defeat, though still uncertain, might incite France to attempt to reclaim the French Canadian provinces. Seasoned French diplomats saw the weak, not entirely reputable, Republic, as a very junior ally in an effort to redress the international balance so drastically upset by Britain and Russia. The most fervent pro-American sentiments were coming from the journalists, from radical clubs, café intellectuals and lawyers, very noisy in Paris, though with an influence not yet ascertainable.

The three American commissioners had still to succeed in persuading Versailles to declare war, an action they calculated would encourage many reluctant neutrals, indignant about Britain's enormous territorial, commercial and strategic gains from the Seven Years' War. With French support, Spain, possibly Holland, might rally against Britain.

Lord Dorset, British ambassador in Paris, devoted to Marie Antoinette and also desiring to introduce cricket to the capital, protested vigorously at manifest French support for the rebels, though London remained cautious, fearing to further antagonise a still uncommitted France. The Westminster disputes – in parliamentary debate, scallywag caricatures (mostly pro-American), street ballads and within thousands of drawing-rooms and coffee houses – redoubled their vehemence. During his last months, Pitt the Elder, Lord Chatham, mastermind of the British wins in the Seven Years' War, was obdurate: 'If I were an American, as I am an Englishman, while a foreign troop was landed in my country, I would never lay down my arms – never – never. You cannot conquer America.'

With their troops already landed, King George and Lord North were determined to show him mistaken.

In Paris, Benjamin Franklin, recognised and applauded everywhere by his brown coat, simple stick, businessman's hat and hair unpowdered among the wigs, steepling coiffures, gleaming satins and velvets, inventor of the bifocal lens, was winning intellectual respect for his novel lightning conductor, of potentially global significance, though feared as witchcraft in some country districts. He was now assiduously transmitting atrocity stories about the British in America, not always with the severe respect for truth he elsewhere so diligently recommended. One such story, of the British rousing an 'Indian' tribe against the colonists, so that the king was subsequently presented with 200 scalps, though unbelievable, was widely believed and deplored. Dorset complained of Franklin, 'He will lie, he will promise, he will flatter with all the insouciance and subtlety that are natural to him.'

An American saying was, 'When in doubt, pray and sing.' At all times, atrocity stories galvanise like an infectious tune. Paul Jones continually inveighed against 'the unmanly Violation and Rapacity that has marked the tracks of British tyranny in America, from which neither Virgin Innocence nor Helpless Age has been a Plea of Protection or of Pity.'

The anti-government *London Evening Post* called the British burnings in Connecticut 'Too shocking to relate. The brutality and cruelty of the soldiers in several instances are too dreadful, as well as unfit, to be printed.' The press licence permitted in London and Paris would have been disallowed by Catherine II, Joseph II and Frederick the Great. A generation later, Ralph Waldo Emerson, though a dedicated admirer of British culture, writing of the earlier time, judged that 'the English could not well read a principle save by the light of faggots and burning towns.'

When Paul Jones was ranging off British shores and winning piratical repute, the *Post* resumed:

What will be the consequences of burning Fairfield and Newark? Paul Jones has done no mischief yet; but had he known of the burning of these towns, is it not probable he would have burned Leith and Hull? They were completely at his mercy. When this burning business comes to be retaliated upon our own coasts, we shall then see the Minister's scribbler expatiating upon the cruelty of it, of it's being contrary to the rules of war etc. It appears that Jones' orders were not to burn any houses or towns. What an example of honour and greatness does America thus show us! While our troops are running about from town to town on their coast, and burning everything with a wanton, wicked and deliberate barbarity, Dr Franklin gives no orders to retaliate. He is above it. And there was a time when an English Minister would have disdained to make war in so villainous a mode. It is a disgrace to the nation.

Dr Franklin never idled and was doing more than deliberating with such as Beaumarchais. He was typical, more of the century ahead, rejoicing in purposeful work and moral precepts, encyclopaedic, solemn as an

Englishman at a concert, though less stick-in-the-mud than some portraits suggest. A versifier, he could be humorous, sometimes satirical. His *Poor Richard's Almanac* was a handbook of axioms to assist righteous self-improvement and virtuous self-knowledge, also their just rewards. He was no stultifying egghead but had been printer, editor, publisher, journalist, founder of a philosophical society, member of the Royal Society, organiser of a fire service, natural scientist, an early example of American knowhow, familiar with varied lives and livelihoods. With Erasmus Darwin, he had devised a speaking machine. Mechanisation had already begun, and with disputes about whether humans themselves were but animated machines. Years before Mary Shelley's *Frankenstein* (1818), Catherine the Great had her greatness sightly impaired when disqualified for cheating against an automatic chess player. Descartes had had a mechanical doll; musical boxes and robot performers were fashionable. Franklin introduced the word 'electrician'.

Of Franklin, DH Lawrence wrote in his essay in, 1928: 'I admire his sturdy courage, first of all, then his sagacity, then his glimpses into the thunders of electricity, then his common sense humour. All the qualities of a great man, and never more than a great citizen,' though ending, 'I do not like him.'

From London, Franklin had supplied Tom Paine with a character reference to assist his entry to America. He was resolute in public support of Washington, even at bleakest moments, and was never deterred from his righteous path by the whims of public opinion.

All this, but more privately, he was also a link in another international institution, as permanent as war and hunger. Espionage had been a stable prop of the Elizabethan state, against Catholic Europe, then of the Hanoverians against Jacobites, Irish dissidents and patriots, English radicals, Scottish malcontents, French agents, and any innocent or guilty, whom London's special investigation 'Bag of Secrets' suspected of conspiring, spying or trouble-making. Espionage was as rampant as speculation, smuggling, forced marriages, wife sale or abduction of wealthy orphans. Its pedigree was as lengthy as all these. Secret agents had supplied England with details of the Armada, and Spain with the ramifications of court manoeuvres. Through a spy, Admiral Blake captured a strong Spanish contingent. Senior officers might buy and retain enemy plans and circumstances, for their private advantage.

Franklin, with his experience, shrewdness and wiles, headed American overseas espionage and naval intelligence, seated above a hushed, grubby sub-world of intricate codes, ciphers, invisible inks, double envelopes, false names, arcane passwords, doubtful beards, tinted spectacles and muffled faces, the surreptitious handshake and covert assignation; also the gibbet, the treacherous thrust into river or sewer, the occasional sensational exposure by which Benedict Arnold and Major André remain encased in American demonology. A realm of mirage, reversed values, uneasy perceptions and risks, easily romanticised, though Franklin's sober vision was not that of Balzac, who saw the spy possessing 'that quality of strange magnificence which never lets him display anger'. Balzac was thoroughly at home among the murky, the dispossessed and declassed, who had several names, queer references, with abstruse contacts with the mysterious that never forced them to lose all hope. Such a predilection, unappealing to Franklin, John Adams, Jefferson or Washington, glints from the strangely evocative opening of his novel, *History of the Thirteen*: 'In Paris, under the Empire, thirteen men came together.'

Much espionage was amateurish; government provocateurs sent to disorganise social and industrial unrest were often the more effective; spies sent from Europe to infiltrate British dockyards, warehouses, barracks and offices mostly fared ill or delivered little of much consequence. Some notables prospered better, with less risk. Franklin's secretary, Dr Edward Bancroft, was a British spy, eventually retiring to London on a £1,000-a-year pension. He played the wartime City market, using inside information of political and military decisions, and passing to London the clauses of the secret Franco–American Treaty, within two days of its signing. Arthur Lee's secretary was a British agent, also Silas Deane's employee, a Maryland sailor, Joseph Hynson, who, in France, secured for Britain important American dispatches to Congress at Philadelphia. The American wife of the first British Commander-in-Chief, Thomas Gage, was suspected of spying for the rebels and betraying vital military plans. In Holland, in 1779, Franklin's secret orders to Paul Jones to convey arms and timber to America were sold to the British ambassador and to Dutch newspapers, ruining the enterprise and forcing Jones to remind the commissioners that all such orders should be confided to the captain alone. 'On no other condition will I ever undertake the chief command, and when I do not command in chief, I have no desire to be in the secret.' Spies betrayed the date of his departure to France on *Ariel*, ensuring, though vainly, British frigates waiting to trap him in the Delaware; and at Portsmouth, Virginia, at his own expense, he had to safeguard the ship from spies and thieves.

To judge past values by the present can only mislead. Eighteenth-century perceptions were casual in financial matters and, unless over-exorbitant, tolerant of others' failings, if only to protect their own. If people were perfect there would be less history, more stagnation. Perfection was the weakness of Eden. Yesterday's perks are tomorrow's sleaze. On a British intelligence file was 'Number 72', cipher of Benjamin Franklin, allegedly used for his wartime dealings with London.

Richard Deacon, British authority on secret service, wrote in 1978:

'There is something about Franklin which makes even the most objective of historians bend his head in a reverence which sometimes blinds him to the truth. More than Washington, more than Alexander Hamilton, both of whom are now seen to have feet of clay, Franklin holds a kind of secular beatitude in the minds of American historians. Yet the question must he asked, shocking though it may sound, was Benjamin Franklin a secret British agent?'

Deacon, whom one hesitates to question, implies Franklin had conflicting traits: reminders of Talleyrand, Milton, Isaac Newton, William Blake, Pierre Laval and the more successful type of medieval Pope. Certainly, Franklin was enigmatic. Arthur Lee, John Adams and Thomas Jefferson reported his assistant, Bancroft, for disloyalty but Franklin always defended him. British Museum papers involving Joseph Hynson suggest that 'Franklin passed on to London information about sailing dates, shipments and supplies to America, and details of cargoes. This act of crass stupidity, if not of downright treachery, caused great losses in American ships and cargoes.'

Hindsight can illuminate, yet be unimaginative in recalling the historical situation, the flavour of dead men's thoughts and motives. Like most of his colleagues in early stages of the war, Franklin would at least have wished to protect himself against probable American defeat and have availed himself of massive and profitable secret information. Deacon interprets him as a 'tool of the British'. Perhaps. Or possibly Franklin wished not only to insure himself but America, by investing in an alternative future in which the defeated colonists would be reconciled to a strong and conservative Britain, rather than to a France weakly governed, even tottering, a condition which he witnessed daily. If he actually was treacherous, this might have been more a betrayal of Versailles; Deacon does reveal that he gave London 'all manner of information concerning France and Spain'. Indisputably, he was wily and self-protective; he may have foreseen an Anglo–American Atlantic Alliance or Commonwealth; might, with the conceit of a celebrity and instructor of western society, have regarded himself as a philosophical arbiter, another citizen of the world, above mere nationality and loftily immune from sordid wrangles, who could fuse commendable profits with moral platitudes, a stance easily misunderstood by lesser minds but in solid Puritan tradition.

Lafayette would see himself with a similar attitude, though in a spirit less mercantile, more chivalrous, striving to balance Crown and Reform under a banner wielded by himself which, in fact, proved mostly invisible, woven with archaic devices in a faded language, untranslatable to those who lustily applauded The Declaration of the Rights of Man, and desiring not only Reform but Revolution.

Throughout, Britain was striving to blockade America, despite commitments in the Pacific and Indian Oceans and the Mediterranean, as well as in the home waters, so that the French squadron's safe arrival in New England was comparable to the American troops in France in 1917. France had objectives far from the altruistic. The Seven Years' War had lost French Canada, Louisiana, Minorca, Senegal and several West Indian islands to Britain, and could be recovered despite the exorbitant costs.

In 1778 France thought itself superior to Britain in shipbuilding and naval theorists, though inferior in guns. Admiral de Suffren was undefeated in the Indian Ocean, though never defeating Admiral Hughes; de Grasse could defy Hood in the Atlantic, though finally outfought by Rodney. The Spanish fleet, reflecting an unproductive aristocracy and sagging empire, possessed numbers, officers in plenty, but limited power, though trusting that Britain and America would exhaust each other; the government was hopeful of regaining Florida and its Caribbean trade monopolies. Washington and Franklin judged that, with Bourbons ruling both Spain and France, a Franco–Spanish–American coalition could withstand even almighty Britain, could the monarchs condescend to declare war. Holland, with her fine naval tradition, but weakened by wars with Britain, remained sullenly neutral, and only a British defeat would encourage further confrontation with the island power. At the Texel, in 1779, Paul Jones noted, in his perpetual sermon, that neglect of its navy could rot a great nation.

The Great Power navies possessed contrasting strategic schools. The English *Fighting Instructions* in 1653 had attempted to co-ordinate a battle fleet within a regular line of attack, strung out to face the enemy's equivalent, each vessel engaging its opposite. Ships of the Line. Intended to discipline the old, haphazard dogfights, the *Instructions* had ossified into an inflexible rule, discouraging individual initiative from the daring, the exceptional, the bloody-minded. SE Morison quotes a French summary of a typical naval conflict: 'One manoeuvres, one encounters, one fires cannon; then each fleet retires. And the ocean is as salt as ever.' Cautious indecision as well as technical inadequacy underlay Graves's failure in

Chesapeake Bay, and failure to assist Burgoyne at Saratoga. Similarly, d'Orvilliers for France, Keppel for Britain, holding too tight on accepted rules, fought a ludicrous stalemate, the battle of Ushant.

New men were challenging the *Fighting Instructions* by encouraging and demonstrating individual enterprise and mobility, rather than a nicely symmetrical battle line. They preferred *General Chase*, which restored impetus, courage, risk, by allowing individual ships to break line to assail chosen targets. This rendered battles more fluid and, if successful, more decisive. Breakaway forays by self-assured, dynamic commanders could excite the entire force into concerted, go-ahead action. Thus Hawke had won Quiberon Bay in 1759; St Vincent, off Quebec, had captured a French warship without casualties, and with only two black eyes – for himself; at the Nile, Nelson, on tactics pioneered by Rodney at the Saints, risked court-martial by anticipating his admiral's orders and, on intuition and clear judgement, shipped inshore of the French and disrupted them. His still unorthodox pulling out of the line gained the day off Cape St Vincent, and Trafalgar was won by his controversial double-line attack on the Franco–Spanish line which would have entailed disgrace had he failed.

Despite his minute resources, John Paul Jones was bound by no hidebound admiralty or petty regulations. He learnt little from manuals, nothing from superiors, but much from the sea itself. He was swift to detect others' mistakes, could switch course for an apparent feint, inveigling a slower craft into the correct tactic, then wreck it by adroit return to his original path, catching the enemy broadside. Or he might approach head on, timing his swerve exactly, thus winning his guns the advantage. Exactitude was always his demand; in steering, signalling, marksmanship and obedience. In strategic novelties, tactical versatility, and fullest exploitation of poor resources, no American surpassed him. In a new and struggling nation largely sustained by French credit and British ineptitude, he must always use the wit of surprise and courage, against numbers, tradition and wealth. Redress of imbalance of inferior vessels needed nerve and, to repeat, timing, that of a great actor or games player. In direct assault, he could fill a single ship with the power of a squadron, so that Melville could write in *Israel Potter*: 'with the impunity of a Levanter, Paul skimmed his craft in the landlocked heart of the supreme naval power of the earth; a torpedo-eel unknowingly swallowed by Britain in a drought of old ocean, and making sad havoc of her vitals.'

7

Liberty and Human Dignity

A Man who aspires to Highest Rank must perform Deeds of Superior Merit.

John Paul Jones

My Roses in this world have not been without a superfluity of thorns.

John Paul Jones

Seldom has daring been more strangely coupled with octogenarian prudence than in many of the predatory enterprises of Paul. It is this combination of apparent incompatibilities which ranks him among extraordinary warriors.

Herman Melville,
The Coming Storm, *c*. 1888

Where's Commander All-a-Tanto?
Where's Orlop Bob swinging up from below?
Where's Rhyming Ned? Has he spun his last Canto?
Where's Jewsharp Jim? Where's Rigadoon Joe?

Herman Melville,
Bridegroom Dick, 1888

For John Paul Jones, war was personal opportunity and professional challenge. His prospects were sound. Work would be offered, and the renegade killer and cool table guest would have no time to study female cosmetics and bath habits. Although still young, he knew all sides of the service – administration, training, strategy, arms – and let others know that he did. Bumptiousness procures no popularity but can sometimes succeed. Already, urged by serving or retired officers, with Jones himself among the loudest, the Marine Committee was planning to build thirteen warships, and to buy, reconstruct and arm whatever else was available.

He was offered command of the sloop, *Providence*, and angrily refused, professing ignorance of so small a craft. By refusing this, and later the even smaller *Ely*, he forfeited some seniority, always rejecting the justice of this, but maintained his right of choice. Finally, in December 1775, he accepted a commission of first lieutenant, under Captain Dudley Saltonstall, of the much larger *Alfred*, of 30 guns. In Saltonstall's absence, but watched by Commodore Hopkins himself, with *Alfred* dressed overall, to music and salutes, Paul Jones was, to his schoolboy satisfaction, claimed to be first to hoist the revolutionary Grand Union flag. In January, *Alfred* sailed into the Caribbean in a squadron led by Hopkins, as part of Washington's strategy of using privateers, the Continental Navy, and ships of individual coastal states to capture British stores from the islands and generally harass British vessels and possessions. There followed relatively easy seizure of guns and goods at Nassau, together with the British governor, but Paul Jones's personal opportunity was delayed until 5 April when, off Block Island, the squadron, with himself to the fore, severely damaged HMS *Glasgow*. This was greeted on shore as a fierce American victory though, in vigorous counterattack, the Britisher escaped. While Hopkins retained all prizes, to be distributed after his own share, the largest, *Glasgow*'s escape eventually injured his own standing, and caused two courts-martial, on both of which Paul Jones sat. He doubtless sat with some complacency, for he had discharged *Alfred*'s lower-deck cannon balls with force and accuracy and was certain that, had he been in overall command unhampered by Hopkins's caution, he would have captured *Glasgow* with some ease. As it was, he gained prize money and a renewed offer of *Providence*, with 70 men, apparently 'spirited'. This time, he accepted and, brashly, perkily, incisively, began haranguing Committee seniors – Hewes, Morris, John Jay and John Hancock – listing deficiencies, suggesting remedies, prescribing new regulations. Fretting for action, he declared that the war could be won, if only men and ships were inspired into total resolution, with what Danton was to thrill Revolutionary France – his clarion call, 'Audacity, more Audacity, always Audacity.' Indeed, such impatience irked the easy-going Esek Hopkins, now 70, and alarmed those unable to shed well-bred or pragmatic respect for Britain and, with many holding investments there, hesitating to offend the mother country too grossly. Jones, with no well-bred respect and with lost investments, could afford to be contemptuous: 'The affairs of America cry haste, and speed must answer them.'

In August he received his first independent American command, 'temporary captain' of little *Providence* with twelve guns. His success was immediate; he evaded the Atlantic blockade by dexterous manoeuvres to convoy supply ships between ports then, free ranging further, he captured eight prizes off Bermuda and destroyed ships anchored in a Canadian harbour. His men were captivated by the 'saucy manner' by which he out-sailed, out-thought such superior British warships as *Solebay* and *Milford*, off Nova Scotia, with teasing mastery of sail, virtuoso judging of distances, eluding, chasing, sometimes bemusing by art or semblance or both, while establishing a handsome position for onslaught by his few gunners. This was notable against *Milford*, a 28-gun frigate, crippling it, but not fatally.

In October he returned, with a row of enemy ships, stores of military clothing, arms, tools and a logbook filled with accounts of fights and landings which, so essential for home morale, proclaimed American valour routing Britain on her privileged territory, the sea. He had begun an American naval style, the humour of conflict; swiftness to exploit unexpected turns in battle; the shifts of current, wind, light, and mist, each giving chances to tilt his angle of attack; confuse, then rake the enemy from the unexpected. However cluttered with grievances and dislikes, in action his mind immediately pared down situations to their essence, perceived the simplest solution, then applied it. He was adept at slanting athwart his opponent, evading counterfire, while delivering his own, like a tennis player intervening with volleys precisely angled, finally conclusive. Even when subordinate to Hopkins and Saltonstall, he had revealed a flair for attack based upon methodical gunnery. Against *Glasgow*, 'I formed an Exercise and trained the men so well to the great guns in the *Alfred* that they went thro' the motions of Broadsides and rounds as Exactly as Soldiers generally perform the manual Exercises.'

William J Norton (1954) is understanding:

His habits in battle followed a pattern. First, instead of pounding holes in the enemy's hull, his early cannonading was designed to destroy the rigging, the masts and spars, in order to make the enemy unmanageable. Second, he posted as many musketeers as possible in his own rigging, with a view to picking off the gunners and officers in the enemy's ship so as to make him impotent. And last, as he strove to fight at close quarters and tried always to set himself to grapple a superior vessel, and board her where his men, fired by his own flaming intrepidity, would be all-conquering.

Like Bonaparte, Jones cherished his guns, and included one when devising his armorial crest. Now, with his flashing batteries, he appeared invincible, though David Saville Muzzey, in *A Patriotic History of Our Time* (1950), must have exaggerated in crediting him with capturing or destroying over 300 British ships. Such reports, nevertheless, reached not only America but Britain, conveying an enflamed image of rebel enterprise and menace. On British streets, ballad-mongers were already creating a legend.

> Come each loyal Briton of Courage so bold,
> As annals can show you would not be controlled,
> It vexes my patience, I'm sure night and day,
> To think how that traitor Paul Jones got away.
> Derry-down, down hey! Derry down!

Once a commander, he could more easily flaunt his opinions, careless of bruising those of others. Washington certainly agreed with his conviction that lack of a navy would prevent the republic assuming true place among the world monarchies. In 1781, the future president was writing to Lafayette: 'Without a decisive naval force we can do nothing definite. And with it, everything honorable and glorious.'

Paul Jones was already in open quarrel with Esek Hopkins, accusing him of inadequate support, and especially of niggardly pursuit of deserters to a privateer, followed by an unsuccessful action against him by the owners. Jones's tone was usually provocative, to such as Hopkins, and the more galling because his complaint was generally sound. 'Be the Consequence what it will, I glory in having been the first who has broke through the shameful Abuses which have been too long practised upon the Navy by mercenaries whose governing principle has been that of self-interest.'

Always that delight in 'the first'. How far he himself was a mercenary is unanswerable. Indisputable, however, was that his cocksureness could be justified only by success. It continued. October 1776 saw him as full captain of *Alfred*, 30 guns, 300 men, a promotion guaranteeing his allegiance, though by now it could not have been doubted. He was given unrealistic instructions to set out with *Hampden* and *Providence*, to raid New Providence in the Bahamas, attack British supply ships on the Quebec run, raid Nova Scotia and rescue American prisoners virtually enslaved in Cape Breton coal mines, and to cut off British ships assisting General Lord Howe at New York. He was fitfully assisted by other ships – *Columbus, Andrew*

Dorio, Cabot, Hornet, Wash and *Fly* – contributing to his command an extra 88 guns and some 800 men. Captain Hacker, on *Hampden*, hit a rock, causing the squadron's return for repairs, Jones's caustic report further exacerbating Hopkins, who had always favoured Hacker. On 2 November, the expedition resumed, though without the damaged *Hampden*, Hacker transferring to *Providence*, only to desert, from cowardice induced by storms. As for Paul Jones, winter seas exhilarated him, and he gained Cape Breton, only to find that most Americans had already deserted to the British. November ice prevented a raid, itself no longer important, but a second descent, on Canso, enabled him to destroy more shipping, warehouses and fisheries. Gleefully cruising at his own will, he sunk, captured or savaged merchantmen, small warships, colliers and a British privateer. Then, wracked by storm, he was pursued by his former adversary, *Milford*, with her superior speed and more numerous guns, while he was slowed by having to guard an array of prizes. On his mettle when challenged, he repeated his ruses of deceptive signals, agile twists, securing escape with all prizes save one, which, to his fury, the officers surrendered, a familiar practice involving bribery, timidity, malice and self-interest shared with the enemy.

The largest prize crammed with military supplies he was determined to retain at all costs, though a new opponent threatened to block him. This was *Mellish*, a heavily armed merchantman conveying not only soldiers and marines but winter clothing for Burgoyne's army trapped at Saratoga. In a short but strenuous struggle, *Mellish* was overcome, a feat which, in boastful reports, further quickened American self-confidence, while confirming the trust of Morris and Hewes in their Scottish protégé.

This trust was needed for there at once occurred a development that aggrieved him for years. Congress issued its ranking list of 24 captains commissioned for the Continental Navy, on which he, Jones, Captain John Paul Jones, was stationed, not first, not second, but eighteenth, beneath even Hoysted Hacker, who had endangered an enterprise through incompetence and, at second attempt, had so cravenly fled. Here was blatant favouritism, rampant influence, corruption at its most flaming.

Rank mattered, a step on the ladder: meritocracy alone could guarantee personal and national survival. Always aggrieved, on the other side of the counter, he protested to Morris, browbeat Hancock, ignored the Dignity of Human Nature. Yet, probably no insult had been intended. Hewes had been absent, Paul Jones had no political base within state factions and little official standing. He was still an outsider with unproven claims to a respectable past and unquestioned allegiance. He was more well known for being combative, intolerant, disrespectful, often intolerable. No less than George Washington was sympathising with homeborn Americans having newcomers put over them, 'whose merit probably is not equal to their own, but whose effrontery will take no denial'.

The only one in step, Paul Jones considered he had proved his merit, without much assistance from the natives, and *Mellish*, safely in dock, was there as evidence. Effrontery was necessary for any 'tarpaulin captain', and to see himself as others saw him would be giving them benefit of too many doubts. More important, he saw himself very clearly and unmistakeably, and he liked what he saw.

The Naval List was insulting: nevertheless, like many Scots and Americans, and like a Cochrane, TE Lawrence, like Orde Wingate, he was usually able to regard rebuffs as moral victories: the art of life, if not the purpose of life, was in transforming loss into capital. After an interval for invective and recrimination, his lowly rating would renew his ambition and, undeterred, he continued with his proposals, demands, tactical flatteries and garish wishful thinking. While acknowledging the performances of a Manley, Biddle, Wickes and Barry, he saw nothing in them to impair the stature of his own.

A contemporary, gifted, often brilliant, dissatisfied with what he considered official slights, angered by tardy promotion and the lack of downright hatred for Britain, and by vindictive accusations of financial irregularities – though never from Washington – was the traitor, Benedict Arnold.

The Marine Committee, when roused from political intrigue and money shortages, recognised that war demanded the skills of a John Barry, Joshua Barney, even of the abrasive Paul Jones, rather than of the inept Hackers and Nicholsons, and was about to dismiss Esek Hopkins. Momentarily, however, all attention was on Saratoga, naval affairs were in a lull. Jones was again unemployed, though richer, and at last with a name, although he had to pay off *Alfred*'s crew from his own pocket, and would not be reimbursed for nearly seven years.

In questions of payments, prize money, recruitment, his methods could be legally dubious but, without them, *Providence*, *Alfred*, *Ranger*, *Bonhomme Richard* and *Ariel* would all have remained in port. Often very publicly, he would scour his conscience over such matters, invariably discovering that he had behaved perfectly.

Morris, Hewes, even Hopkins, were asking him to wait, promising important work which seemed never to come. He made plans, they collapsed; he wrote long, sometimes over-elaborate letters, replies were vague, sometimes never written, sometimes perhaps stolen. Then, in life's abrupt exchanges, he resurfaced, all confidence restored. In June 1777, Congress formally replaced the Grand Union flag, with its small Union Jack, by the Stars and Stripes, symbol of absolute sovereignty, and appointed Captain John Paul Jones to mount it on the new, though unfinished sloop *Ranger*, eighteen guns, with splendid directions: 'We shall not limit you to any particular cruising station, but leave you at large to search for yourself where the greatest chances of success presents.'

Once again, this was the mission he most relished, exactly suiting his independent temperament and chosen needs, even though little had yet occurred in his new career without accident, delay or hostility. He may, or may not, have suspected that Congress's motives were ambiguous. The inescapable duo, Sam Adams and Arthur Lee, probably hoped he would never return, others might have welcome respite from his unremitting attention to their own duties.

No matter. *Ranger* was unfinished; so much the better, he could the more expertly complete it himself. His appointment had been contested. Excellent. The chance for extra gratification in proving others wrong.

The proof would be neither headstrong nor mere bombast. He could see that America, still without fighting allies, would never overcome the Hoods, Rodneys and Jervises, by random privateering and the flourishes of a novice navy. His message never altered: it was repetitive, maddening, accurate; summed up in 1780:

'It is absolutely necessary to destroy the Foreign Commerce of the English, especially their Trade to the Baltic, from whence they draw all the Supplies for their Marine. It is equally necessary to alarm their Coasts, not only in the Colonies abroad, but even in their Islands at home. These things will distress and distract the Enemy much more than many Battles between Fleets of equal force.'

He also recognised that, whatever the British administrative deficiencies, there was always what Walt Whitman afterwards called 'the surly English pluck'. Against this, America must bang down, as if upon nerves, the smaller hinges upon which the British mechanism turned, reproducing in miniature the strategy by which Lord Chatham had so lately won an Empire.

With so much of John Paul's private life and personality obscure, cryptic or disfigured by legend, poets and novelists have attempted to flesh him out. The 'other' Winston Churchill, the American novelist (1871–1947), in *Richard Carvel* (1899) offers a glimpse of 'Captain John Paul' at this period:

'But a navy must be organised, sir. It must be a unit,' objected Mr Carroll, 'and you would not for many years have force enough, or discipline enough, to meet England's navy.'

'And I would never meet it, sir,' he replied instantly, 'that would be the height of folly. I would divide our forces into small, swift-sailing squadrons, of strength sufficient to repel his cruisers. And I would carry the war straight into his unprotected ports of trade. I can name a score of such defenceless places, and I know every shoal of their harbours. For example, Whitehaven might be entered. That is a town of fifty thousand inhabitants. The fleet of merchantmen might with the greatest ease be destroyed, a contribution levied, and Ireland's coal cut off for a winter. The whole of the shipping might be swept out of the Clyde. Newcastle is another likely place, and in almost any of the Irish ports valuable vessels may be found. The Baltic and West Indian fleets are to be intercepted. I have reflected on these matters for years, gentlemen. They are perfectly feasible. And I'll warrant you cannot conceive the havoc and consternation their fulfilment will spread in England.'

If that divine power of genius ever made itself felt, 'twas on that May evening, at candle-light, in the Annapolis Coffee House. With my own eyes I witnessed two able and cautious statesmen of a cautious province thrilled to the pitch of enthusiasm by this strange young man of eight and twenty.

8

Paris and Whitehaven

I had no fear but the sea was clear as far as a sail might fare,
Till I met with a lime-washed Yankee brig that rode off Finisterre,
There were canvas blinds to his bow-gun parts to screen the weight he bore,
And the signals ran for a merchantman from Sandy Hook to the Nore.
He would not fly the Rover's flag – the bloody or the black,
But now he floated the Gridiron and now he floated the Jack.
He spoke of the Law as he crimped my crew – he swore it was only a loan;
But when I would ask for my own again, he swore it was none of my own.

Rudyard Kipling
The Rhyme of the Three Captains, 1890

> He came to Selkirk Hall
> Did he not? Did he not?
> And stole Rings and Jewels all,
> Did he not?
> Robbed the Plate and Jewels all
> Which did his Conscience call,
> Did it not?

Anon

Not until October 1777 could *Ranger* sail, and Paul Jones spent long weeks disputing with the New Hampshire naval agent, Colonel John Langdon, who was also an important politician and businessman, hitherto responsible for building and equipping the ship and partly responsible for choosing its officers. With his impulse to scorn the work of others, Jones demanded modifications here, redesigns there, better sails, extra gear, tougher nails and screws, all costs disregarded. Poorly funded by the indigent Marine Committee, Langdon had duties elsewhere, and was considered dilatory where his private interests were less involved. He did find time to insist on the appointment as first lieutenant of Thomas Simpson. His qualifications? These were considerable, though, to Paul Jones, offensive. An older man, without fighting experience, he was nevertheless a cousin of the important administrator, John Hancock, also cousin of the influential New Hampshire dignitary, John Wendell and, as a tidy bonus, brother-in-law to none less than Colonel John Langdon.

Outvoiced, Jones was allowed the baser toils of collecting the non-commissioned crew. By smoothness, quick talk and ambiguous promises, by his glowing reputation, he mustered a quorum for which, given his nature, would be an eventful but hazardous venture.

Nothing is ever certain: what should happen, often does not, the inevitable can fail to occur. Unexpectedly, Paul Jones's happy marauding prospects collapsed, for, on 17 October 1777, at Saratoga, Lord Burgoyny surrendered to the American field-commanders, Daniel Morgan and Benedict Arnold, though the nominal victor was the gifted, if morally dubious General Gates, who secreted hopes of supplanting George Washington.

Saratoga was briefly offset by Admiral Lord Richard Howe's capture of Philadelphia, crucial for the colonists. Congress was forced to retreat to New York with Washington left to a gloomy and painful winter at Valley Forge, the British gaily celebrating in Philadelphia, the rebels' abandoned capital. During the Valley Forge ordeal, Washington was frequently abused for Fabian caution: politicians, venal, uninformed, partisan, or quietly honest, could mistake sensible tactics for irresolution or indecision, too often judging their leader by themselves. They were shortsighted when urging his replacement by the brilliant but erratic Gate, whose political gifts were negligible. Washington, having to manage not only an army but a government, possessed the purposeful, unspectacular stamina of the long-distance runner. In the field, he had to stimulate and discipline a few regulars and state militia, many roughnecks of uncertain dispositions, volunteer, amateurs, foreign idealists and adventurers and a number of drifters. The previous year he had informed Congress that to rely on militia was assuredly to rest upon a broken staff.

The British defeat at Saratoga was thus a thrilling blaze when Republican fortunes were at low tide. Disobeying Washington, General Charles Lee, acting on his own, had been captured by the British, with whom he had been treacherously corresponding. He subsequently benefited from an exchange of prisoners.

Underground conspiracies against Washington continued and desertions were plentiful, scores of New Jersey soldiers accepting offers of a royal Pardon. Tom Paine was writing *The Crisis* in camp at Valley Forge with Washington. During the dire winter of 1777, only Washington's skills in handling forces depleted by sickness, capture, desertion and of dwindling morale, coupled with British mistakes and mental lethargy, culminating at Saratoga, averted probable defeat.

Congress had now to exploit the victory at home and abroad. The news must reach France with all speed, giving impetus to Franklin's diplomatic proddings. Surely King Louis would cease hesitating, and declare for French entry into the war, probably accompanied by Spain? Great Britain seemed to be at bay. Holland might follow. Moreover, the Scandinavian governments were restless, grudging British naval superiority and arrogance. Beaumarchais's supplies continued to dodge the British blockade.

The obvious messenger to France was the fearless, always eager to serve, and perhaps expendable John Paul Jones. Another American ship was already bound for Europe, setting him a challenge. His prospects of free-wheeling aggression must be postponed but he already had half-promises across the Atlantic; a warship, the frigate *L'Indienne* was being built in Holland, secretly financed by France, and promised to America. Apparently, he might be its captain.

Behind his back, Congressmen may well have been winking, from faces ashine with jocular complacency. Once in France, responsibility for the rumbustious captain would pass to Franklin, Deane and Lee, with France persuaded to foot the bills. Paul Jones, hastening his preparations, would at least understand that, in his absence, he would need his few supporters: Morris, Hewes, Jefferson and, more remotely, the commander-in-chief.

Despite interferences, quarrels, obstructions and non-deliveries, *Ranger* was ready by 1 November 1777, leaving for Scotland's traditional ally. Jones crossed the Atlantic by 2 December, racing through all weathers and a wild squall but was delayed by his failure to resist halting to fight and capture two British brigantines. This ensured that, by a few hours, Captain JC Austin beat him, who so loved to be first, to Nantes, with the news of Saratoga.

No matter. He had the exciting onus of driving to Paris to meet the commissioners, to convey Congress's needs, to assess the personalities American and French and relay British defeat to the volatile streets. He had also to probe for any details of his promised campaign, preferably not on *Ranger* but on the larger *L'Indienne*, strongly manned by 36 eighteen-pounders. One of the negotiators was the smiling Dutch nobleman, Prince

Charles de Nassau-Siegen, whom Jones, in relative amiability, was to call 'almost a sailor'.

The prince was sophisticated in the intrigues which passed for diplomacy, spoke several languages, was at ease in foreign courts, and claimed to have seduced the Queen of Tahiti, a feat which amused his intimate, Prince Potemkin, and to which Jones, while professing scepticism, might not have been indifferent. An agile global traveller, the Dutchman was always in need of ready money, and his larger exploits never quite succeeded; he failed to acquire an African kingdom, to capture Jersey, and secure the noisy but futile Franco–Spanish assault on Gibraltar.

With Holland still neutral and wishing to gratify France without offending Britain, *L'Indienne*'s future remained indeterminate. However, Jones quickly established a cordiality with Franklin sufficient to arouse suspicion from Deane and Lee. He also met John Adams, now assisting Franklin's attempts to entice France to begin hostilities against Britain.

Adams (1735–1826) was Washington's successor as president. He was no grandee like Jefferson, but a small landowner and lawyer, vain but public-spirited, fair-minded, as ready to defend British soldiers shooting at Boston rioters as to protest against British taxes. Like Cromwell, like Washington, he was respected but scarcely renowned until the critical moment, the challenge of a cause he first vigorously inspected, then deemed righteous. He was incorruptible, more so than Robespierre, who was corrupted by power and self-delusion: he was unwavering in his belief in American independence and the necessity for loyalty to the supreme commander.

Adams's assessment of Paul Jones was cooler than Abigail's: 'A smooth, plausible and rather capable adventurer' with a postscript, 'of a ferocious temper'. He also suspected that he had been enlisted by Franklin in an intrigue against himself. Jones's respect for him was tepid: 'A wicked and conceited upstart.'

Vigorous, widely read, a no-nonsense counterpart of a Lady Mary Wortley Montague or Lady Emily Eden, Abigail was of the type praised in Alexis de Tocqueville's *Democracy in America* (1835–40), for 'happy boldness' of thought and language, seldom fooled by the specious and meretricious, and who could see that the greatness of many 'heroes' consisted merely in the greatness of the opportunities they missed, like Byron's estimate of Wellington. In *Don Juan* (1821) he castigated 'Villainton':

Never had mortal man such opportunity, except Napoleon, or abused it more.

Dealing with the commissioners Jones found less satisfying than dining at the Adams's table, and their own relations were frayed by rumours of Franklin and Bancroft profiting on the markets by early news of Saratoga.

Of the French outside the Versailles parade of silken knee-breeches, embroidered belts, satin coats and curled, glistening perukes, the most important for Paul Jones were Sartine, the Marine Minister, and his all-purpose agent or accomplice, Le Ray de Chaumont. On advice generally believed to have come from Franklin, who had once called women 'sleeping dictionaries', a term inconcise but scarcely designed to flatter, Paul Jones was soon paying court to Madame de Chaumont. Anxious for regular access to her husband, he employed the charm he reserved for ladies, but may have over-estimated her influence.

A third and more curious Frenchman, also with an attractive wife, was the king's cousin, the Duke of Chartres, son of the Duke of Orleans. Rated, if only by himself, as a naval expert, Chartres was still scheming for the supreme command, through lineage and influence exploited at its most blatant, though the duke was soon removed from Paul Jones's attentions in unfortunate circumstances.

Jones was optimistic. Saratoga must have convinced Louis and his Foreign Office of the decadence, even decrepitude, of the great enemy. The London newspapers were declaring as much, the opposition rejoicing. The French war party was ascendant and, despite London's outcries, Dorset's reproaches and concern for the queen, French loans and supplies to the rebels increased monthly. The actual declaration of war was delayed only by protracted negotiations with Spain and the nervous Dutch. Beaumarchais was delighted with his own efforts. 'The success of the Americans, reducing our rivals to nothing more than a second-rate power, puts us back in the front rank, and gives us long preponderance over Europe.'

Such were general expectations, the British goose was being methodically cooked, the golden eggs were ranged for all hands that could dare a fight. Paul Jones was determined to have place at the table, within the chatter and boasts. He would not, though, have a place on *L'Indienne*. Fed by spies' reports, the British Foreign Office announced that were Holland to allow its deliverance to France for lease to America, this would breach Dutch neutrality and give Britain a legitimate excuse for war.

Holland shrank from this but, on 8 February 1778, gently but persistently urged by Jefferson and Franklin, majestic France formally declared war on Great Britain, followed shortly by Spain. Holland continued to waver, but the Russian empress and the Scandinavians were envisaging a pact of armed neutrality, to resist the British arrogant right of search, to enforce its blockade of America. With the first Franco–Spanish victories, this might coalesce into direct warfare and a purposeful division of spoils.

A Gibbon might have gloomily murmured that Britain seemed threatened by perils, worse than those of 1066, reminiscent of AD 367, when Roman England was assailed on all sides, by Irish Scots, northern Picts, Scandinavians and Teutons, in a mysteriously organised, or possibly imaginary 'barbarian conspiracy'.

Here was what Chatham so dreaded: European and Latin American ports, protected by Spain and France, open to American commerce, British fleets outnumbered, the City bankrupted, Antwerp and Amsterdam regaining position, the Empire doomed.

Despite this glistening promise, Paul Jones had been enduring weeks of frustration, in which he had to coerce and appease, feed and sustain his ragamuffin following, uncertain of why they had come, uneasy about their future destination, and in a foreign land, lively but unwelcoming. Nevertheless, suspense and delay can, while mortifying the temper, intensify the will and Jones strenuously continued his efforts to convince French officials of his importance and skills, to spike the sceptics, diagnose and assess the disorders already apparent in France, while royalty continued a routine at Versailles that had begun to creak rather painfully.

In late January, indecision ended with the commissioners repeating that offer of a roving expedition, financed by Chaumont to follow his long-digested plan to harry British shipping and coast, provoking alarm and perhaps disturbances in England, Scotland and Ireland.

It could be done, and again he would not be first to enact it. Lambert Wickes and Henry Johnson had already dared British waters, setting the pace though accomplishing little. He must do more.

Whatever he did, it would be a sideshow, for Admiral d'Orvilliers and the Duke de Chartres were at work designing a full Franco–Spanish descent upon England. He could not thus expect any French officers, auxiliaries or French sailors of spirit to volunteer for an American captain of a puny ship, which was preparing for some amorphous project without guaranteed spoils. Denied *L'Indienne*, he must venture alone on *Ranger*, with its eighteen guns, though, always tenacious, he continued several years to intrigue, bargain, then merely hope for, the large, almost ideal vessel lying unused in Holland.

To exhibit his calibre, he confided to Silas Deane a daring plan, praised by the American naval historian, Admiral Mahan, for a French surprise attack on Lord Richard Howe's blockade of the Delaware, a lethal enterprise exploiting Howe's over-confidence and Jones's predilection to strike where least expected. Deane promptly submitted it to the king as if it were his own, receiving some affable remarks though nothing was done until Admiral d'Estaing's summer expedition, itself too late for likely success. Here, the Dignity of Human Nature and Philanthropy was missing in Deane's machinations and Jones's indignant responses.

More happily, Sartine confirmed *Ranger*'s cruise and, on terms advantageous to himself, Chaumont settled details of supplies, wages and prize money. Franklin was encouraging though the American seamen were suspicious. Most wished, not to adventure off enemy coasts within range of heavily armed British warships, but merely to return home, claiming, with some justice, that this was their legal due. The officers, led by Thomas Simpson, if not frankly mutinous, were apathetic, save for Edward Meijer, a Swedish volunteer. Only the chances of capturing prizes gave cohesion to a group of men at best unreliable. Paul Jones himself remained sanguine, writing to the Marine Committee that he had in mind several enterprises of some importance. Of these, he disclosed nothing further, either to the Committee or to his men.

Despite the Breton pirates, he would risk embarking from Brest. While France prepared for the glory of the Great Design, d'Orvilliers's grand invasion, *Ranger* left Nantes for Brest, disregarded, unescorted, to undertake plans known only to Jones and Franklin. At sea, on 14 February 1778, ever tenacious of rights, he three times insisted on French vessels giving the Stars and Stripes the most formal salute yet received in Europe. Another 'first'. The last, with guns, flags and eighteenth-century regalia, was delivered off Brest from the flagship of d'Orvilliers himself.

The ageing admiral received John Paul Jones on board with all honours and courtesies, offering support from himself and his colleague, de Castries. He also offered the protection of a French commission, to save Jones, if captured, from a British trial for treason. Doubtful in law, this was rejected, but d'Orvilliers's friendliness and outward respect gratified, indeed moved Jones, who was always responsive to official deference. Before rejoining *Ranger*, he spoke sadly of *L'Indienne*, which by now he regarded almost as his personal property, stolen by the greedy and treacherous.

In other ways, he was markedly dissatisfied, particularly in directives from America: 'If I have been instrumental in giving the American flag some Reputation and making it Respectable among European Nations, will you permit me to say that it is not because I have been honored by my Country either with proper means or proper Encouragement.'

He had then to pass several weeks, not outward bound, glory bound, but in convoying merchantmen between local ports and reporting any British movements. One more aggressive scheme, leaked to Britain by spies, perhaps by an officer, had to be abandoned, but in April he was free to experiment in wider seas. His intentions would now have been more pointed, for he was flying not Stars and Stripes but the Union Jack, and a Dutch ensign and, stacked below, were scores of British uniforms. To pose as an honest merchantman, with guns concealed almost to the moment of attack, was a ruse customary, if not knightly, and gratified the Scot's pawky humour.

To date, this was his most considerable venture. His status had improved, for he had now met personally French and American statesmen, officials, naval and military personalities. To associate with Franklin, be in correspondence with Lafayette, made him the *arriviste* who had arrived. Now he was taking risks barely appreciated by those who sought naval eminence without wetting their feet. He had always bitterly despised venal and conceited stay-at-homes and in this he was one with Washington who, after winter agonies, had spoken to Congress in a tone shared by many on active service. 'I can assure these gentlemen that it is much easier and less distressing to draw remonstrances in a comfortable room by a good fireside than to occupy a cold, bleak hill, and sleep under frost and snow without clothes or blankets.'

Jones's peril was not only that of battle and storm. Not only had he that murder charge still outstanding but, in 1776, London had ordained that American sailors captured in arms were traitors, pirates and felons and that soldiers, in some legal persiflage were merely rebels. This always rankled with Jones, in his eagerness to complain and resist. 'This Circumstance, more than any other, rendered me an avowed Enemy of Great Britain. Never before had History furnished the example of a People arrogant enough to assume sovereignty with such deliberate cruelty.'

To his officers, Simpson, Lunt, Meijer and the rest, he had soon to disclose some, though not all, of his intentions, in excess as they were of the others' expectations. The commissioners had given him leave to use his own judgement about how best to 'distress the Enemies of the United States'. In this he desired more than seizing easy prizes. Primarily, America must be established as a naval power. From this, he constantly repeated, all else must stem, at whatever cost. This credo he kept to himself: though sound, it would discourage those to whom sensational schemes promised sensational risks.

He needed to demonstrate, not only by personal valour but by objective analysis, that the vaunted British ships could be worsted in free fight. He furthermore desired to accomplish some resounding feat, 'to put an end, by one good fire in England, of shipping, to all the burnings in America.' He also planned to affect an equitable exchange of prisoners-of-war, to prevent Americans being consigned to fouled jails and brutal conditions.

As in so much else, he was not fair-minded, and would have known, as his two major biographers noted, that most American captives were from privateers, whom Washington had forbidden to be exchanged, yielding the greater advantage to Britain with its far larger able-bodied population. By agreement, British sailors, on release, could return to their fleet, American privateers only to their homes.

Ranger had now reached the Irish Sea, the captain speaking expansively though vaguely of lucrative prospects and the joys to be purchased when once British shores were reached. Fortunately, his flair continued. One merchantman was sunk off Carrickfergus, then several smaller ones. Another, with the gratifying name *Lord Chatham*, was captured, and Jones's cannonades scuttled an armed, inquisitive revenue vessel. Against actual invasion, some 8,000 Irish volunteers assembled, soon to be feared by London as a possible seditious nucleus. But he had no real quarrel with Ireland and, with dozens of British prisoners held below and with old associations astir, he was steering north, aiming at Whitehaven, so close to his family and neighbours. 'Every man,' Dr Johnson allowed, 'has a lurking wish to appear considerable in his native place.'

Beneath its cliffs, Whitehaven Bay, which had once served Agricola's Romans, had prospered on trade with the Isle of Man, Ireland and the New World, its quays bearing such telling names as Sugar Tongue and Lime Tongue. A year previously, it had lost four ships off the Solway to the intrepid Lambert Wickes but, with true English unconcern, had not prepared itself against further American intrusion. Lightning, it is said, erroneously, does not strike twice. Since Viking days, no invader had risked a landing.

Paul Jones, of course, had special memories of the town, where he himself was remembered as slaver, suspected smuggler and murderer, manic captain and now traitor to His Majesty.

The harbour, always crowded with shipping, was defended by guns on piers north and south, and by a small barracks. The guns would be loosely guarded; only the eastern English seaboard anticipated any attack, and that, not from madcap Americans but from the Franco–Spanish grand invasion. After sunset, they would probably be abandoned. Jones's plan had daring simplicity: a surprise night attack, a fire assault on those quiet, wooden masses, a British harbour in flames, the population terrorised, speedy escape by dawn, the world left wondering. Melville wrote: 'Whitehaven, the mining town, now about to be assaulted by a desperado, nursed like coal, in its vitals.'

By 19 April, adverse winds prevented access to the harbour. Flying British colours, *Ranger* lingered outside, evoking no alarm, even interest. Prisoners, willing, bribed, or coerced into being pilots, divulged that one ship sheltering from the wind was the warship *Drake*, with 20 guns.

After four days, the wind swung back behind *Ranger*, which Jones, by nightfall, had steered back to undefended Whitehaven harbour, *Drake* having gone, leaving it an open target, though what was easy on the surface might in practice be less so.

Paul Jones spent so much time waiting, bargaining, arguing that physical activity was always a downright necessity. The sea, conflict and leadership all purged his mind of frills, inessentials and imorbidity: action was freedom from forms, invoices, instructions and from prolonged tensions. To dare was sensation at its most primitive, the ballad world reaching exultation in raw, barely satiable appetite, though he thirsted, not for blood but for name, honour, to be gathered in the hot dance of life and spirit as he sailed at his own will, under the enemy's flag over the darkened sea.

Nevertheless, with England within gunshot, its merchant ships slumbering, he could issue no direct orders to fractious officers inclined to mutiny. Diplomacy was needed, to deal with those anxious not for glory or death, merely for safe return with bulging pockets. Captain though he was, he was backed by no long tradition that Rodney and Hood could manipulate. His sinkings off Ireland might already be known on shore, starting rumours and fears, and only a few days previously, after warnings from Meijer, now proved trustworthy, he had had to quell unrest at pistol point. At this instant, with all staked, he could only plead for volunteers.

Led by Simpson, a majority of officers confessed sickness, the rest remained sullen, convinced that behind them, out in the spring night, privateers would be amassing booty in bulk. Their own captain's plan promised little save probable capture, possible death. A Dumfries letter asserts that *Ranger* carried some 150 men: 'English, Scots, Americans, French, and smugglers who were acquainted with the country; one of those who landed was said to have lately been a waiter at a tavern in Kircudbright.'

A solitary harbour beam was unwelcome but Jones was now approaching a pier. Meijer at once joined him, then two more officers and 29 reluctant men – these he distributed in two small boats stacked with combustibles. In one, he headed through glimmering darkness, as Whitehaven remained soundless, its boats rocking by quays, its guns deserted. Unexpectedly, the wind turned around, the going slowed. This and ill temper threatened the raid, for dawn was aglow before they reached the stone steps.

If others hesitated, Jones did not. Ignoring mutters, pleas and threats, he must once more be first, the first United States officer to step armed on English soil. Leaving the Swede to guard the boats, he hurried one group down the south pier, ordering the other to the north, to torch as many ships as possible.

A small fort contained soldiers, but all were within, leaving no sentries. Jones reached a guardhouse, knocked the door open and, nervously followed, captured its inhabitants, then hastened on. Encouraged, his men arrested the lighthouse keeper with drawn knives while Jones himself spiked all 36 harbour guns. (A cannon, discovered in the sands in 1963, is now exhibited as one of these.) Beneath, the ships remained defenceless against the fire bombs.

But nothing was happening. The north flank was quiet and he soon discovered that he had been disobeyed. The men had broken open the nearest grog shop and gone no further. And an Irishman, David Freeman, a traitor, was off to rouse the town. Despite his own lot's renewed hesitation, Jones had time to set ablaze one ship, *Thompson*, vainly hoping that the fire would spread from hull to hull across the entire harbour. Several more ships were soon adrift, but most were saved. Jones wrote afterwards:

'The inhabitants began to gather in their thousands and individuals ran hastily towards me. I stood between them and the ship on fire, and ordered them to retire, which they did with Precipitation.'

It suggests a melodramatic tableau; the flames, fire-lit faces, a drawn sword or gun, the threats and cries, a stampede. But eight o'clock was sounding, shots were starting from streets and windows and the little force hastily clambered down to rejoin Meijer and the rest, few sober, Jones's mood ugly.

Back on *Ranger*, alone with Meijer, he discovered that his officers and men had not only disregarded his orders but had discussed abandoning him on shore, while they sailed away under Simpson, to privateer.

His situation was precarious, outnumbered by mutineers and with Whitehaven now alive with scared or angry Cumbrians to whom he was a proscribed traitor. His captaincy had been betrayed, his enterprise mocked, his life endangered. He was one to whom exposure to ridicule outweighed death itself. He was also John Paul Jones, in his own eyes incapable of being defeated by a Simpson, a mere politician's pet, who shrank from real war and the hard edges of life. He resumed the bridge, relied on smoothness to tame, though not to forgive, the crew, gave orders to sail and was, at last, rather too eagerly, obeyed.

He did not yet know the clamour he had aroused far beyond Whitehaven. Such a raid, magnified in the telling, had been unforeseen by King George, the Admiralty, the public, and by insurance syndicates whose rates promptly doubled. Not since a rare barbary raid, and Dutch ships in the Medway in 1667, had the nation been so affronted. Whitehaven, shivering from reports of Jones setting Liverpool in flames, began building expensive defences. In Cumberland, John Paul Jones was never forgotten; people still alive heard in childhood the excitement of his raid which, in August 1977, was re-enacted by two dramatic clubs. In local lore, girls, hearing his name, would 'rush to the arms of the nearest stranger', or, at undesired attentions, invoke the irresistible pirate, John Paul Jones. He had gone some way to confirm his pledge to Robert Morris: 'When an Enemy thinks a Design against the improbable, he can always be surprised and attacked with Advantage. It is true, I must run great risk; but no Gallant Action was ever performed without danger.'

Though Paul Jones surely never performed in a theatre, he never lost something theatrical in style and imagination.

Like a Lafayette, Landais, Nassau-Siegen, a Paul Jones survives by resilience, obstinacy and cunning, is ever brimming with new hopes, fresh plans. Alternatives always exist. Alone in the Solway, he devised a surprise, belonging more to the ballad than to Augustan rules: a project of blackmail by abduction, effective if not gentlemanly.

Though Kirkbean was closed to him, in reluctance to imperil his family, there remained the Selkirk's great house on St Mary Isle, on which so many childhood fantasies had centred. Wistful expectations, magnified by time, exaggerated the territorial grandeur, and the influence at court – actually negligible – of the bookish, exclusive earl. To kidnap the nobleman, parley as between equals, then ransom him for American seamen rotting in Portsmouth and Plymouth jails, attracted all that was humane, ambitious and snobbish in the gardener's son. It was understandable; even today, not all Americans instinctively shrink from earls.

Ranger's company must, despite the captain's reticence, have sensed more likely pickings than a few drinks in a Whitehaven cellar. When, in early morning, he mustered the ranks, *Ranger* was still outside the harbour, its identity muffled. He could win to his side only fourteen volunteers, two officers among them, Simpson himself consenting to join. These followed Jones into a cutter, sailing to shore with *Ranger* primed for instant departure, under a British flag.

Safely on land, unobserved, they hurried along paths familiar to Jones, into the wide Selkirk property. When halted by estate hands, with his usual hard wit and love of a ruse, Jones announced that he was a press-gang officer, leading a posse on behalf of His Majesty. This scared the Englishmen into spontaneous flight. The little expedition advanced through trees and gardens towards the mansion. They were, however, disappointed. The great Lord Selkirk was absent, the militia were far away, and the intruders found their weapons and ferocity suddenly absurd, to be brandished only against a pregnant countess breakfasting among her women.

Disconcerted but cool, Jones insisted that they all remained outside. He disdained to make war on 'the fair', less marketable than their lord and whose maltreatment would impugn his boasted Honour and Philanthropy.

The others, less detached, desired plunder, instant riches, if not rape. Their courage was marvellously kindled when, through windows, they saw the enemy lair, opulently furnished, luxuriant details open for looting. Jones ordered restraint, but they threatened him with violence so that, unsupported by Simpson and the other officer, he was forced to compromise. He refused to the leave the garden and push his way indoors; it was inglorious, unthinkable, that an American officer and gentleman should be reported throughout Britain as a blustering thief. He thus permitted the two officers to enter and commandeer, with utmost courtesy, the family silver.

They consented, obeying with surprising punctiliousness, an achievement of Paul Jones, which some historians, through lack of imagination, have sometimes under-estimated. Simpson could have very willingly shot him, releasing the rest to ransack the house with impunity. By killing a rebel, a virtual outlaw, Simpson must have believed that he obeyed British law. But the frightened ladies were blandly reassured and, while Paul Jones controlled the seamen outside, the silver was collected, a considerable haul, all else remaining undisturbed. Then the group re-formed, hastening back to the cutter and the safety of *Ranger*.

Lady Selkirk, inconsistent in her several accounts, wrote to Mr Craik that the people really behaved 'very civilly'.*

There does appear in Paul Jones some residue of the boy brooding outside the forbidden garden, the amateur gentleman scratching on the doors of the highborn. On 8 May 1778, back in Brest, he laboriously composed his letter to the countess, of which he made many copies, displayed in operatic manner to the great and powerful – or those who appeared to be.

In the letter, he disclaims personal desire to injure or plunder, while confessing surrender to his officers' demand for retaliation for the atrocities which the British and their German associates had, even in winter, robbed Americans of their farmyard stock, even to the last cow. Having ordered them to respectfully accept nothing but the silver, he pledges himself to eventually buy it back and restore it. He assures her that he wages 'no war with the Fair', is ambitious for her ladyship's esteem and friendship, begs a line from her hand to reassure him about his own men's behaviour and to inform him of any service he might render her in France.

This is very much how Paul Jones chose to see himself, considerable sincerity and hopefulness mixed with calculation and the sentimental humbug of the age, perhaps, though the language changes, of all ages. In his view, he had risked his neck against the British, in a just cause; had risked his back against his men, on behalf of civility and culture. Save for Meijer, he was quite alone in his beliefs and values, throughout the expedition, he was also, as his few friends must have realised, more emotional than he usually cared to reveal. Suppressed for long periods, his deeper feelings occasionally gushed out in extravagant self-indulgence:

'Tho' I have drawn my Sword in the present generous struggle for the Rights of Man, yet I am not in Arms as an American, nor am I in pursuit of Riches. My Fortune is liberal enough, having no Wife nor Family, and having lived long enough to know that Riches cannot ensure Happiness.'

To modern ears, much of this is platitudinous or hypocritical though it is fair to repeat that in everyday affairs, his concern and efforts for American prisoners remained undeviating throughout.

At this period he liked to style himself 'citizen of the world', a term fashionable in the Enlightenment, sometimes adopted by Goldsmith, Gibbon, Jefferson and Montesquieu. He uses a typical period strain of moral clichés, literary allusion, decent-minded rhetoric and special

---

*The full text is given on pp. 247–9.

pleading lip-service to civilisation perhaps, though lip-service can be better than no service:

> I profess myself a Citizen of the World, totally unfettered by the little distinctions of Climate or of Country which diminish the Benevolence of the Heart and set bounds to Philanthropy. Before this war began, I had, at any early time of life, withdrawn from the sea service in favour of calm Contemplation and Poetic Ease. I have sacrificed not only my favourite scheme of life, but the Softer Affections of the Heart; and my prospects of Domestic Happiness. I am ready to sacrifice life with cheerfulness if that Forfeiture could restore Peace and Goodwill among mankind.

He never admits that war can be a godsend to youngish males unsatisfactorily employed and discontented with domestic bliss. His unrealistic, even pathetic hopes of acceptance by the aristocratic caste, even that of the Selkirks and England, unctuously strive to convince the countess:

> As the Feelings of your Gentle Bosom cannot but be congenial with mine, let me entreat you, Madam, to use your Soft Persuasive Arts with your Husband (an influential Aristocrat) to endeavour to stop this Cruel and Destructive War in which Britain can never succeed. Heaven can never countenance the barbarous and unmanly practices of the Britons of America, which Savages would blush at; and which, if not discontinued, will soon be retaliated in Britain, by a justly enraged People.

This threat, he repeated almost identically, in the ransom demand he intended to deliver to Leith next year, as an alternative to destruction from the cannon of *Bonhomme Richard*.

In a dream of his own, he added: 'Should you fail in this (for I am persuaded you will attempt it, and who can resist the Power of such an Advocate?), your endeavours to effect a general exchange of Prisoners will be an Act of Humanity which will afford you Golden Feelings on a Death Bed.'

This prophecy was both tactless and unappealing. Unwilling to relish the reference to her death bed, the countess did not reply, contenting herself with vivid dispatches to friends in terms more vehement than those to Mr Craik: 'A great villain as ever was born, guilty of many crimes and several murders by ill-usage, was tried and condemned for one, escaped and followed a piratical life until he engaged with the Americans.'

The reply she left to the earl, though war conditions prevented Jones from receiving it. In it, Selkirk exercised the polite condescension of his breed towards underlings, suavely disdainful of Jones's attempted eloquence, denying his own influence with the king, doubting British atrocities, mentioning that home opinion blamed the colonists for 'the unusual and cruel practice complained of', then candidly rebuking the ill-judged policies of British ministers. He was dignified, forbearing and civil and without warmth:

> It was certainly fortunate both for Lady Selkirk and me, that I was from home, and it was also fortunate for you, sir, that your officers and men behaved well, for had any of my family suffered outrage, murder, or violence, no quarter of the globe should have secured you, nor even some of those under whose commission you act, from my vengeance. But, sir, I am happy that their welfare enables me to inform you that the orders you mention in your letter were punctually obeyed by your two officers and men, who in every respect behaved as well as could be expected on such an occasion...
>
> Your genteel offer, sir, of returning the plate is very polite, but at the same time neither Lady Selkirk nor I can think of accepting of it, as you must purchase it you say for that purpose, but if your delicacy makes you unwilling to keep that share of its value which as Captain you are entitled to, without purchasing, I would in that case wish that part to be given to those private men who were on the party, as an encouragement for their good behaviour. You, sir, are entitled to what is more honorable, viz: the praise of having your men under good discipline, which on all occasions I take care to make known...
>
> Your letter is wrote like a man who means well, and who wishes to be considered a man of honour. Your behaviour, then and since, has in so far as regarded my family been genteel, and though your intention in taking me was certainly absurd, yet as it was so from mistake I therefore will not allow myself to think with those people, that a man who professes honorable sentiments, and is acting under an honorable commission for what he thinks is supporting the rights of mankind, would for the sake of a pitiful ransom degrade himself to the low and vile character of a Barbary private, which would be

the case if these people were right in the opinion they give, but I chose to judge more favourably of you.

Privately, the serene patrician wrote with considerable fair-mindedness:

He is such an odd fellow, by what I hear of him, that it is not easy to know how to write to him, nor yet very proper to neglect answering him. He seems to he an enthusiast, absurd and ignorant of the springs and actions of our affairs...

If he is the man whom the people here believe him to be, he is both a dangerous and worthless fellow, said to have committed no less than three murders, and that in absconding from the West Indies after the last one, he fled to America, and so commenced heroic vindicator of the rights of mankind and officer of fine feelings. I have made my letter to him intolerably long, but I could not well help it, unless I had given him a very short answer, which might have made him burn my house at his next trip to these coasts; but we shall give the devil his due, he certainly, be he who he will, behaved well at my house, notwithstanding some plate was taken away. His letter was so long and so absurd that it has forced me to be very diffuse also and perhaps as absurd, to think of arguing with the captain of a privateer.

The episode always stayed with Jones. In the account he inserted in his memorial to Louis XVI, it had so enlarged that he described Lady Selkirk's invitation to dine with him after the raid. Precise truth was not in him, his imagination fed greedily on success and failure. He kept his promise about the silver, buying it from the men for some 600 dollars and having it returned after the war. *The Gazeteer* (1832) reported that the silver teapot, snatched from the breakfast table, still contained the original tea leaves, while offering no proofs. In a final letter to the earl, in February 1784, Paul Jones declared: 'As I have endeavoured to serve the Cause of Liberty through every stage of the American Revolution and sacrificed to it my Private Ease, a part of my Fortune, and some of my Blood, I could have no Selfish Motive in permitting my People to demand and carry off your Plate.'

This is characteristic, histrionic, calculated, with some self-deception yet with an urgency to shed accusations of common theft, the ungentlemanly action.

Selkirk wrote a second reply, shorter, courteous, again praising the sailors' extraordinary discipline ascribed wholly to Paul Jones, 'which I have mentioned to many people of fashion'. This, at least would have gratified Jones. In all, though, despite enterprise and prizes, the venture, initially considerable, seemed crumbling into farce. Armed intrusion on defenceless women, purloined silver, no grail of destiny but a useful teapot were no Saratoga. Washington, Lafayette and d'Orvilliers, need fear no eclipse. Coarse hilarity could follow the spectacle of doughty Americans not mastering British stalwarts but bargaining among themselves over cutlery and candlesticks. Hector, tamer of horses; Paul Jones, stealer of teaspoons! With sensitivity picked raw, he was isolated. Whitehaven had not been ravaged, its ships were mostly intact, the Earl of Selkirk roamed free.

Nevertheless, hindsight shows that SE Morison erred when delivering judgement that Paul Jones had made a fool of himself. Tories jeered, rivals chuckled, but most contemporaries did neither. A sensational advertisement had been won against odds for American daring; wild reports of landings, fire and roving made graphic propaganda. That a solitary American vessel could elude British warships, mock British defences, land unopposed, having scared Ireland and alarmed London, was a barely credible fillip to the colonists' morale, their will to persist and conquer. Not only this; it would further bolster Franco–Spanish enthusiasm for the grand invasion, the Great Design to crush Britain in the Channel, land an army and hearten Irish dissent.

History thrives not only on what people do, but on what they are thought to do. Shakespeare allows Rumour a speaking part in *Henry IV*. People to this day can model themselves on the imaginary or misunderstood, and the most influential heroes – Thor, Baldur, Orpheus, Hercules, Odysseus, Arthur, Robin Hood – may not have literally existed but, embalmed in myth and ballad, they encapsulate human desires, fears and wonder. Alexander the Great modelled himself on Achilles; many French radicals were envisaging themselves as likenesses of Plutarch's heroes.

The landing of a handful of New World rebels in England had one further implication. Paul Jones had given a prophetic message to the world, an intimation that one day, however distant, American troops, for better or worse, with singular mingling of altruism and venality, might intervene in Europe. Indignation, bribery and faulty memory can inflate stories, facts, language itself. Sir Walter Scott lamented 'an Act of wickedness, more surely diabolical than any hitherto upon record.' He was referring not to the Seven Years' War, the burying of Russian prisoners alive after Frederick the Great's victory at Zondorf, not to the Austrian theft of Galicia, the English excesses in Scotland after Culloden, not to the Slave Trade, but to the publication of *The Complete Works of Lord Bolingbroke* between 1753 and 1754.

Many discordant voices ensured that Paul Jones had squarely fixed America on the British map, and had he lingered he would have seen improvised beacons flaring, heard of great houses abandoned, couriers speeding south. Out at sea, he still held cards. Some gallant action was demanded and he knew where to find it. Belfast Lough was a haven for many prize pickings and, notably, His Majesty's *Drake*, 20 guns, might be there.

He set due helm and, off Carrickfergus again, sighted this powerful warship. His delight was not shared. To the consternation of all save the Swede, he set course, direct towards it, ordering the guns to be manned, while aware that the greater enemy was commanded by Thomas Simpson. For Simpson's doggish following, to overcome colliers, trawlers, merchantmen and register their share was well enough, but to gratuitously seek out a warship was suicidal. Almost all rebelled: 'I ran every chance of being killed or thrown overboard . . . the mutiny almost reduced me to the necessity of putting some of them to death.'

They could not withstand him. Elated, the stolen silver forgotten, gun in hand, he threatened Simpson, shouted down the rest, hustled all gunners to their posts. Drawing closer to *Drake*, ignoring Simpson's protests and excuses, entrusting essential directions to Meijer, he ran up British colours and, the enemy as yet suspecting nothing, summoned his crew around him. With long-tried versatility, he praised, cajoled, promised, joked, appealed to their manhood, their cupidity, spun out visions of their acclaim back home. He gained hearing, a sort of acquiescence, a hang-dog submission, then roused them by confiding his battle intentions, his spirit infectious, touched with a guile that was almost fun – then won them completely, 'tickled their caprice and soothed them again into good humour'. His relations with such men were always chancy, and to have secured their quiescence and silenced Thomas Simpson implied the extent of his smoothness.

Drake's Captain Burdon was now curious about the approaching stranger, then apprehensive, though not doubting his capacity to question a smallish, apparently defenceless merchantman. He waited, while Paul Jones set the trap, unobtrusively stationing musketeers behind bulwarks and prepared to mount riggings; the cannon were trained on *Drake*'s masts and bridge, though less on its hull: prize money apart, he needed to capture, not sink, so as to exhibit *Drake* to French eyes, crow over his enemies, perhaps give an addition to the Continental Navy, certainly enthuse America itself.

Ranger was soon within gunshot but Burdon still hesitated, giving no order until startled by the first explosions on his own ship, around and above him.

An hour later, the action, described by Jones as 'warm, close and obstinate', watched by astonished and volatile Irish harbour crowds, was over, with Burdon and his first lieutenant dead. In a favourite tactic, Paul Jones had crossed *Drake*'s bow, hurling forward shot before tacking for broadsides. These speedily left 'her sails and rigging entirely cut to pieces; her masts and yards all wounded, and her hull also very much galled'. *Ranger* then lay alongside almost with impunity, positioned for boarding, all levels of *Drake* covered by cannon and musket.

Paul Jones described the contest in the letter he wrote to Lady Selkirk pledging to return her silver, employing what he thought was a requisite literary flavour, unlikely to be much appreciated. He noticeably modified the actual savagery of the opening attack.

Jones's jubilation was justified: he had not toppled mere hobbyhorses and gingerbread clowns, scolding loudmouths and gentlemen captains appointed by politicians and carteliers. Lincoln Lorenz has just appreciation:

'The engagement was not only without parallel as the first victory of an American Continental vessel over an English ship of war, it also stood in marked contrast with most European encounters...Obviously Jones neither followed inflexible rules nor feared to fight at close quarters. He had struck adroitly and hard, weighing contingencies and seizing opportunities in the endeavour, according to his own expressed resolution, if not to insure success at least to deserve it.'

By sailing to France with *Drake*, and six other captives, John Paul Jones had secured what could not be sneered at by Arthur Lee, Samuel Adams and Silas Deane in their comfortable offices, nor Jemmy Twitcher at the Admiralty deny. He had justified the faith of Franklin, Morris and Hewes, gratified Chaumont and Sartine and, a wonder, extracted applause even from his crew, who might remain loyal could but their considerable prize money be screwed from the shifty French.

More important than these, he could praise himself, the poor boy from nowhere, male Cinderella. In an hour he had joined captains Barry and Manley, Wickes and Johnson, Conyngham and Barney, hitherto more renowned. He had seven prizes, 200 British prisoners to exchange for

American. He had carried his belief that 'not all their boasted navy can protect their coasts; and that the scenes of distress which they have occasioned in America may soon be brought home to their own door.'

In Ireland, the volunteers reassembled, soon to be deflected into nationalist politics, a bishop and a woman among their leaders. English volunteers gathered in Derbyshire and in Middlesex, the militia in many districts were called to arms, City prices slumped and insurance rose yet higher. Horace Walpole wrote to Horace Mann that the summer would not lack sights, each county would become an armed camp, 'the coasts amused with sieges', now that 'an American privateer has attacked Whitehaven and plundered Lord Selkirk's mansion'. The Paul Jones legend was already in being, a web of distortion, exaggeration, fear and ignorance floating around a kernel of truth.

Samuel S Griffith, in his *In Defense of Public Liberty* (1977), claimed: 'Captain Jones had brought his war to Britain's door and fractured the myth of inherent British superiority. Ship to ship, gun to gun, man to man, American sailors could hold their own on the seas.'

In long winters of ebbing and recovering fortunes, almost always uncertain, the British could still be considered to be prevailing on land, so that General Washington could write: 'The common interests are mouldering, and sinking into an irretrievable ruin, if a remedy is not soon applied.'

Vying in popular superstition almost with Saratoga, the name of John Paul Jones sounded loud in the spring of 1779, as part of the remedy.

9

Lord of the Sea

Along the lower'd eve he came horribly raking us.
We closed with him, the yards entangled, the cannon touch'd,
My captain lash'd fast with his own hands.

We had received some eighteen pound shots under the water,
On our lower-gun deck two large pieces had burst at the first fire
Killing all around and blowing up overhead.

Fighting at sundown, fighting at dark,
Ten o'clock at night, the full moon up, our leaks on the gain,
    and five feet of water reported
The master-at-arms loosing the prisoners confined in the afterhold
To give them a chance for themselves.

The transit to and from the magazine is now stopt by the sentinels,
They see so many strange faces they do not know whom to trust.

Our frigate takes fire,
The other asks if we demand quarter?
If our colors are struck and the fighting done?

Now I laugh content, for I hear the voice of my little captain,
We have not struck, he composedly cries, we have just begun
Our part of the fighting.

Walt Whitman,
Song of Myself, 1855

Flamborough reapers, home-going, pause on the hill-side, for what
sulphur-cloud is that that defaces the sleek sea; sulphur-cloud
spitting streaks of fire. A sea cockfight it is, and of the hottest, where

128

British *Serapis* and the French American *Bonne Homme Richard* do lash and throttle each other, in their fashion; and Lo the desperate valour has suffocated the deliberate, and Paul Jones too is of the Kings of the Sea.

Thomas Carlyle,
The French Revolution, 1837

In a word, luck – that's the word – shortly threw in Paul's way the great action of his life... the unparalleled death lock with the *Serapis*.

Herman Melville,
Israel Potter, 1855

Paul Jones's career is a graph of periodic success interrupted by misfortune or malice, sometimes self-induced; enforced idleness necessitates dogged striving for renewal, often successfully.

Back in France on *Ranger*, with his captive ships and Britons, on 8 May he immediately received requests, or apparent requests, from Franklin and Sartine, to remain for some new venture, to assist the mighty descent upon England planned for the summer. In Paris, at Brest, his deeds in whatever telling were being hailed as the heroic prelude to Great Britain's downfall. 'I am inclined to agree,' he remarked to such praise. On evidence, Britain was effete, corrupt at home, her fleets and armies overstretched abroad.

There was work ahead: to refit *Ranger*, redouble his efforts for *L'Indienne*, develop intimacy with Franklin and, urgently, to settle accounts with First Lieutenant Thomas Simpson.

His nature was fixed, unforgiving in a process older than Presbyterianism, obdurate, unsusceptible to special pleading. That a question might have two sides he almost never admitted. In the Age of Reason he could be perverse and unreasonable. He wasted no time in reporting the delinquent to the commissioners in tones almost intolerably familiar:

'I have faithfully supported and fought the dignified cause of Human Nature ever since the American banners first waved on the Delaware and on the ocean. This I did when That Man did not call himself a Republican but left the Continent and serviced its Enemies. And this I did when That Man appeared, Dastardly backward, and did not support me.'

In thorough Presbyterian mould, he believed, if not perhaps in revenge, but certainly in retribution, as justified as the payment of debts and the flogging of defaulters. Contracts must be honoured, penalties exacted for failure, rewards distributed for honest toil. He had no concern with the blissful idealistic, the grossly mercenary, the incapable, tormented, the devious and the downright silly. Certainly not for the treacherous who, in the Bible, in ballads and moral tales, deserved almost the worst. In his *Inferno*, very deep among the damned, Dante placed the infamous traitors, Brutus, Cassius and Judas. Jones very speedily demanded a court-martial for Simpson, but with so few American officers available in France, this was difficult. He did persuade local authorities to imprison the lieutenant but, rather surprisingly, agreed to his parole. Then, with the young delinquent openly sneering at his erstwhile chief in cafés and taverns, orders arrived for *Ranger* to return to America.

At this, Paul Jones resorted to another of the simple yet dextrous moves that so delighted him, assisted his interest and briefly appeased his pride. Deciding to remain in France, he sought and received permission from the Commissioners to dispatch *Ranger* home, with as many of the crew, still unpaid, as wished to go. The commander was to be none other than Simpson.

At first inexplicable, this was soon recognisable as good sense, pleasing all parties including himself. The agreement removed all present dilemmas: he was rid of a traitor, rid of surly and difficult men, rid of the responsibility of collecting their dues, and furthermore, acquiring some repute for magnanimity towards the disgraced. He could now anticipate new freedom, prospects of adventure offered by France while still holding to American contacts.

He could, if not very easily, forget Thomas Simpson, who reached America safely, was later promoted captain, serving well enough until captured by the British. On release, commanding a merchantman, he was drowned. Very possibly, this *Ranger* episode shows Paul Jones at his weakest. He may have disliked Simpson at first glance: he was never willing to delegate authority or display trust, affection or appreciation of others, and could not, or would not, extract the best in the younger man.

He had no time to brood upon psychology, Simpson's or his own. Inevitably, new grievances had started. The *Drake* victory had not been instantly followed by a Congress citation, a medal or promotion, even money to cover wages and general expenses. Few men could have been treated worse. Plainly, the American Revolution had determined to maintain independence on the cheap and nasty.

If he could not yet sail and fight, he could write without restraint. Ceaselessly his letters were delivered to the commissioners, to the French Marine, the American Marine, to Robert Morris, forceful reminders of his needs, of his very existence; he presented fresh plans, novel strategies, imaginative theories for the overhaul of dockyards, ships, officers, purveyance methods. Much must be reformed, perhaps more should be scrapped.

All was unavailing. The commissioners quarrelled among themselves, Franklin a soothing diplomat when he should have been a ruthless corner-cutting dictator; Morris was comfortably reassuring, but preoccupied with an almost bankrupt Treasury. That Lafayette, not yet twenty, had been promoted general, enduring with Washington the glories and agonies of Valley Forge, would not have mollified Jones, despite his regard for the Frenchman. He himself remained only Captain No. 18 on the Navy List. The attentions of titled ladies, the acclaim from the streets, the fears and vilifications reported from England, could not atone for an indifference, for an insult so perverse, so mule-headed, so intolerable.

In Paris, the three feuding commissioners, living well on insufficient means, were, like Chaumont, ignoring or disputing his financial demands: for wages, prize monies, expenses. Even before leaving America, he claimed, he had spent 1,500 of his own dollars on the Republic's behalf, had been reimbursed none of them, receiving only evasions – a deplorable way of managing war and revolution, and of treating the gifted and valiant.

Such matters, however, were negligible in Franklin's thoughts besides France's own war effort, prodigious though expensive. Twelve warships, 4,000 soldiers, 800 guns were in transit to America, with British blockade and ships everywhere threatened and, furthermore, the grand invasion, Great Design, was being vigorously prepared in Paris and Madrid. With troops dispersed in Gibraltar, in Canada, and fighting in America, Britain itself must be largely defended by retired or amateur officers and incompetent militia. Rumours multiplied, favourable omens abounded and, in England, Horace Walpole was pronouncing with easy complacency and without loyalty to the Union: 'France has a right to humble us. The true English who are in America have behaved like Englishman, without any Scots ally. The victories of France will be over Scots. Dr Franklin's triumph has been over a Scot ambassador.'

Paul Jones's decision to remain in France already appeared unwise. For ten months, despite *Drake* and the universal British panic, he was jobless, forgotten or best forgotten, with a hungry, grumbling remnant from *Ranger* regretting their refusal to depart with Simpson, accusing as fraudulent the legally worded agreements which their captain had induced them to sign. From *Drake*, large, valuable, but now possessed by Chaumont, they had won what they might never get.

To Chaumont and Franklin, Paul Jones confessed shame at appearing in public. Life in a provincial seaport was narrow, monotonous, and hampered by his disorderly sailors frequently at odds with the locals. In Paris, whatever the patient encouragement from Franklin, the graciousness of John and Abigail Adams, he was humiliated in ministerial anterooms by the thin smiles, well-considered bows, discreet apologies, the graceful shrugs barely concealing boredom. The atmosphere was too far from the sea, the fresh and bracing, the challenge of a worthy antagonist. He found patronising insolence in Franklin's well-meant suggestion of accepting a privateering commission. Simpson himself was faring better than the man he had betrayed. Preferring 'a Solid to a Shining Reputation, a Useful to a Splendid Command', Jones was eclipsed, becalmed, while American campaigns still fluctuated and all glory and honour were being reserved for France, now upstaging Britain itself.

Jones could see final victory resting less with Washington than with the Franco–Spanish descent upon England, while he languished in a France that ignored its obligations to himself, whose motives were slippery, and where a Beaumarchais in his counting house was more formidable than the heavy, powdered king in his palace. At no time since Tobago had he felt such a castaway. 'The Suspense is hell,' he lamented to Dr Bancroft. France and America appeared better at obstructing his future than providing it.

He could only continue pleading with Franklin, accosting the commissioners with lists and figures, badgering Chaumont who was once goaded into threats to demand his recall. 'He has treated me like a child, five times,' Jones raged, while still flirting, perhaps injudiciously, with the Frenchman's wife. He hurried from one well-disposed acquaintance to another: d'Orvilliers, completing plans for the design, the Duke de la Rochefoucauld, the Duke and Duchess de Chartres, the duke with a future so strange, though the American must have seen only a talkative Frenchman anxious to share honours with d'Orvilliers in the coming, flamboyant invasion. All were probably less intimate with Jones than he himself fancied. He now requested a place with d'Orvilliers to at last witness the operations of a great fleet, and the first large-scale invasion of England since the Dutch Stadtholder, later King William III in 1688, and the Jacobite rising in 1745. Though the admiral happily consented, Sartine did not, though assuring Jones that he was essential for other activities, while not disclosing their nature.

Never diffident in petitioning the highest, Paul Jones finally completed his memorial to Louis XVI not, of course, forgoing mention of his need to uphold 'The Violated Dignity and Rights of Human Nature'. He concluded: 'I am persuaded that you will not disregard my situation nor suffer me to remain any longer in this Insupportable Disgrace.'

Silence. King Louis, like King George, was beset with his own difficulties. But the onus of waiting, to sit out anxieties, temptations, bureaucratic procrastination was always a captain's lot between sailings, while having to maintain crews, bribe officials, satisfy purveyors and harbourmasters, awaiting Admiralty payments always tardy, often overlooked. It was gambler's territory that could induce despair, sometimes suicide; or strengthen obstinacy and anger and, between bouts of loud language, Paul Jones knew that he had no choice. Similar exasperation, with real or imagined conviction of lack of respect and promotion, together with numerous quarrels, prompted the sensational treachery and flight of the charismatic and gifted Major-General Benedict Arnold, the most famous traitor in American history.

Weeks went drearily by. Still Paul Jones agitated for *L'Indienne*, now completed in Holland, still Franklin reassured him, still Nassau-Siegen smiled, appearing and disappearing like a weatherman, fluent in grandiose but unmethodical schemes and with annoying reference to his influence with Alexander Potemkin, the one-eyed Russian empire builder, Prince of the Tauride, intimate, or more, of Catherine II, the small but mighty German who, everyone said, had murdered Tsar Peter III, her husband.

Could *L'Indienne* but be procured, Jones promised the engaging Dutch prince an exciting commission and, in return, was offered a subordinate part, which he spontaneously rejected, in Nassau-Siegen's proposed capture of Jersey, a difficult project that was to end in ludicrous defeat. Two conceited men with origins widely disparate were swapping insincere compliments and angling for positions in improbable ventures while behind them lurked Mr Thornton, the British spy. Learning of *L'Indienne*'s possible sale or loan to France, Thornton informed London, the Foreign Office protesting so angrily that the Dutch hurried to dispose of her to a French privateering syndicate without the sympathies of America and, indeed, which regarded French, American and the British alike as legitimate prey. Dutch neutrality was thus preserved until the British downfall with d'Orvilliers's high festival.

Sartine, immersed in momentous preparations, but anxious to silence the importunate Jones, suggested another ship to replace the one irredeemably lost. This was the *Duke of Duras*, a converted merchantman, 900 tons, some thirteen years old, probably neglected, even unseaworthy.

After the newly built *L'Indienne*, the offer did not dazzle and Paul Jones, distracted and dogged by the sickness that so often overcame him when under pressure, was thoroughly dejected, writing, December 1778: 'I am for the first time in my life in a disposition to doubt almost all the world.'

In America, the friendly Joseph Hewes was dying, or already dead. Franklin's precept from *Poor Richard's Almanac*, 'He that lives on Hope will die Fasting,' so fitting for the sober, diligent and rising professional classes, did not, at this instant, exhilarate John Paul Jones. Yet hope remained while Franklin supported him. The older man, exemplar of Puritan ethics, scientific curiosity and political acumen, yet retained some imaginative instinct for the unorthodox, the singular, even the risky. Overworked and unwarlike, he could yet discuss with Paul Jones experiments in ship design, technology and strategies to employ after the allied victory, though he does not appear to have envisaged the British Grenadiers mutinying, Parliament in flames, the king scuttling towards the Isle of Man. He remained steady, patient with Jones's expense accounts and self-centredness, uttering only an occasional sorrowful reproach. He earned one of Paul Jones's very rare effusions: 'I know the Great and Good of this Kingdom,' he had written to Hewes, 'better, perhaps, than any other American who has appeared in Europe since the Treaty of Alliance, and if my Testimony could add anything to Franklin's Reputation, I could witness the Universal Veneration and Esteem with which his name inspires all Ranks. Envy itself is dumb when the name of Franklin is mentioned.'

It suggests a relationship almost familial and, for once, Jones never retracted it. After Christmas, while he languished in Brest, within sight of French vessels preparing to outnumber, outgun and out-manoeuvre Great Britain, his fortunes brightened. Though Chaumont continued to withhold *Ranger*'s prize monies, doubtless for his own speculations and the commissioners delayed in confirming his expenses, they were now subsidising, if frugally, himself and those remaining with him. Chartres and d'Orvilliers entertained him, with sufficient respect and distinction, spoke of his future with flattering optimism, backed his credit. From Chaumont came more talk of *Duras*, still privately owned and, despite its deficiencies, he meditated attempting to purchase it from his own funds before, on rumours that the French Marine was contemplating securing it for transfer to America, he again hastened to Paris.

Here, all was not, as it were, shipshape. With prices rising, constant bread shortages and bad harvests, political agitation at good news from America and Lafayette's prowess, an absentee court regarded as wilfully, selfishly, extravagant, an unpopular queen, and ministers weak, helpless, or obstructed by the privileged and anachronistic, the Paris crowds were beginning to demand a role. They were being enflamed by gifted, idealistic demagogues, who combined exciting rhetoric with an often insecure grasp of realities, helped by provocateurs, a vindictive, often scurrilous press, and a group of able, radical politicians, headed by the energetic Mirabeau, who was idolised yet remains controversial even today.

A very young and talented journalist, Camille Desmoulins, intimate fellow pupil with Franklin's admirer, the lawyer, Maximilien Robespierre, a coming man, was dreaming aloud of 'a new Tahiti', a society born not from James Cook's notebooks but from an imagination generous and somewhat absurd. For Camille, Tahiti was a society still in the Golden Age, itself a fable powerful though illusionary, a society of what human nature could achieve, free of the unreason, greed, hatred, factions and despotism, which were the outcome of antique and tyrannical institutions. From his book-lined study, the admirable and sensitive Condorcet issued well-reasoned, well-balanced, ill-informed reminders that human nature was in essence pacific, benevolent, just, impaired only by lack of education, a dated administrative apparatus, and the corruption of those who had usurped power and held it too long.

Paul Jones wasted no time with café rhetoric and obscenities, or dram-shop virulence; he was at once grappling with Chaumont and Sartine, their multiple, sometimes contradictory plans and explanations. Chaumont did confide that his superior was considering allowing Jones not, of course *L'Indienne*, perhaps not even *Duras*, but some other ship, 64 guns no less, though the captain must find the crew. He would be given some roving commiss:.n, akin to what he had enjoyed on *Ranger*, dangerous, but important, a clause in the Design, a footnote to resounding victory.

Jones considered this too vague, part of the wavering fug enveloping Paris cabals and Versailles indolence. He continued to visit Madame de Chaumont but showed no enthusiasm for the deal with her husband. Nevertheless, he had now inspected *Duras* and began tirelessly assuring Chaumont that 'It will answer our Purpose'. In this he was resolved; he must have it, he would have it. She was no mere sloop, he could alter, lighten, rerig, provide for at least 40 guns, more than he had yet commanded. Money? Franklin would find it. All arrangements? Chaumont could make them. Tact, dignity, fine manners must be discarded in impatient, all-out efforts to win over king, navy ministry, commissioners. Let the gentleman be forgotten, the captain must have his ship.

Considerable opinion would back him. Britain was angering all nations, particularly neutrals, by its unilateral fiat by which its navy imposed universal right of search, boarding any vessel, under whatever flag, suspected of carrying goods to rebel America.

Finally, the French authorities submitted. Despite the turmoil of the supreme enterprise, the Great Design, Sartine's ministry consented to acquire, arm, generally equip *Duras*, with Captain John Paul Jones licensed to muster volunteers, and to decide with the commissioners how best to exploit his second European adventure under the Stars and Stripes. His delight shot up like the flag itself. He rushed to L'Orient with plans for alterations – spars, rigging, guns – and, as a tribute to Franklin, renamed her *Poor Richard*, *Bonhomme Richard*: not classical, not aristocratic, but of the civic virtues recommended by Franklin.

Sartine promised that the American would lead a squadron, with tried French captains under him. In all but name – though name was important – he was admiral, with flagship and a free hand against the British. He wrote to Congress and the Marine Committee in language which would have shocked Tom Paine, to whom monarchy was 'a poor, silly, contemptible thing':

> It shall be my Duty to represent in the strongest terms to Congress the Generous and Voluntary Resolution which their great ally, the Protector of the Rights of Human nature, and the Best of Kings, has taken to promote the Honor of their Flag, and I beseech you to assure His Majesty that my heart is impressed with the Perfect Sense of Obligation which I owe to my highest ambition to merit, by rendering every service to the Common Cause. I cannot insure success, but I will endeavour to deserve it.

In this abnegation of worthy American slogans and popular rights, he was not alone. Though Jefferson had testified that a republic was the only government not eternally at open or secret war with the rights of mankind, future French terrorists were not yet convinced. Collot d'Herbois published an 'Ode to Marie Antoinette'; Mirabeau still had hopes to reconcile and ultimately to control the Crown. Though Robespierre had few such hopes, he was shrugged off by Condorcet as a flea that would vanish in the winter.

February 1779 presented a further, more concrete possibility for Jones. In America, the war threatened stagnation; it demanded yet more effort from France, and who better to help negotiate it than Lafayette, future Hero of Two Continents? With projects lit by youthful bravado, having returned to France to help engineer the French declaration of war, the marquis would soon be again crossing the Atlantic on a new frigate, *Alliance*, under Captain Pierre Landais.

In Paris, discussing Franco–American strategy wlth Franklin, Lafayette had revealed a spirit of such scope that a third party, John Paul Jones, was co-opted. The French nobleman and the Scots villager mixed well: both were adventurous, brave, enjoying challenges. A plan was promulgated, conforming exactly to Jones's pleas for raids on Britain. Jones was to be active on sea, Lafayette on land, 'for whatever share of Glory'. Fending off Arthur Lee, wrangling with creditors and huddled in diplomatic exchanges with France, Spain and Holland, Franklin, was supportive, and this, Paul Jones exclaimed, would make a coward brave. Writing to Lafayette, Franklin pronounced: 'On the whole, it may be encouraging to reflect on the many instances of history which prove that in war attempts thought to be impossible do often, for that reason, become possible and practical because nobody expects them.'

Paul Jones had been insisting on this throughout. He and Lafayette corresponded, eager minds with generous, attacking vision. Part of the plan envisaged Paul Jones threatening to bombard British towns from the sea, unless they paid ransoms, which would replenish French and American funds. By March, Franklin was suggesting a levy of 48 million livres on Liverpool, twelve million on Whitehaven and Bath, six million from Lancaster. In judging distance, he was, for once, inexact.

Liverpool was the chief target, Britain's centre, with Bristol, of the slave trade, a mass of wooden warehouses and windmills, its quays stacked with cloth and cotton bales, its waters holding over 100 privateers, as many merchantmen, nearly 2,000 guns. To fire Liverpool would, metaphorically, set England alight and convince the Europe of Louis and Maria Theresa, Joseph II, Catherine and Frederick, of American might. But within days, spies alerted the Liverpool Fathers, who at once implored arms and soldiery from London, completed a Merseyside fort, erected beacons along the coasts and on the Isle of Man. Paul Jones was returning. The name was sufficient but, betrayed, the plan was aborted.

Down south, with the French and Spanish fleets reported in collusion, the grand invasion nearing paper completion, but with George III and North unable to rally patriotic fervour for an unpopular cause, Horace Walpole bemoaned 'the ruin brought upon my country by both as worthless and incapable a set of men as ever had the front to call themselves politicians. They hurried us and blundered us into a civil war, a French war, a Spanish War. America is lost, Jamaica, the West Indian islands, Gibraltar and Fort Mahon are scarce to be saved.'

Ireland, he foretold, would fall next. As for England: 'I should have little fear if men who have conducted themselves so wretchedly were not still our governors.'

France, despite the glitter of the Great Design, was in no way superior. The previous year, French society, sophisticated yet chauvinistic, weakened yet frivolous, had been dismayed and amused by the battle of Ushant, a masterpiece of inept signalling, grotesque co-ordination, lordly inexperience and common ill discipline, in which the rival commanders August d'Orvilliers and Augustus Keppel, obedient to the *Fighting Instructions*, formed their lines, banged a few discharges, scarcely did more, then sailed away. Though more blame attached to his joint-commander, Keppel was court-martialled, acquitted, and was raised to First Lord and a viscountcy in 1782.

This fiasco magnified the necessity for spectacular success in the Great Design. To help repair the damage, a scapegoat was procured in the Duke of Chartres, who was accused of disobedience or cowardice, and to a barrage of caustic witticisms, was removed to the army, with a new grudge to add to those he already cherished against his royal cousin and the Austrian-born queen.

The grand invasion had to be hastened. Agreement with Spain had been reached for the division of British possessions, thefts of the Seven Years' War. Sixty-six allied ships of the line were to join off Finisterre, then bear down upon England in an assault to match that of the Conqueror himself.

On 4 June 1779, d'Orvilliers, aged 70, sailed to meet the Spanish fleet, with 30,000 soldiers and massive artillery, against an enemy with widely dispersed fleets. Neutrals and hesitant friends blithely awaited the preliminary dispatches: the storming of Wight, dragoons abandoning Portsmouth Hard, home ships sinking, Plymouth in flames, Drake's memory desecrated, London rioters sacking Lord North's mansion, City banks and insurance offices bankrupted overnight, George III on his knees amid the trembling Cabinet.

The experts were sanguine. In three years, Sartine maintained, he had enlarged 36 ships of the line to 64, while Britain was reported able to deploy only 54 against the allies and, in the Atlantic, British transports, merchantmen

Right: John Paul Jones: a king of the sea.

Mary Evans Picture Library

Below: The pirate of popular infamy, glamour and pantomime.

Mary Evans Picture Library

Opposite (above): That strange midnight battle under the moon.

Mary Evans Picture Library

Opposite (below): Stand by for boarding.

Bettmann/Corbis

Left: King Louis XVI, reluctant friend of America.

Michael Nicholson/Corbis

Below: Naval manoeuvres: John Paul Jones, American naval commander, in the 'Bonhomme Richard' attacks the 'Serapis'.

Mary Evans Picture Library

Above: American naval
heroes of the Revolution.
Hulton/Getty

Above: The Paul Cottage set in the village of Kirkbean (below).

Above: George Washington: Never a desk-bound general.

The Houdon bust: 'The slightly lidded and averted eyes confessing his secret pondering and aspiration, his circumspect searchings and his canniness'.

and warships were being assailed by French squadrons and fierce New England privateers.

This new momentum wrecked the Lafayette–Jones project, whatever its genuine seriousness. Suspicious of the liberal marquis, Versailles tried to consign him to a mere regiment, persuading him that his future lay with the freedom lovers overseas. Paul Jones was thus left to plan elsewhere, borrowing and recruiting as best he could, relying most on Franklin. He was not to forget those few, high-spirited weeks of discussion, notions, vision, and the young Frenchman's natural courtesy and ardour, corresponding with him for some years until Lafayette became engulfed in the French revolutionary turmoil. Jones did not live to realise the extent of Lafayette's moral weaknesses and vanity.

Although fretful and opening his purse wider, Paul Jones remained eager to scoop fame by the 'brilliant action' of his daydream. Back at L'Orient, he was at once transforming *Bonhomme Richard* to an armed frigate, rerigging the three masts, collecting 40 guns 'of greatly different calibre', gathering a crew, while realising that Chaumont's obligations would be meanly fulfilled. He soon had 380 men, with officers likely to be more reliable than those on *Ranger*. The company made an amalgam of mixed languages, mixed motives, or no motives at all, the last resort of drifters in an inhospitable foreign land. There were dockside opportunists, cosmopolitans unemployable elsewhere, some tried sailors and 40 English and Irish renegades. He was glad of the Frenchman, Colonel Wiebert, and his 140 marines lent by Sartine, a vigorous arm of attack and precaution against mutiny.

As first lieutenant was no Simpson but Richard Dale, of known courage and resource. An Englishman captured at sea by John Barry, he had been persuaded into becoming first mate; captured by the British he had escaped from prison in America and rejoined the Republicans.

With *Bonhomme Richard* were to sail the French frigates *Pallas*, 32 guns, under Cottineau; *Alliance*, 36 guns, under Landais; the smaller *Vengeance*, 12 guns, under Ricot; the cutter *Cerf*, 18 guns, under Varage, together with two privateers, from which Jones expected little and received less.

Cottineau, Ricot and Varage were Frenchmen, not wholly dependable but with respectable experience, even though more often from privateering from which they had not wholly disassociated themselves. Pierre Landais's reputation was less savoury and his crew contained a considerable proportion of Englishmen.

Paul Jones could not have been wholly sanguine, especially after examining the contract handed him by Chaumont. In this, the disposition of prizes was again reserved for the French agents and, though worded imprecisely, appeared to limit Jones's absolute authority to *Bonhomme Richard*; not a recipe for total success of a squadron, more likely a guarantee of disaster. The disadvantages of his own position, being responsible to Congress, the Marine Committee, the Paris commissioners, the French marine ministry and to Versailles were increasingly patent. He saw, correctly, that his French consorts would obey orders only when it suited them, their ultimate plans likely to be different from his own, none more so than those of Captain Pierre Landais.

Today's intelligence, with more elaborate equipment to analyse human nature and scrutinise the reality, even desirability, of loyalty and discipline, is apt to query notions and values of failure and success. Sceptical of the actuality of polar opposites, we can find them closer than the less humane Paul Jones would have suspected, and some doubt the reality of either. Right and wrong, good and evil, foul and fair, share too much. Psychologists can find Landais one of those fascinating, though unendearing, misfits that move the imagination. Such are Loki; catalystic god of mischief, Hermes, patron of thieves and practical jokers; Titus Oates, Rasputin, Benedict Arnold in the field; Groucho Marx on the screen. They might acquit Landais of unseemly behaviour, and indict Jones for failure to communicate and show unflagging sympathy, which, with a Duncan or Nelson, would not have occurred. A contemporary historian, Robert Harvey, who brusquely dismisses many misconceptions and fantasies about the American War, concludes that, while Paul Jones possessed extraordinary courage and seamanship, 'circumnavigating the British isles and thumbing his nose at the British,' he was not one of the greatest commanders, 'exerting virtually no authority over his squadron'.

A novelist might see Landais as a Dostoyevskyan clown, cursing the God he loved, craving to be thrashed by a devil he hated; or deflate him to a theatrical Dickensian villain twisted by jealousy and tormented by obsession with injustice. He may have been a freak of nature or circumstance, one of those judged by Byron as 'warp'd by the world in Disappointment's school'.

A Breton, he had sailed round the world in Bougainville's great voyage (1755–9) and returned, though according to Paul Jones, still ignorant of the existence and function of the compass. Ejected from the French navy for disobedience and incompetence, he was given, through Silas Deane, a captaincy in the American in 1777. His mixture of bullying and taciturnity, together with what appears wilful mismanagement, incited mutiny.

Congress, however, accepted his stories at face value and, inclining to regard Frenchmen as prestigious additions to the cause, gave him command of *Alliance*, currently their best ship. He accepted American citizenship and was soon claiming to be the only true American in Paul Jones's force. When sailing to France with Lafayette as passenger, he faced another mutiny, his eccentricities, endearing or comical in print, no advantage in mid-Atlantic, disqualifying him from control of himself and others. John Adams, an observer neither mendacious nor biased, reported in 1780:

'He is Jealous of Everything, of Everybody, of all his Officers, of all his Passengers. There is in this man an inactivity and an indecision that will ruin him; he is bewildered – an absent bewildered man, an embarrassed mind.'

Such was the captain selected to accompany Paul Jones into human and elemental hazards that could be mortal. He would never have been chosen by Jones himself, who thought only in stark contrasts. In support of Landais were Chaumont, Deane, Arthur Lee, the Americans gullible, and possibly anxious to counterbalance or discredit Jones, so favoured by Franklin, whom they resented and envied. As against Chaumont's well-phrased ambiguities, Franklin's orders to Landais were explicit: 'You are to join Captain Jones, put yourself under his command as your senior officer, proceed with him on the cruise he is about to make, and, obey his orders until your return to France.'

The squadron had a short, preliminary mission from 19 June, escorting French merchantmen through British ships watching the coast. Though successful, it began with an American privateer refusing any co-operation, and with a junior officer, steering *Bonhomme Richard*, colliding with *Alliance* when scarcely out of port. A court-martial cashiered the officer though evidence suggests that Landais was more to blame. The incident aggravated the already uneasy relations between the two captains.

Convoying continued, and not until 14 August 1779, while Europe awaited the triumph of the Design, the invasion, did Commodore Jones's somewhat forlorn little group sail from Croix to 'distress the enemy as best it can'. Landais had been anxious to be seen first in the lead, but failed by a few minutes.

Chaumont had stipulated that the expedition must end in September, in neutral Holland, where more French vessels would be awaiting an armed convoy.

The collision suggested an expedition beginning badly and ending worse. Within days, quarrels flared, about objectives, prize money, discipline, Landais usually ignonng staff conferences and, when present, disputing Jones's prohibition of individual prize hunting, and shouting insults at him from *Alliance*. Even Cottineau, stalwart enough, while unsympathetic to Landais, seemed reluctant to risk very much for what might end in very little. Privateering, or savaging Britain within the safety of the overwhelming Great Design, were more attractive.

Few, then, would have wagered on much success. While Jones wished to assist d'Orvilliers and humiliate Britain, his subordinates, abetted by Chaumont's desire for a quick return on public and private investments, were lukewarm, the crews themselves unmoved by feelings that shook Franklin into a plaint to Congress: 'Will no one under a commission from the United States retaliate on the coasts of Britain for the burning of our beautiful Fairfield?'

Paul Jones had already given the first answer and, now braced for a second, was further dismayed by realising that, of all the squad, *Bonhomme Richard*, the heaviest, was also the slowest, unable to head the chase, and not always able to follow. He and Dale were isolated above a brigade of cosmopolitan mercenaries, incapables and cut-throats, with himself still popularly derided not as an allied commander but a mere escaped murderer on the run.

A storm on 26 August sent one privateer scuttling back to L'Orient, its captain excusing himself by stating that the devil himself could not have kept a ship at sea. *Cerf* had also vanished. Jones, to whom storms were never as dangerous as his fellow men, kept his ship intact, with no human losses, and kept his course, 'the devil in a Scots bonnet'. He had already taken one substantial prize, and gale and wave were less menacing than the threat of plunder by the remaining auxiliary privateer.

Events largely followed the naval tradition. Off Ireland, in calmer waters, *Cerf* reappeared, but on *Bonhomme Richard*, some men, mostly British, contrived to abandon ship, and the loyal third lieutenant, in pursuit, got himself captured with a score of others, mostly due to blunders by Captain Varage on *Cerf*. Jones was undeterred, easily gaining several more prizes, so that *Cerf*, satiated with spoils, again turned back to France, followed by the privateer.

Worse succeeded, Paul Jones making a culpable and uncharacteristic mistake. He attempted to conciliate Landais, with a generosity probably insincere and certainly overdone. Landais had already shown himself a past master of disloyalty, timidity, incoherent abuse and bad seamanship. By nature adverse to accepting advice, particularly poor advice, Jones now accepted it in conference with Landais, against his private judgement but in an effort to conciliate, for the larger plan, thereby missing a big British West Indiaman, incurring anger from all crews. A few days earlier, Landais had endangered Jones's success in taking *Union*, a privateer filled with stores for British Canada, by hoisting the wrong flag. Compounding this, he filched both *Union* and another prize, *Betsey*, from Jones, 'even under my nose', while the captain was supervising the prisoners. As if in his own right, Landais dispatched these two ships to Chaumont's agents in Bergen, then held by neutral Denmark, thus helping bedevil Danish–American relations for almost 80 years.

Henceforward, Paul Jones relied on himself alone. The seizure of six more prizes restored some amity and appeased natural cupidity. Mahan, distinguished naval authority, was mistaken in alleging that Jones preferred destruction to capture. The Scot recognised the importance of capture; partly as visible propaganda for American vitality, partly for prize money as insurance against mutiny and as contribution to France's expenditure and to retain Chaumont's favours, and partly because such large vessels as *Mellish* and *Drake* could enlarge America's own navy, still far too small.

With August ending, strong seas and desertions had scattered the squadron, leaving Jones on *Bonhomme Richard*, accompanied only by *Vengeance*, with fierce Scottish waters ahead. Far from base on the edge of their known world, with its legendary whirlpools, mythical sea monsters, gigantic cold, and mysterious lights, flaming and billowing, but with prizes registered, the grand invasion presumably accomplished, Britain open for despoiling, the majority of his followers must have felt they need accomplish no more. Their mission finished, they must now set course either to ransack some British town or to sail homewards before the onrush of autumn storms.

They were mistaken. Down south, the inevitable had again failed to occur and, on an awesome, operatic scale, though with gusts of high comedy, the historic invasion had collapsed almost before it began. The Spanish fleet had rendezvoused too late, combining this with ignorance of French flag signals and making dignified refusal to learn. Chaumont's incessant and versatile activities overlooked the provision of fresh fruit, cleanliness and physicians, presumably deemed unnecessary in a brief, decisive voyage, though, almost overnight, as if by a sorcerer's cliché, the ships were racked by the atrocious trinity of scurvy, dysentery and smallpox. The grand invasion dissolved in disgrace, disillusion, mocking epigrams, despite its pomp of ships of the line, its 400 transports, its 40,000 men. Some did sight Portsmouth, before sudden squalls caused havoc, confusion, wreckage, collisions and finally, catastrophe, all vessels in flight and reeking with casualties, including d'Orvilliers's own son. The British Channel fleet, despite its shortcomings, had never been accustomed to allow enemies a free hand.

This was the end for Paul Jones's old friend and, when the allies dared reunite in the Atlantic in 1782, they were routed by Rodney at the battle of the Saints, then, yet again, by Nelson at Trafalgar in 1805.

During this tragic absurdity, Paul Jones's squadron, the reserve, the second eleven, disregarded by all save Franklin, the distrusted Chaumont and a few consistent enemies, was still thrashing through Irish, then Atlantic, waters, seeking to damage King George's property. To posterity Jones's situation was bizarre, in his unwieldy old ship, with those others which he nominally commanded appearing and disappearing at will. He was a tiny digit in the larger campaign. Though British opposition seemed negligible, Cottineau, Ricot and, on occasion, Landais, were bargaining over prizes like rival undertakers.

Paul Jones remained intractable, clutching his silent purposes. With a sinking here, a capture there, prisoners taken, he was, unlike d'Orvilliers with his golden chain and collar, his ornate decorations and magnificent hat, actually afloat, free from diseases, pushing on with Ireland passed, and leaving behind new rumours and alarms on both sides of the sea, on into the unknown north.

Despite expostulations and fears, though manfully supported by Richard Dale, he ignored the Hebrides, rounded perilous Cape Wrath, turned south off the eastern Highlands and, by 7 September, sighted the Orkneys, the British now attempting to shadow him,

Jones's guns were serving him well. Already Britain had a trail of lost ships, magnified by false reports and invasion scares, from himself, France, Spain and lesser scavengers. No more than Jones himself did the Admiralty know how many ships he led, how many he had defeated. His intentions were obscure. Lord North, in Downing Street, was urging Lord Sandwich, in the Admiralty, to give absolute priority to safeguarding the nation against 'a squadron, or perhaps two, and prevent the mischief he intends against the coasts of Great Britain and Ireland'. With their native 'pirate' back on the warpath, small Scottish sea towns sought cover. At Kirkcaldy, the minister knelt on the shore praying for wind to blow the terrorist away. The Lord hearkened, the wind obeyed, rain fell, but Jones scarcely noticed, and had no interest in tiny Kirkcaldy. Off Orkney, *Pallas* and *Alliance* rejoined him after an illicit bout of privateering, and he disclosed to the wary Frenchmen plans of dressing the three ships and crews with British flags and uniforms, all guns screened by canvas. Landais at once refused co-operation, then threatened the commodore with a duel to the death, scandalising his two fellows.

In London, relief for the débâcle of the Great Design was countered by fears of Paul Jones, goading the press to revive the Mungo Maxwell story: 'As the Carpenter was in one of the hot days fast asleep upon deck, Paul anointed his head plentifully with turpentine, after which he laid a trail of gunpowder at some distance, which, setting fire to the Carpenter, he instantly bounded up, and in the confusion jumped overboard and was never heard of more.'

In thus navigating round most of Britain, Jones accomplished a considerable feat of seamanship. He was now reported sailing, on 15 September, into the Firth of Forth, followed uneasily by *Pallas* and *Vengeance*, resolved to spare the town of Leith, where his grandfather had once kept a market garden and tavern, from bombardment, on £50,000 payment. Here occurred his mild sport of terrifying the man sent to beg a powder keg by the worried baronet, and the Englishman confiding to the harmless-looking captain in British uniform that Paul Jones should be hanged as the greatest pirate that ever was, Jones smiling agreement.

Volunteers regathered in King George's three kingdoms. Leith, then Edinburgh, shuddered with drums, Hogarthian uproar, horrendous messages, reports of explosions, burlesque militia exercises, emergency measures completed only weeks later, creating an uproar of outsize drinking, hysterical ladies, strutting half-pay officers with excuses to depart, outraged patriots, sharp-fingered hangers on, and the rumble of opulent coaches that soon jammed the highways west. From Walter Scott himself, Fenimore Cooper heard of the Paul Jones furore, comparable to that at the start of the 1745 Rebellion. Troops were rushed from Edinburgh to Dunbar past improvised diggings, batteries, and shouts of a pirate landing.

> All was then hurly burly, from Leith to Dunbar,
> With trenches, pallisadoes, and long guns to shoot far,
> Out marched the brisk sailors to man their platoons,
> All sweat, dust and foaming, in march'd the dragoons,
> In dread of Paul Jones and his horse-stealing loons.
>
>   Anon

At the Admiralty, Lord Sandwich was alerting ships to the north, but contrary winds saved Leith, also the officers' angry opposition to bombardment of that town and Newcastle. Easy pickings among unarmed colliers and supply ships remained more attractive. With Landais within sight, but aloof, Cottineau and Ricot remonstrated that they had surely done sufficient, and could legitimately remind their captain of Chaumont's order to soon assume duties in Holland, and that they were now almost overdue.

Jones listened, though his demeanour was not reassuring. Convoying, mere police work, was no real test, no challenge to his self-belief. He needed the 'brilliant action' by which to be acclaimed and remembered. Yet winds still debarred him from raiding and bombarding Edinburgh, Leith or Newcastle, or receiving substantial money from threats of assault. He could not force Landais to conferences or prevent the others from deserting, or maraudmg on their own. Without Landais, he temporised with the others, with his customary mingling of bluff and half-truth, leaving himself options not always disclosed. The captains regained their ships and, while they hesitated, he set course south, towards the Humber and fortified Hull. By 22 September, he was seen approaching wealthy Scarborough. Again, the drums, florid exhortations, turn-out of militia and volunteers, gentry uneasy in great houses, horsemen speeding towards London with news that swelled at each post station.

The wind swerved, keeping Jones close to land. Nearing Flamborough Head, he sighted, further to sea, a sight to stop the heart, a long row of top sails. If only for himself and Dale, the prospect was so stupendous that he at once ordered his pilot boat to capture a roving brigantine, for storage of goods that would impede fighting, and for the reception of prisoners, those already held and those he was now determined to take. However, he swiftly ordered recall when the quarry hove into full view, and he realised its magnitude: 44 Baltic merchantmen in convoy.

These were protected by two warships: Thomas Piercy, commanding the sloop *Countess of Scarborough*, with 22 six-pounders, and Richard Pearson, captaining the more formidable *Serapis*, a frigate deploying 50 guns on two decks, including 22 eighteen-pounders. At most, *Bonhomme Richard* had 40, on a single deck, with but six eighteen-pounders. Inferiority in weaponry, however, had never daunted Paul Jones and his 'wild, lonely heart'. Rage against Landais and disillusion with his French colleagues would not stifle the clamour within him; he had only to rouse his motley, discontented crew.

Landais was ignoring action signals, hovering on the margin with uncertain movements, but *Pallas* and little *Vengeance* were standing by, perhaps prepared to fight, more probably to withdraw after the first salvoes, from which *Bonhomme Richard*, slow, almost cumbersome, must have small chance. They had little concern for France or America, their first duty was to themselves.

Drums beat to quarters, marines and musketeers ordered to their stations: below, the prisoners waited. Behind hatches, the guns were loaded. Momentarily, as he had done on *Ranger*, Jones addressed the men, above them on the bridge and, by fluke of personality and the quivering pressures of mortal crisis, the sight of looming hulls and glint of cannon, he made them listen. With Dale beside him, he gave commands, he gave assurance, stirred the blood. He had never known defeat, their old ship was piled with British spoils: fortunes could be made, all could be heroes. Perceptibly, the polyglot mob was coalescing into a unit, desperate but not despairing, setting itself against the two warships, every minute larger, taller, heavier, with thickets of masts and British flags. All knew that their captain alone would determine the night's outcome: he controlled fate, his and theirs. To support him would be dangerous, to refuse might be fatal.

At last John Paul Jones had what he loved, an audience. The approach of the great Baltic convoy, rumours of strange ships and of the pirate himself, had roused citizens in their thousands, sent them flocking up to the steepling head, with a late afternoon view over miles of long, white-capped waves, 'skipper's daughters', the long trail of merchantmen, and the converging warships. A staging marvellously theatrical, with darkening clouds and attendant moon. With folk memories of Viking invasions, Yorkist champions in the Roses Wars and legends of the Whitby hero, James Cook, Yorkshiremen loved strong personalities and doughty contests.

For Jones, an additional danger must be anticipated, from his scores of British prisoners beneath hatches. Should he appear to fail, the treacherous or cowardly might release them, leaving him with only Wiebert and his French marines. He trusted Wiebert, rightly, and had no time to reflect more. To win himself a few moments to manoeuvre correctly and instruct his gunners, in his old sleight, he ran up, not the Stars and Stripes but the Union Jack, calculating that it would make Pearson pause, momentarily to hold his fire.

It succeeded, allowing time for hailings, evasions, lies and mounting British suspicion, while Jones angled for position, to diminish the odds, until *Serapis* and *Countess*, disregarding the convoy, realised their own peril and hoisted 'the bloody flag' for battle, drums hustling men of Old England to their stations, guns hastily primed, Pearson judging distance, seeing *Pallas* and *Vengeance* hovering out of range, but *Bonhomme Richard*, without doubt the American freebooter, drawing closer.

Walt Whitman was to demand in *Song of Myself* (1855):

> Would you hear of an old-time sea-fight?
> Would you learn who won by the light of moon and stars?

It was 6.30. Haze thickened with sundown, distorting sails, hulks, spaces. A full moon was still hidden by cloud. Behind the warships, the merchantmen were crowding sail in anxiety to reach the shelter of cliffs and land fortifications, the guns of Scarborough Castle. These were forgotten, mere extras obliterated by smoke and flame, as bloodlust and fear, the primitive, surged as the first shots crashed, sails and flags gusted, gulls screamed and fled and the massed onlookers sighed and shouted, marvellously content.

Jones could see *Pallas* and *Vengeance* heave away to safety, *Alliance* invisible, presumably turned towards France. He was never a hit-or-miss fighter, but had the instincts of a bullfighter, adept in feints and goadings, timings, calculated thrusts and dodges, sudden flourishes, fripperies of violence, before delivering the death blow. He could improvise like Nelson but disliked trusting to chance. *Bonhomme Richard* was difficult to manoeuvre in the small area now left around *Serapis*. Marines were ranged on the poop, marksmen thick in the rigging, gunners stationed at their cannons, and he had to hold them to the last instant while straining all he could to evade the murderous barrage from barely 30 yards off, and employ the angling tactics he so often found irresistible

Yet almost at once he appeared to have lost: 'At first we took a Pounding.' As the moon rose over Flamborough, the watchers saw the explosion as, on the first order to fire, two of his heaviest guns blew up, toppling, maiming, crippling; survivors stampeding below, refusing to return. After the second round, only three guns of any size were left him so, while shouting orders to Dale to draw still closer to *Serapis*, Jones rushed to whatever guns remained. One was on the wrong side, he dragged it over, manning it himself, while determined to draw alongside the enemy, grapple, board her, fight it out, throw blue French marines against British redcoats.

Seldom easy, this initially failed, despite support from musketry above, and Pearson must have sensed victory, but then under-estimated his opponent. This was understandable. His own guns were shearing down the

French marines, Jones attempting to rally them, while not daring to abandon his gun, with none yet willing to replace him.

All, elated or despairing, realised that *Bonhomme Richard* was holed, listing, on fire. At the wheel, Dale desperately strove to close, matching Pearson's every turn and twist without quite pulling alongside, while musketeers raked both ships. Yet only the grapple could save Jones, then he must urge his men not only to resist but to attack, fighting as if on land. Several gunners then ventured back, freeing him to regain control. Yet his survival seemed impossible. Scarcely one of his guns was firing, devastation surrounded him. Behind, the *Countess of Scarborough*'s guns were blazing, further decimating the marines. *Alliance* was nowhere, *Pallas* was anywhere, *Vengeance* remained a silent and ignoble witness throughout. Jones was wildly outnumbered as moonlight made torn sails spectral and flames infernal; yells and screams were incessant and officers, save Dale, recognised defeat. But not Paul Jones, though he could not prevent *Bonhomme Richard* clumsily lurching to within grenade range almost of its own will, in position the worst for boarding.

Pearson tried to counter across her path but miscalculated distance and angle, knocking against Jones's bowsprit, briefly entangling with his rigging, both ships swaying, shaken by waves and red-hot cannon balls. Grappling irons were thrown, then missing, or wrenched away. Straightening, escaping Jones's first attempts to board, *Serapis* had slowed almost entirely, without space to avoid the American's assault. Jones, at first vainly, was trying to grapple with *Serapis*'s stern, yelling for the irons, then for man to man onslaught.

Battles neatly described even by participants, especially by participants, are suspect, insufficiently catering for confusion, the half-seen, plain error. Paul Jones could log no running commentary, his recollections are vivid but perforce subjective. 'A Person must have been an Eye-witness to form a Just Idea of this tremendous scene of Carnage, Wreck and Ruin that everywhere appeared. Humanity cannot but recoil from the Prospect of such finished Horror and lament that which should produce such Fatal Consequences.'

Probably – necessary word – at this crisis, frantic to escape his burning, lopsided, shattered vessel by storming *Serapis* with all hands, he uttered his famous cry, though, from the mauling, demented turmoil, accounts differ. In one, Pearson, seeing *Bonhomme Richard* fatally stricken, called to know whether Jones had surrendered, only to receive the retort: 'Surrender! I have not yet begun to fight,' in tones maddened, exultant, contemptuous or in instinctive bravado, but not quite silenced yet. In another, a master-gunner, Henry Gardner, at a cry that Jones and Dale had fallen, attempted to grab command, ordering the release of the prisoners and rushing to haul down the flag, by now the American, only to find it already lying at his feet, so that he could only implore the British for mercy. Then, seeing the infuriated Jones still alive, begged him, 'For God's sake, surrender,' Jones later claiming to have flailed him with a hand gun while bawling the great defiance. Then he recovered the flag, tattered, discoloured, and grimly nailed it back on what remained of the mast. The story might not be strictly correct, but Paul Jones knew that by such rags, men live.

In the shifts that determine crowds and battles, he suddenly succeeded, against all Pearson's calculations. With British grenades exploding around him, his own last shots smashing into *Serapis*, smoke dense and choking, flames almost everywhere at the tar and timbers, water filling the hold, prisoners scrambling up in bewildered disarray seeing compatriots and rebels shooting to the death, most pumps fouled, canvas flaming, corpses everywhere – back at the wheel, Jones at last managed to ram the British stern head on, the shock again entangling the rival masts. Pearson's jib boom was gripped, Jones and Dale rushed forward with grappling irons, Wiebert and his marines ready to leap into *Serapis* at Jones's order, while he yelled at the few surviving guns to give them ingress by firing straight. They obeyed and, as if on dramatic cue, could once again, through foul air, amid screams and hateful thuddings, see *Pallas* back with them, Cottineau nerving himself to attack *Countess of Scarborough* and silencing its guns, which had been supporting Pearson throughout.

With gun muzzles almost touching, the two listing flagships were as one, Paul Jones himself seizing an enemy forestay, lashing it to his own stump of mizzen mast, then driving in the nails and uttering the gist of that apocryphal call: 'Well done, brave lads, we have her now. Stand by for boarding.' An order was certainly given and the irons held. Despite Pearson's exhortations, Wiebert's onrush briefly mastered the British, the American snipers giving what support they could in a last fire before leaving.

Dale had been among the first to jump ahead, and others, so often rebellious, had zestfully followed, joining the marines in impetuous clashes. The ships, all aslant, swung almost full circle on the tide, the headland crowds watched breathlessly, transfixed by the din, the fires, the smoke, the dim but blooded figures slashing, tackling, hurling grenades, flashing knives, firing pistols, while British upper-deck guns still pounded the derelict *Bonhomme Richard*. To the Flamborough multitudes, vast on the glimmering cliffs, momentous political issues and the Rights of Man had dwindled to bullet and blade, raw fists, to fire, water and metal.

Jones wrote later to Gouverneur Morris: 'The Enemy's stern opposite to our bows and the yards being locked...in that Situation the action continued two hours and a half, both ships being on fire for the greater part of the time.'

Sure of Dale, he had rallied his three intact cannon and whatever else available, had somehow controlled the floundering prisoners, but knew that *Bonhomme Richard* would scarcely last until dawn. In agony to survive, men on both ships could only go forward, lost in unstoppable killers' rage, barely upright on tilted decks slippery with blood. Attack or extinction, the dead and maimed distorted by flame and moon, while others strove for a ladder, a gun, to unbolt a hatch, ward off blows struck at them from the indistinct and formless, seen as if through reddened tissue. Officers and men, all nationalities, merged in a common mêlée, shrouded in fumes from flesh and powder. Woodwork was pulverised, metal shrinking, on all sides hung the pungency of rich life becoming rich meat, luridly transformed by the bland moon, oozing, stinking.

On *Serapis*, Jones's men held ground, were almost victorious as Cottineau, having eliminated the *Countess*, was moving to confront *Serapis*, more explosions rocking the night.

The burning *Serapis* was also holed, though less drastically than *Richard*. Jones and Cottineau must then have thought they had won, but they were mistaken. Abandoning his own ship, ready to personally overcome Pearson, Jones saw that defeat might come, had perhaps already come, not from the fighting British, not from volunteers from the convoy or from Yorkshire, but from another ship now firing at the backs of himself and his men, blows from life at its meanest, to snuff him out in failure, all hopes dropping overboard with his body.

Hoarse shouts and gasps of hope and relief at once died as Pierre Landais, lord of treachery, prepared to trample on the losers. Out in the moonlight, its fresh guns aiming at the fiery chaos, *Alliance* was unmistakable, with its pack of crowing French and Britishers. Astounded, in near panic, his erstwhile associates cursed, threatened, then implored him to desist. But, ignoring the *Pallas–Countess* duel, Landais, visitant from outer darkness, in manic glee or cold deliberation, revenging himself from whatever torments, had twice circled the four battling ships then, despite his officers' protests, hurled his broadsides at Jones and Cottineau, while the undefended Baltic merchantmen, a fortune for the taking, lumbered towards safety but still open to his attack. 'I beg you not to sink us,' a cry reached him, Jones vainly displaying signals of identity as best he could. Cottineau shouted for Landais to accept *Countess of Scarborough* as prize or join in against *Serapis* but the Frenchman ignored him, still firing on Jones then withdrawing as soundlessly as he had come, perhaps at last perceiving, though late, the convoy escaping, covered by smoke.

John Paul Jones fought on, regardless of prizes. Some half of his men were out of action: on *Richard*, but one pump was still usable, all was near foundering while on *Serapis* men with unnatural strength wrestled with flames and each other. Musketeers, marines, seamen, officers, almost exhausted, staggering towards a common end.

Captain Pearson retained strength enough to seek the master blow, despite his own dangerous situation. For Lincoln Lorenz, this was the moment of his demand for Jones's surrender. Perhaps, but no matter. The conflict continued, the watchers aloft on the cliffs, seeing the two ships atrociously embracing, disfigured by bulging smoke and weird lights, appearing a booming, flame-spitting sea monster, glowing crimson, fading, reviving in blossoms of sparks and in retching convulsions as it tore at its own guts. In the unfocused welter of fire and explosion, living and dead, blood and gristle, Paul Jones and Richard Dale rebuffed Richard Pearson and again drove and cursed their men into attack. 'The Scene was Dreadful beyond the Reach of Language,' Jones wrote. His prisoners, released by the master of arms, still on *Richard*, unable to knife or overpower him or join the raving fight, were bailing, douching, swamping, anything to keep alive, though timbers were fatally loosening. Yet it was from the wreckage of one of its masts that deliverance came. Forestalling British cheers was a flash of terror, a dreadful quake, as a Scot, overhanging *Serapis*, lobbed a grenade down the open hatch of a gunroom still loaded with powder. In the explosion, some 40 men fell, all cannon halted, commands ceased and, in a stillness both sickening and inspiring, Jones took his last chance. Could he force his men to endure but a few moments more, be first to break from the paralysis of the explosion, he must conquer. His snipers had matched his orders, Wiebert still lived, fearless above the stricken, a slow British counterattack was viciously repulsed, though numbers could scarcely keep their feet and the final say was being relinquished to the captains, Richard Pearson and Paul Jones. With *Bonhomme Richard* half-sunk, *Serapis* in danger of being dragged down with it or, if battle continued, of itself being downed by water flooding the hold, one man had to outstare the other, and the Englishman flinched.

Richard Pearson's courage was never questioned, but his mainmast had gone, the others were broken, he had had three hours of evil whines and bangs, shakings and screeches, of unremitting bloodshed. *Alliance*, which could have saved him, had vanished, the *Countess* had surrendered, his ship barely alive, supporting agonies, flares, and the peril below. Also, he had accomplished his mission: he had saved the 44 ships entrusted to him. He had done enough and, surrounded by several hundred casualties, American, British, French and the rest, he surrendered his sword to John Paul Jones, who summoned the grace to return it, with requisite courtesies.

Between the now immobile ships and Flamborough Head, fog fell swiftly, like a curtain. The moon withdrew, as if satiated. A sort of groaning silence enveloped the water. Trim vessels had become hulks for the dead and for surgeons bending over disgusting wounds.

Whitman concluded his description:

> Serene stands the little captain...
> stretched and still lies the midnight,
> Two great hulls motionless on the breast of the darkness.

By morning, *Serapis*, though battered and scorched, was still afloat, flying the Stars and Stripes, as Paul Jones's flagship *Bonhomme Richard* was lying on the sea bed, where it remains.

'No action,' Paul Jones considered, 'was ever, in all respects, so bloody, so severe, and so lasting.' He exaggerated, of course, addressing an age of exaggerated manners, ideals and diction, in which the manipulation of a snuffbox had the intricacies of a marriage contract, a smile contained a score of insinuations, a bow was a graceful opportunity for a multitude of deceits. Nevertheless, he had procured Washington a considerable American feat. Kings and emperors would know of it; Chaumont, Arthur Lee and Sam Adams would haggle over it, Franklin rejoice, Dorothea Dandridge dream of it and, because of it, Pierre Landais would fill himself with more hate. Paul Jones had justified the belief of Hewes, Morris, Jefferson, John and Abigail Adams, of Lafayette: he had forced his name into the consciousness of Selkirks and Craiks. The dead – his father in a Presbyterian heaven – would hear of him. His mother and sisters must applaud him. The jealousy of other captains was splendour in his blood. He, landless John Paul, had reached deep into himself and drawn out the prize that had waited there, and an English commander sat prisoner in a cabin no longer his own, allegedly never bringing himself to speak to his captor.

Herman Melville later judged that the great fight would 'involve at once a type, a parallel and a prophecy – sharing the same blood with England, and yet her proud foe in two wars – not wholly inclined at bottom to forget an old grudge – intrepid, unprincipled, reckless, predatory, with boundless ambition, civilised in externals yet a savage at heart, America is, or may be, yet the Paul Jones of Nations.'

Latter-day objectivity may judge the fight, like the Whitehaven landing, of no great historical significance, though it would be magnified by broadsheet and street ballad, fear, patriotism, deranged reports. For Britain, a minor defeat had been redeemed by the preservation of the convoy. For America, however, Paul Jones, heroic as Washington at the Delaware, had given immediate tonic, by the only celebrated defeat of Britain at sea by one of its own. By valour. Once again, tavern gossip, schoolyard rhymes, coffeehouse rumours, pothouse wiseacres, molly-house wits contributed their quota. Great liars, Hitler was to declare and demonstrate, are great magicians. Such a battle repolished tribal symbols, picturesque, true, or false, but cluttering the imagination. Symbols of national success, like gods, heroes, witchdoctors and prophets, made people feel at home in the world, part of a larger society, apt to venerate or seek the paradisial, the ideal, the impossible. Truth was not the main factor. Daniel Defoe had already remarked that 100,000 men were always ready to fight Popery, though undecided whether this was man or horse. A few generations ahead, Russian crowds were bawling for 'Constantine and Constitution', imagining the pair were man and wife.

The twenty-first century has no cause for complacency. Technology can reinforce popular credulity by more widely distributing falsehood, promoting superficial celebrities and cheapening language. GK Chesterton was to reflect that it takes an age which has nothing to say to invent the loudspeaker. Imagination craves to invent or embellish.

A twentieth-century gardener gained an extravagantly circulated reputation for piety by continually reiterating 'Trust in the Lord'. Only the insiders knew that he was invoking Lord Northcliffe, a founder of the *Daily Mail*, owner of *The Times* and, in 1918, director of wartime propaganda. An admirer of Napoleon, he allegedly chose his title so that he could use as his monogram, 'N'. Not quite forgotten is his querulous rejoinder, 'If he wants a title, why can't he buy one, like any other honest man?' Another tiny flake of social history concerns a traveller on the early London Underground. He stepped out at a disused station, then, realising his mistake, stepped back. This was enlarged into a national report of him remaining imprisoned in the empty station for several months, surviving by chewing torn-off posters.

To foster cohesion and self-respect, the new nation and possible Great Power of America still required traditional rituals, symbols and institutions, inherited through centuries of British growth, from England, Scandinavia, Franks, Anglo-Saxons, Common Law, individual rights; tolerant philosophy, independent judiciary, customs allowing for the sporting chance – to be refurbished for the needs of a small, lively but serious population amid the huge opportunities of seemingly limitless lands. The Republic incorporated immemorial totems: flag, oath, icons, song, with a written constitution, supreme court, and, dispensing with another sacred object, the Crown, swearing fealty to an elected president.

In a decor of heroes and victims, struggle and victory, sacrifice and paeans, Flamborough Head had a place – in the growth of an American imagination and the almost legendary origins of an American navy, with some part to play in the defence, spread or defeat of civilisation.

The commonplace must replace the sensational, otherwise the latter would not exist. Once in command of *Serapis*, Paul Jones had to turn from the heroic to the mundane but essential.

From *Pallas*, *Vengeance* and even, in some accounts, *Alliance*, now that hopes of scavenger pickings on *Serapis* had been extinguished, the seamen, some doubtless shamed by their comrades' bravery, had attempted to retrieve *Bonhomme Richard*, but Paul Jones himself finally acknowledged this as useless, waters had almost reached the deck, fires still smouldered and, 'with inexpressible grief' he ordered total abandonment, leaving the ravaged vessel to sink, the only ship he ever lost.

He had no leisure, or inclination, to lament in his new quarters. Immediately, he was supervising restoration of *Serapis*'s masts and bulwarks, repairs to the hull, draining the hold, the arrangements for the wounded, the prisoners and the disposal of the dead, all this quieter and surely more eerie than the moonlit contest itself: the burning shrouds, toppling masts, the explosions, the glimmering cliffs, bloodshot waters, the ghostly crowds. All equipment must be inspected, even in the anxiety to leave British coasts. Most guns were wrecked, ammunition was virtually spent. Jones had also to deal with his prisoner, Richard Pearson, with his snapped-off career, dejection, though not humiliation. He had fought well, saved the convoy, sacrificed his prospects and risked his life. From his lost flagship, he wrote to the Admiralty:

'I am extremely sorry for the misfortune that has happened – that of losing His Majesty's ship that I had the honour to command; but at the same time, I flatter myself with the hope that their Lordships will be convinced that she has not been given away, but that, on the contrary, every exertion has been used to defend her.'

Serapis, despite all repairs, was in no condition to reach France. Trailed by a few British auxiliaries, Paul Jones steered for the Texel, *Pallas* accompanying him. Despite victory, much was sombre. He had lost some 150 men, the British slightly less.

The voyage safely accomplished, he must winter through long, difficult weeks in neutral Holland, amid wrangles, intrigues, and diplomatic flurries. His ego was gratified, nevertheless, by the welcome awarded him. To the indignation of the British ambassador, the local population acclaimed the American, singing:

> Here comes Paul Jones, such a nice fellow,
> Does his job well and still plays the hero.

Of the Dutch and daily conditions, he had no complaint: the son of Mr Craik's housekeeper could appreciate not only his popularity on the streets but the streets themselves, daily cleansed of dung and garbage, the orderly crowds and, overall, the sober workmanship, religious tolerance, the enterprise and apparent honesty.

Information reached him of American jubilation over the battle, France itself rejoicing in some share of the credit, to offset miseries of the d'Orvilliers fiasco. Paul Jones had presented the only allied success of 1779. John Adams was unusually stirred, and Benjamin Franklin, now sole minister plenipotentiary in Paris, wrote to his sister:

'Tho' we have burnt none of their Towns, we have occasioned a great deal of Terror and Bustle in many of them, as they imagined our Commodore Jones had 4,000 troops with him for Descent. He has, however, taken and destroyed upwards of twenty sail of their Merchantmen and Colliers, and is indeed arrived safe in Holland with some 500 prisoners.'

Paul Jones was soon bedevilled with abstruse issues and complex negotiations. Holland was no more politically homogenous than any other Great Power. The political situation was worried over by a pro-British Orange faction, by neutralists scared of Britain and by interventionists eager to join France and America and avenge the afflictions of the seventeenth-century Anglo–Dutch Wars, though their bellicosity, and urge to despoil the British carcase had been wrecked by the failure of the Great Design.

The Hague authorities were mostly anxious to be rid of Jones, to force him back to sea. Vengeful British warships were hovering off the Texel, waiting to trap him, and in London, Lord Sandwich was imploring his subordinates: 'For God's sake, get to sea instantly... If you can take Paul Jones, you will be as high in the estimation of the public as if you had beat the combined Fleet.'

The public itself was humming the latest catch song:

> If success to our Fleets be not quickly restored,
> The leaders in office we'll shove from the boards,
> May they all fare alike and the Devil pick the bones
> Of Germain, Jemmy Twitcher, Lord North and Paul Jones.

Paul Jones now had prisoners to oversee, *Serapis* to repair, prize money to demand from France – $27,000 for himself – and he must have cursed Landais for so promptly obeying Chaumont and relinquishing those prizes to the Danes, a guarantee of interminable negotiations and ill temper.

Scarcely realised in the fury of battle but not overlooked by Chaumont, already shocked by casualties among the French marines, was the loss of the convoy which Landais could at least have halted. Landais himself was due for court-martial, his perversities and treachery had to be completely nailed but, though shunned by many, he nevertheless had defenders. Captain Cottineau and some of *Alliance*'s crew, though aggrieved by loss of the Baltic spoils, were already excusing him. Not so Captain Ricot, of *Vengeance*: 'Landais is a madman from whom there is all to fear.'

The delinquent, still at large in Holland, was publicly taunting and baiting Jones, claiming the Flamborough Head victory as his own and, surely, if reason had any place in his behaviour, he must have planned to destroy the American, capture the Englishman, and take the profits. Jones, however, brusquely commandeered *Alliance* unopposed and in righteous wrath, demanded the traitor's arrest and trial from Franklin.

'His conduct has been Base and Unpardonable. Either Captain Landais or myself is highly Criminal, and one or the other must be punished. I forbear to take any Steps with him until I have the Advice and Approbation of Your Excellency. I have been advised by all the Officers of the Squadron to put M. Landais under Arrest; but as I have Postponed it so long, I will bear with him a little longer, until the return of my express.'

Without ship or status, abandoned by whatever confederates he had had, Landais managed to reach Paris, bristling with complaints, explanations, boasts, denials and accusations, to which Chaumont might well have listened, with his own misgivings about Paul Jones and, possibly, about this own wife, but the staid Franklin for once lost restraint. 'I think you so imprudent,' one of his most censorious epithets, 'so litigious and quarrel-some a man, that peace and good order and consequently the quiet and regular subordination so necessary to success, are, where you preside, impossible; these are within my observation; your military operations I leave to more competent judges. If therefore, I had twenty ships of war in my disposition, I should not give one of them to Captain Landais.'

With profounder curiosity than Paul Jones, Franklin nevertheless had small concern for the 'maladjusted', a term he would have regarded, as Churchill did 'shellshocked', as a shirker's charter. Landais remains an interesting case history, in its way, a form of triumph.

Paul Jones behaved among the Dutch with modest tact, while awaiting events, involved as he was with the raddled *Serapis*, cleansing *Alliance* from slovenly neglect and keeping creditors at bay. A year later, in 1780, a bill for £20,000 'fresh expenses' would descend upon the wearied Franklin. Jones had to placate and reassure, with crew and prisoners, and those on *Alliance*, and deal with the restive and morose Pearson. He was also enjoying sentimental passages with the schoolgirl daughter of an American delegate, Dumas, of whom little is known.

Chaumont's agents were assiduously collecting, without distributing, all prize monies, while those who had earned it lingered almost destitute. Lord North, Lord Sandwich, and the ambassador were demanding the surrender of the ships, crew and prisoners of 'Paul Jones, of Scotland, who is a rebel subject and a criminal of the State'. They made threatening accusations that 'in direct and open Violations of the Treaty', the Dutch had allowed 'an American Pirate to remain several weeks in one of their Ports, and even permitted a part of his crew to mount guard in a fort in the Texel'.

There were suspicions, perhaps well grounded that, on orders from Franklin and America, Jones was prolonging his sojourn to further aggravate Anglo–Dutch relations and, by infringing Dutch neutrality, ensuring Holland's joining France and Spain in a coalition that might attract Denmark and Sweden.

The Texel fort contained the British prisoners and actually the privilege permitted him in thus holding them on neutral soil was, Lorenz comments, 'without precedent in diplomatic annals'. He remained even after rendering *Serapis* fit to depart, thereby forcing Holland to recognise the American Republic. 'Huzza America!' he crowed, confident that this was preliminary to war.

The Dutch were being precipitated into crisis not only by America. The British were stopping and searching Dutch vessels, confiscating any goods suspected as intended for the rebels, all existing treaty privileges were suspended until finally Britain itself declared war on Holland in 1780, the favours being granted Paul Jones prominent in the formal proclamation. A plan for him to escort a fleet conveying timber and war supplies to France, for American use, had already been discovered by spies and betrayed to London.

After several months, Chaumont's ministry accepted entire responsibility for Paul Jones's squadron and prisoners, Franklin promising a small wage payment on account, though the French suggestion that, in leaving Holland and breaking through the British watchdogs he should adopt French colours, Jones rejected as 'a most Impertinent Proposal'. His pen darted into action on behalf of 'the flag' in a letter to the Congress president:

'I claimed and obtained the first Salute from that of France, before our Independence was otherwise announced in that Kingdom, and no man can wish more Ardently to support its Rising Glory than myself.'

At a further suggestion of escaping Holland in a French privateer, he stormed:

'My Rank from the beginning knew no superior in the Marine of America . . . It is a matter of the Highest Astonishment to me that the Court should offer the present Insult to my Understanding and suppose me capable of disgracing my present Commission. I confess I never merited all the praise, bestowed on my past Conduct, but I also feel I have far less merited such a Reward.'

To others, and not overlooking Franklin, he agitated about being asked 'to disgrace the Stars of America by accepting a dirty Piece of Parchment'. Hearing of a murder plot against him, the Dutch peremptorily ordered him out, despite the dozen British ships offshore. At various times, 42 such ships were on the lookout, patrolling almost the length of eastern Britain, a diversion welcome to America.

On 28 December 1779, Paul Jones left harbour on *Alliance* with *Serapis* and other prizes with him. A newcomer on board was the doughty American captain, Gustavus Conyngham, for whom, before his escape from a British prisoner-of-war camp, Paul Jones had pleaded for mitigation of his hardships.

Once again, exploiting his zest for the challenging with the least expected, he reached the Channel, dared the Solent and, sailing almost under the guns of Portsmouth and Wight, he evaded all pursuers with feints and dodges almost debonair in their precision, while resuming gunnery drill, confident of a towering future opening for him on golden hinges. Reaching France without mishap from sea or foe, he was assured of a cordial greeting, not only from Franklin but from those still reckoned to be of higher social grandeur.

> The prisoners he brought were from Britain and England,
> He does things with skill, has made a fine prize.
> From Texel to Brest, let them see his stern only,
> He's like a swan on the sea, shoots cannon-balls like currants,
> Carries sword on his hip but looks like a student.
>
> Anon

On Flamborough Head is a memorial: 'reminder of the famous sea-fight off the headland between the American colonist, John Paul Jones and Captain Sir Richard Pearson, RN. John Paul Jones is regarded as the founder of the U.S. Navy.'

Bonhomme Richard still lies somewhere off the Head. Plans to locate and lift her for the 1979 bicentenary were frustrated by the funds having been spent on preliminaries. More proposals by Clive Cussler, author of *Raise the Titanic*, helped by the National Ocean Industries (USA) and Decca Navigation (UK), accumulated a larger amount, and the marine archaeologist, Sydney Wignal, director of Atlantic Maritime Foundation, co-operated by trying to discover the ship's whereabouts, assisted by the American Bi-Centennial Association, but results remain disappointing.

> The two British captains suffered court martial but were acquitted and became great heroes. Each had conferred upon him the freedom of the Borough of Scarborough and also that of Kingston Upon Hull. A silver casket lined with heart of oak, which was presented to Captain Thomas Piercy of *The Countess of Scarborough* by the Council of the Borough of Scarborough on 25 October 1779 to mark the 'freedom' ceremony has been in the possession of the Royal Navy for many years...The other casket, presented to Captain Pearson of *Seraphis* was auctioned at Sotheby's in 1978 and sold for £3,780.
>
> Scarborough Borough Council Tourist Information Centre

10

Trials and Rewards

Here richly, with ridiculous display
The Politician's corpse was laid away.
While all his acquaintances sneered and slanged
I wept; for all I had longed to see him hanged.

Hilaire Belloc,
Epitaph on the Politician Himself, 1923

In the course of near seven years service, I have continually suggested what has occurred to me as most likely to promote the Honor of our Marine and render it Serviceable to our Cause; but my voice has been like a cry in the Desert. The whole result to counterbalance the Dishonor of the Flag and the loss of the navy only appears to have augmented the Purses of the Agents, besides enabling a few of the Actors, perhaps not the first in merit or abilities, to purchase farms etc.

John Paul Jones,
Letter to Marine Office

The mildest Monarch who has ever filled the French throne.

Gouverneur Morris,
A Diary of the French Revolution, 1939 edition.

In America at least, France was winning some revenge for decades of defeat. Paris society still crackled with wit, often spiteful, Versailles still glittered, though Franklin was aware of a crown trapped in protocol and tradition; an archaic administration that obstructed its attempts of reform; further energy rotted by bored, devitalised courtiers and dishonest flunkeys usually unpaid for years. Its chronicler, G Lenôtre, wrote in 1894 of 'This crowd of useless and expensive servants, this complication of the most menial services, these parasitical excrescences thrust upon the royal power, stifled and exhausted it. It was from that that it died, but so little did it understand its malady that it deemed it indispensable to its life.'

The elaborate pacings and insincere inclinations, fatigued expressions and slow winks; the anterooms of insolent officials and perplexed ministers; the stuffy, candle-dripping boudoirs and malodorous passages; the inert routine of cards, hunt, chapel and intrigue; the caustic grins of underlings watching complacent patricians exploit costly sinecures, while the bourgeois administrators, industrious but unprivileged, waited their chance...all that had evolved to awe rowdy streets and control the professional classes, was becoming dangerously unreal.

Society had accepted with a straight face the claim made by de Quélen, Archbishop of Paris, that not only was Jesus the Son of God but, on his mother's side, came from very good family, but the weary parade of wigged elaborate ladies and gentlemen no longer convinced. Louis XIV's bankrupting defeats, Louis XV's loss of India and Canada, Versailles itself, were not yet paid for. The bills for the American War would alarm the stolid, worried king, who, like all monarchs, breathed too much flattery. What Mussolini was told, that the deadliest gas was incense, was true of Bourbon France.

In the Paris of the spring of 1780, a few savants might have pondered the prophecy of Nostradamus in 1555: 'A great King captured by a young man, not far from Easter: confusion: a state of the knife.' Others could contemplate with equanimity the apparent weakness of oligarchical Britain, ringed by the coalition of France, Spain, Holland and the Scandinavian powers uniting in armed neutrality to guard against the hated Royal Navy.

Despite problems at L'Orient where *Alliance* lay unused and Landais clamoured for redress, Paul Jones was much in Paris, savouring the social felicities of a great European capital: 'No woman was in fashion unless she had kissed me. ' At the opera, he received an ovation. From Versailles, he was awarded the title, 'chevalier', that for sturdy American Republicans he cherished too fervently. Also, a royal gift given to no other American officer, not even to Washington, the Order of Military Merit, *Pro Virtute Bellico*, with a gold-hilted sword inscribed in Latin: 'Louis XVI rewards the Brave Upholder of the Freedom of the Seas.'

Such adulation was toxic. The opulent and modish saw the suppleness, grace and modesty of a gentleman twinned with the glamour of a Byronic corsair, 'Man of loneliness and mystery', a splendour of roving, wanton, original personality that had astonished the British on moonlit waters. The

Nine Sisters Masonic Lodge, whose members included Helvetius, Voltaire, Franklin, Sieyès, Condorcet, Chamfort, Danton and Desmoulins, welcomed him, commissioning the Houdon bust, praised in the 1781 salon: 'A strong, sea-faring face, prematurely aged, with an expression of decision and self-will.'

Prince de Nassau-Siegen complimented him and apparently introduced him to an expensive courtesan. Accommodating husbands presented gracious wives. He indulged in an affair, on both sides somewhat calculating, with 'Madame T', Aimée de Telison, (or Théresa Townsend, or both), and Countess de Lowendahl, whose brother had naval ambitions, and who painted his miniature, now in the American Naval Academy. He accepted the favours of 'Delia', Scottish-born Countess de Murray de Nicolson, who was sufficiently enamoured to propose leaving her husband, leaving Paris, and joining the captain in his 'small cabin'. Never before, she wrote, had she felt a love 'so dear and fatal to my peace when fate revealed you to my ravished sight; That moment fixed my destiny for ever'.

She was wrong. Meanwhile, she received his verses, scarcely Byronic:

> When Jove, from high Olympus goes
> To Ida and the fair below,
> All Heaven laments – but Juno shows
> A jealous and superior woe.
> In vain to her all Power is given,
> To female weakness ever dear,
> She scorns the Sovereignty of Heaven,
> Her God, her Jove, seems all to her!

She desired to be goddess for a man to whom beauty was an inadequate challenge:

'You ask my indulgence for your verses, adorable Jones. How dear is your Modesty in my heart. But never had anyone less cause for it; everything belonging to you is enchanting. Those incomparable lines which portray your noble mind and all its elevation, made me shed a flood of tears. Dear Jones, you are unequalled in your perfections, and never was mortal as adored as you are worshipped by my devoted heart.'

He did not demur. Titles are apt to be despised by those who have failed to acquire them or by those already in possession. Chevalier Paul Jones was not yet critical of countesses – de Lowendahl – who claimed to be a daughter of the sexually spendthrift Louis XV, a claim to be more thoroughly investigated, with disappointing results. It was more gratifying to be accepted by Franklin's admirer, the Duke de la Rochefoucauld. His supporter, Chartres, though professionally discredited, was also prince of the blood.

To the son of a Scots villager, Louis-Philippe Joseph and his duchess must have been romantic and provident. That Chartres was weak and selfish, not generous, but extravagant and over-impulsive, was unscrupulous, toadying to egalitarian journalists and seeking popularity from fickle crowds, for the moment was not obvious. Paul Jones might not yet know that when his duchess underwent a dental operation, Philippe announced that had the surgeon pulled off her entire jaw, he, the duke, would not have moaned if the tongue had also gone. Chartres was listed in a secret police dossier as habitually using language at which the most shameful would blush. A womaniser like Paul Jones, he considered a woman well-dressed only when naked.

Nakedness was to be thought a form of equality. To demonstrate his egalitarian beliefs, a revolutionary deputy, Charles Javogues, like to parade himself naked. He also issued another undesirable creed: 'I recognise as a Patriot only he who, if necessary, would denounce his father, mother and sister, and drink a glass of their blood on the scaffold.' During the Red Terror of 1792 to 1794 and the subsequent White Terror, such behaviour and rhetoric was insufficiently deplored. To such as Chartres and Javogues, civilisation owes no debt, in comparison with the moderation of Washington and Adams, Jefferson and Franklin.

Of Chartres's mistress, the intellectual Madame de Genlis, Talleyrand mentioned that to escape the indignities of coquetry, she always yielded at once. Governess to the ducal children, she strove to cure Louis-Philippe, the future Citizen King of the French, from being a bore, a task possible but arduous.

Already, eyes keener than his own were watching Chartres, soon to be Duke of Orleans, as if from a betting shop. Like his fellow Mason, the anti-clerical, professedly liberal Lafayette, Chartres, with his several contra-dictory ambitions, may never have been certain of what he actually was.

Despite social high-flying Paul Jones had work to do, both in Paris and L'Orient. Prize money must be wrangled from Chaumont, wages contrived for an impatient or dejected crew, soundings be taken with Sartine for another and larger expedition. Reputation, once founded, must be mounted upon.

All so often, officialdom procrastinated. Enraged by delays and excuses, counterproposals, he posted back from L'Orient and awoke Franklin at four in the morning with a stack of complaints.

This situation was familiar even to Nelson, who would later write to Emma Hamilton: 'My time, ever since I arrived in Town, has been taken up in attempting to get the wages due to my good fellows for the various ships they have served in the war.'

Franklin had confirmed his commandeering of *Alliance*, forbidding Landais to attempt to regain it, but Jones's request that Congress should both refit it and rescue *Serapis* from French claims dismayed the commissioner, so renowned for restraint and economy. Franklin responded: 'The whole Expense would fall on me... I therefore beg you to have mercy on me. I have no money... for God's sake be sparing! Unless you mean to make me a Bankrupt!'

Eventually, Jones was promised the frigate *Ariel*, in addition to *Alliance*, now in charge of Richard Dale, and perhaps *Serapis*, though Congress soon ordered the first two to hasten to America with supplies for the hard-pressed armies.

Paul Jones remained too long in Paris, with its opportunities for conferences, interviews and allurements. In L'Orient, his men, disheartened, bewildered or indignant, were feuding with Landais's lot, who welcomed the absence of the formidable American. Encouraged by Arthur Lee, himself anxious for passage home, Landais was noisily maintaining that he was still captain of *Alliance*. Jones's men were ill clothed, badly fed and ignorant of their future. Many, illiterate, or speaking no English, had volunteered for the usual short spell and felt fooled by Jones's meticulous contracts into an indefinite and meaningless imprisonment in a strange town where foreigners were disregarded or disliked.

The French authorities seemed resolved to keep hold of *Serapis*, which they were ostentatiously repairing. Congress, insisting on the immediate sending of the supplies, was also demanding full accounts of the late expedition's expenses and debts, without reference to its own obligations and those of France. Jones informed Franklin: 'Unless the prize money is paid, my throat will assuredly be cut... I engaged these men, they fought bravely, and I must see them done justice.'

He must have known that gratitude is seldom a foible of the powerful. The only gratitude known of Frederick the Great was to the horse on which he fled after a battle.

Paul Jones also had visions more than those of money and justice: of a navy totally reorganised, of St Helena captured, of Britain's eastern commerce disrupted, of British Indian trade routes patrolled. Also, never relinquishing hopes once grafted, he was still wanting *L'Indienne*, now in America as a private merchantman.

He parleyed with officials. contractors. purvevors and attended irritable mass meetings on *Alliance*, but unwisely lived on shore, allegedly with 'Delia', though more is inferred than documented. Worse, in complicity with Lee, for whose private baggage, valuable war materials had to give place, Landais had seized *Alliance*, ejected Dale, manacled those still loyal to Paul Jones and thrust them into the verminous hold. He then hoisted sail for America, prepared for the congratulations of Congress and the commendations of Arthur Lee for delivering the supplies.

By alerting the harbour master, Jones could have stopped him, but he desisted, 'to avoid bloodshed'. Such scruples may not have been his main reason. Transporting supplies was routine, almost menial: better chances remained in Europe, he had no great affection for *Alliance* and he was as well rid of Landais as he had been of Simpson. He did lament the abduction of his *Bonhomme Richard* men. 'How shall I face those poor fellows in America, who, for Attachment to me were carried away in irons on the *Alliance*?'

Landais's vainglory was swiftly inglory; lurching about the Atlantic, he had a stand-up row with Lee about the great man's eating habits, followed by indiscriminate rages against officers and passengers, which provoked two mutinies. He then abandoned all command, retired to his cabin and, reaching port, had to be dragged hysterically ashore. Court-martialled under John Barry, on Lee's evidence he was judged insane, and he was dismissed from the service for usurping *Alliance* and mismanaging government stores. His story, however, was not altogether complete.

After more delays, renewed demands from Congress, even from Franklin, who was now resolved to rid himself of naval affairs, Paul Jones finally submitted, storing *Ariel* with guns and powder for the American army. Before sailing on 8 October 1780, he gave a flamboyant party on board, in which scenes from the *Serapis* battle were performed. Laden with vulnerable arms, he could not risk gratuitous prize seeking. Also, he was in haste to counter Landais and his high-placed confederates, then gain new contacts, now that Hewes was dead, and Robert Morris more concerned with the Treasury than the Marine. He could probably rely on John Adams, but Lee and Samuel Adams, high in the Republic's councils, would be defending Landais.

Leaving France, he almost at once met a hurricane off Brittany, one of the fiercest storms of the century, surpassing, he wrote, 'the reach even of Poetic Fancy, and the Pencil'. In darkness, his masts smashed, the hold awash, granite cliffs and rocks ever closer, in such crisis he could reach a personal summit, at one with himself in contest with the impersonal and the elemental, dependent on no one else in a brute struggle to live. With its perilous currents, rocks, massive winds and waves, the sea could be overcome by sheer will, adamantine concentration. Human duplicity and perversity now had no part: he was complete in his loneliness, the loneliness of a master craftsman, relying on his own nerve and capability. His obdurate, ungenerous nature was his ultimate sanction. The sea, nature, knew nothing of generosity and decency, and could destroy a man given to second thoughts and prolonged consideration. It was not an idle distraction or a phrase from Thomson's verse, but an immediate challenge, which he accepted without thought.

He mastered the tempest, outriding it while other ships perished by the score. 'The entire Breton coast,' an American historian records, 'was strewn with wrecks, and the bodies of drowned men; even in landlocked harbours vessels had to be dragged ashore.' A passenger on *Ariel*, Samuel Wharton, praised 'the matchless skill and unshaken intrepidity of Captain Jones... who rode the whirlwind and directed the storm.' Years afterwards, Richard Dale testified that he had never seen 'such coolness and readiness in such frightful circumstances as Paul Jones showed in the nights and days when we lay off the Penmarques, expecting every moment to be our last; and the danger was greater even than we were in when the *Bonhomme Richard* fought the *Serapis*.'

Not a man was lost but the damage necessitated two months' repairing, to Congress's annoyance, during which Jones unsuccessfully sought another command, through the new French navy minister, de Castries, through Chaumont, even through Lowendahl's brother, William. By Christmas, he and Dale had to return to *Ariel*, now refitted. He was soon playing old tricks: in one fight, with *Ariel* flying British colours and with guns concealed, Jones challenged *Triumph*, 20 guns, in a game of bluff and counterbluff. He interrogated the English captain at some length, with persuasive charm, intending to entice him on board *Ariel* to prove his credentials. This failed, so, changing expression, he ran up the Stars and Stripes, giving the Englishman five minutes to surrender. The other stubbornly refused, so Jones steered his ship broadside, allowing his guns full target. At this, *Triumph* surrendered, but the Americans lost time in cheering and self-congratulations and, when at last they were ready to board, the enemy crowded sail and with superior speed, soon disappeared. Paul Jones, master of surprise, was now himself surprised and, the biter bit, was unamused.

Resuming, quelling some unrest, evading two British frigates that had sighted him, he reached Philadelphia, now again in the rebels' hands, on 18 February 1781, where Congress was battling with near bankruptcy, with sedition and military reverses, though these were less serious than was thought. While accepting congratulations, meeting old friends and enemies, he had to beat off attacks from the Lee–Adams cabal, assess the place-seekers, the honest, the discouraged and defeatist, and prepare financial statements for Congress. For insurance, he sent explanations to the commander-in-chief, who returned his satisfaction with Jones's conduct and merit. Praising his American officers, Washington added:

'Delicacy forbids me to mention that particular one which has attracted the admiration of the world and which has influenced the most illustrious monarch to confer a mark of his favour which can only be obtained by a long and honorable service or by the performance of some brilliant action.'

Such delicacy might not have been wholly appreciated, but the letter was a valuable addition to the captain's testimonials and, thus fortified, he set himself to submit accounts, claim payments and to find a new ship. From France, he had already pleaded with Washington to be 'instrumental to put the naval Force that remains, on a more useful and honorable footing', though what the generalissimo wanted was *Ariel* and its supplies. However, with citations from Sartine, de Castries, Franklin and Lafayette...he wrote replies to 47 questions demanded by Congress concerning his foreign activities. Most were routine but a few were insulting, inserted by those hostile to Franklin and himself, insinuating that he had enriched himself by privateering, and had connived with Landais to avoid responsibility for *Alliance*. In this last, he shrewdly shifted the answer to Arthur Lee, who had himself illegally sailed with Landais and could thus accuse no one else.

Within days, Congress formally confirmed his 'distinguished bravery and military conduct...attended with circumstances so brilliant, as to excite General Applause and Admiration', and permitting, at a sparkling reception, the French minister to invest the Chevalier with his Cross of Military Merit. Another resolution gave thanks to 'the Zeal, Prudence and Intrepidity with which he hath supported the Honor of the American Flag; for his bold and successful enterprises to redeem from captivity the Citizens of these States...and in general for the Good Conduct and

Eminent Services to which he had added Lustre, to his Character and to the American arms.'

This was gratifying but, unaccompanied by practical rewards, not gratifying enough. French entry into the war, useful for America, was a setback for Jones himself, for Congress was virtually abandoning its Continental Navy, negligible beside de Grasse's powerful fleet, yet, withal, expensive. Eighteen months passed, during which, admired but unemployed, he had to borrow from Robert Morris for personal expenses before he could collect some 20,000 dollars of back payment, though for the more recent prize monies he had still to await signs of French goodwill. As for Richard Pearson, now released, his gallantry had already won him knighthood, Paul Jones sourly commenting that, next time, he would make him a lord.

He himself, though 'Chevalier', officially remained only a lower-ranked captain, despite, since a naval defeat at Charleston, South Carolina in 1780, five superiors having been cashiered. Always indifferent to, or unaware of, solecisms, he suggested for himself the award of a Congressional Gold Medal, to match the one from Louis XVI. Predictably, this was most emphatically opposed by his old adversary, Captain James Nicholson, himself shortly to face court-martial for incompetence. On this, Paul Jones was invited to sit, though, surely to his regret, sickness prevented it.

American military fortunes were recovering; the British blockade remained, but the French deftly evaded much of it and, at Chesapeake, de Grasse was worsting Admiral Graves. The land campaigns were proceeding with the lack of magnanimity habitual to civil war. Congress permitted the hanging of some Quakers for pacificism, a form of treason, and in the Carolinas the British had executed deserters. Both sides were threatened with exhaustion, but advantages lay with those engaged on their own terrain, and Washington, with Lafayette and Rochambeau, was preparing to converge on Lord Cornwallis at Yorktown.

George Washington was not infallible – he made mistakes, endured misfortunes, could be distracted by self-interest – yet the century, with its high stock of talents, produced few men and women entitled to stand beside him. His words reported as his last, in 1799, deserve attention: 'It is well, I die hard but I am not afraid to go.'

If true, they are appropriate; if not, they still express the man. He achieved far more than those still revered by many revolutionaries and political scientists: Paine and Wilkes, Mirabeau, Danton, Saint-Just, Robespierre. If he lacked the glamour of Catherine and Potemkin, the easy charm of Fox, the depths of Johnson, Montesquieu and Diderot, he could have won their private approval and public respect. Despite his toleration of slavery, he left no bad smell. All this but, in an American survey of 55 universities in 2002, only 42 per cent knew anything of Washington, while 99 per cent were familiar with such cartoon favourites as Beavis and Butt-Head.

Paul Jones, who has not been recorded as objecting to American slavery, watched events without realistic expectation of being present at the kill. One award he did ceaselessly crave as his due was promotion to admiral, despite the present absence of a navy. There was, however, a flagship, and it must be his: *America*, largest of the Republican warships, ordered several years back, though still on the stockyards and supervised by another old opponent, Colonel Langdon. Though promotion to admiral was blocked, on 23 June 1781, Congress unanimously elected him to command the new ship, with even Arthur Lee assenting, and with instructions to Morris to hasten the launching. John Adams, immersed in political and constitutional labours, found time to write that the command 'could not have been more wisely bestowed...I assure you that, if I could see the prospect of a dozen ships of the line under the American flag and commanded by Paul Jones, I apprehend that the event of a battle with the English of equal force, would redound to the glory of the United States.'

Paul Jones sped to New Hampshire to galvanise the dilatory Langdon and, in full uniform, high court, held a Franco–American reception on the decks of *America*, to celebrate the long-awaited birth of a son to Louis XVI and Marie Antoinette. Energy and tenacity then procured him a set of eighteen-pounders originally cast for *Duras*, together with a hoard of smaller guns captured from the British, though his abuse of Langdon's rigging, timber, cables and masts was constant, as were his abrasive complaints of shortage of materials, money and workmen. Once, in person, he had to stand sentry on board, against pro-British saboteurs. By day, he took charge of completing the ship according to the latest naval require-ments, achieving a masterpiece of line, power and concealed batteries, to equal the toughest that Britain had sent to the Atlantic and Caribbean.

Notwithstanding his tongue and handiwork, delays continued. He raged, but could only see life as a parade of others to blame, at times a search for defeat. Despairing, he once offered himself to Lafayette, outside Yorktown. Worse, in July 1782, he received the knockout: *America* followed *L'Indienne* as a lost hope: an accident to a French warship forced Congress, already alarmed at *America*'s expenses, to hand it to France as replacement.

The man 'of ungovernable temper' was surprisingly stoical. He had fervently longed to mastermind *America*, then lead her to sea followed by a French and American squadron, but he was now asked to superintend the last details and effect the launch, but on behalf of the French Admiral de Vaudreuil.

Though aggrieved, he consented: the launching, a difficult job, he achieved to acclaim, and saw, impassively, the tricolour flutter at the mainmast.

In this sad chapter, his spirit slumped, convinced of betrayal by, of all men, Robert Morris, though, by restraining his feelings, he achieved self-mastery to a degree of greatness. This was admitted by Morris, who appears sincere in regrets for an actual necessity. The captain's loyalty and resignation, he declared to Jones, would always 'reflect the highest Honor upon your Character. They had made so strong an impression on my mind that I immediately transmitted an extract of your letter to Congress.'

If slightly mollified, Jones must have seen himself as a Ulysses, his career one of making, through courage, shrewdness, ruthlessness and resourcefulness, the best of a very bad job. 'It was thought that Act of Congress would give me great Pain, but those who were of that opinion did not well know my Character... it was a sacrifice I made with the Pleasure to testify my grateful regard for France and my invincible attachment to the Interest of the two Allied Nations.' No doubt, though immaculate sentiments seemed to be their own reward, they were otherwise disregarded. 'However,' Richard Bickford wrote in 1993, 'he spent much of his time pressing the Authorities to modernise and improve standards of naval training and efficiency; and out of this the Annapolis Naval College was born.'

What next? *L'Indienne*, renamed *South Carolina*, was for sale and, helped by Robert Morris, Paul Jones once again almost acquired her, only to hear of her capture by the British. At this, his future seemed made negligible, 'the small farm' the only likelihood. The American navy was now little more than *Alliance*, captained by John Barry, and a sloop, *Deane*. He could only revive an old desire to at least witness the actions of a real fleet. Admiral de Vaudreuil was soon to lead 16 French warships in West Indian waters that the young John Paul had once known so well, and he requested permission to accompany him as an observer. 'I had the flattering hope of finding myself in the first military school in the World, in which I should be able to render myself useful, and to acquire knowledge very important for conducting great military operations.'

De Vaudreuil heartily consented. So did Congress, once again glad of relief from their bouncy Mr Know-all, whose zeal was as exasperating as his incessant suggestions. Paul Jones soon recovered health and cheerfulness, after being welcomed on the flagship as a fellow-professional by the admiral and the army commander, Baron de Vioménil, despite news that Rodney had overwhelmed de Grasse off Les Saintes Islands. De Vaudreuil successfully evaded Hood's superior squadron but, once again, failure of the French and Spanish to collude caused the wrecking of a French ship with scores of unnecessary casualties.

Paul Jones could only watch and restrain his feelings. Almost at once he succumbed to a severe and lingering fever. Even his own body was liable to rebel and disobey orders. It was often over-taxed. 'The state of your health alarms me,' 'Delia' had written in their happier days.

In October, before de Vaudreuil could retrieve position, Lord Cornwallis, hoping for relief from Southern loyalists, was trapped at Yorktown between American and Lafayette's French troops, and de Grasse's 24 warships blocking the Chesapeake and repelling British attempts to land men and supplies. With his expected Southerners in retreat, Cornwallis, with the last effective British army, was forced to surrender, the war formally ending with the Treaty of Versailles on 21 January 1783.

Paul Jones wrote: 'The most Brilliant success and the most instructive experience in the Art of War could not have given me a Pleasure comparable with that which I felt when I learnt that Great Britain had been compelled to recognise the Sovereign Independence of the United States of America.'

War seldom assuages international venom and social strife but it can often help solve personal dilemmas. It had released Paul Jones from inaction to fame. He was now in a stalemate which peace could not guarantee to resolve. He had been unable to assist either de Vaudreuil or de Grasse in their achievements and he had had no part in defeating Cornwallis. On shore, among the exultations and handouts, he had to recognise that Congress had lost all interest in naval reorganisation. The sea could be left to the French. His election to the Order of Cincinnatus (an order of wartime officers, including Washington), was a gratifying compliment devoid of political influence. Still not wholly recovered from sickness, he was again jobless and grouchy, still fretting about his rank – only ninth senior captain – 'miserable and dishonored by being superseded without any Just Cause assigned, ' after having 'fought and bled for the purpose of contributing to make millions happy and free.'

The future was blank. Sex and dalliance, social compliments, were nothing. The millions already had more to consider than heroes of a war won only by foreign help. To Morris, Jones confided: 'If I have been Instrumental in giving the American Flag some Reputation and making it Respectable among European Nations, will you permit me to say that it is not because I have been Honored by my country either with proper means of support or proper Encouragement.'

In France, Condorcet was starting to enthuse over America as 'Immune to prejudice and disposed to study and reflection.'

11

The Gold Medal

A politician is an arse upon which everyone has sat except a man.

EE Cummings, *Complete Poems*, 1973

> The politician dead and turned to clay
> Will make a clout to keep the wind away
> I am not fond of draughts, and yet I doubt
> If I could get myself to touch that clout.

Hilaire Belloc,
On Another Politician, 1923

Personal Advantage never was the spring of my public acts; I had more noble motives; and far from enriching myself by the Revolution in America, I have consecrated to this Great Object the Ten best years of my life without interruption, as well as my Tranquillity, a portion of my Fortune, and my Blood.

John Paul Jones

In time of Peace it is necessary to prepare, and be *always prepared*, for war by sea.

John Paul Jones

The war had ended with the ill-will expected between allies, the French claiming to have given more than they received, which was negligible, and accusing America of blackmail over an immense French loan. They suspected Franklin of being more anxious to placate Britain than to support French and Spanish needs.

The peace, negotiated by Franklin, John Adams and John Jay, gave Europe a taste of American wit. A French diplomat toasted Louis XVI, as

'The Sun in Splendour'. An Englishman desired glasses to be raised to George III, 'The Moon who Rules the Waves'. Benjamin Franklin gave them the man who, like Joshua, had halted both sun and moon – George Washington.

In grief and chagrin, King George, had twice contemplated abdication and had assured Charles James Fox that he would ever think badly of any Englishman who accepted the post of minister 'of that revolted State', but he finally received John Adams, as the first American representative to Great Britain, with dignified kindness.

'Mr Adams, I will be very free with you. I was the last to consent to the separation, but the separation having been made and having become inevitable, I have always said, as I say now, that I would be the first to meet the friendship of the United States as an independent Power.' Words that have affected the king's latter-day defender, Charles, Prince of Wales.

Hated by colonists, Whigs, and his own heir, butt of Junius and Wilkes, scorned by most historians, prey to a disease in which he mistook Wellington for a tree and himself for a loaf and seeking comfort in Handel, the former monarch of America gained some respect, even love, from his people during his long, painful years of isolation, blindness and derangement.

The British Empire had been shaken, but less catastrophically than many had feared, or hoped. Canada was reinforced by thousands of loyalist immigrants. Supreme in Bengal, the East India Company was ranging further into the subcontinent, consolidating its position as a global financial force. The West Indies, and the South American markets, were intact, British African companies about to establish themselves, through explorers, traders and missionaries. British Australasia was in being, and the younger Pitt was mistaken in lamenting that the loss of America in 1783 was the sun setting on England's glory.

Spain was beset with problems internal and external, France was suffering continuous economic crisis and political divisions, but British imperturbability resumed with 131 ships of the line; Britain held Gibraltar, smashing the Spanish off Cape St Vincent while, back in health, Rodney had scattered the French in the Atlantic. Against Revolutionary and Napoleonic France, Britain would win the most sustained and costly war it had ever undertaken and leading to what was largely thought a temporary expedient, income tax. It resembled the Danegeld of Ethelred II, an emergency measure that nevertheless persisted for two centuries.

British commentators had small fear of independent America, which might yet collapse under interstate feuds, political graft or economic naïvety. As late as 1889, Kipling rejoiced in San Francisco's vulnerability to British warships, and reflected that the Royal Navy could still capture New York.

For Paul Jones, peace, a relief to humanity, was unpropitious for himself. He was ready for offers, but the outlook was dull. In Britain, he would be a proscribed killer and traitor; France was near bankruptcy and Holland was angrily regretting its brief contest with Britain. He was now 36, 'Delia' dismayed by his dwindling letters. An American flag command on a foreign station was impossible. Slightly less so were plans to rescue American sailors, victims of Barbary pirates and lying almost forgotten in Algerian jails. In the forefront, of course, was his vision of organising, training, ultimately commanding 'a Respectable Navy'.

Impatient with protocol, tact, good taste and common politeness, Paul Jones would lecture or write to the great men of the Revolution – Washington, Jefferson, Adams, Franklin, Jay, Hamilton, Morris... discharging his omniscient, irritating personality and irrefutable thesis, with an inflexible and embarrassing persistence: 'The navy has, upon the whole, done nothing for the Cause, and less for the Flag. The Public has been put to a great expense, yet the poor Seamen have almost, in every instance, been *cheated*, while the Public has reaped neither Honor nor Profit.'

His demands were inflexible, and he never lost belief that the baby who makes the noise gets the milk. His convictions centred on the necessity for a centralised Admiralty, which owed nothing to the privileges of individual states but, as a unit, would interlock like a machine, controlling the ships, dockyards, personnel, maintenance, supplies, general administration and, very much not least, new training schools. 'A General Reform is indispensable... the great mass of the officers were never intended by Nature to fill such important places; and what I have said from the beginning has been proved true. They cannot support their Rank with Honor to themselves or their country. Our Navy has not only been put into bad hands, but it has been unwisely employed. It has served to enrich a few Ignorant Individuals, and has done almost nothing for our Cause.'

However annoying, Paul Jones was prescient. He had noted the French neglect of cadet training, he knew the prevalence of influence and cash in class-ridden Britain and, almost alone, he pleaded for an American Academy, which would hold regular examinations, particularly in mathematics, and with expertise in navigation, ship management and gunnery, to create an officer corps in which a Landais had no place, nor the caprice of a wealthy politician or regional celebrity. Of his numerous recommendations, Lincoln Lorenz judged: 'The establishment of naval academies aboard ships and at stations, for the training of officers was typical of his foresight. His most valuable proposal... was the thorough study of foreign naval systems as a valuable background for the newly born nation.'

The opportunities to avoid social and professional stratifications were prodigious in a mobile meritocracy. In his standards of provisioning, equipping, arming and of manning ships and yards, and in his meticulous demands of contractors, navigators and gunners, Jones was far in advance of current, nepotistic improvisation, and geared to a time when 'America must become the first Marine Power in the world.' SE Morison, finest of his biographers, adds: 'Jones showed great acumen in pointing out the absolute necessityfor clear and quick communication between a flag officer and his fleet.' In this, even the British had lagged. Paul Jones was seldom too arrogant to learn from those he respected, such as the French signals expert, du Pavillon, whom he had met and whose system, with 1,600 signs, he adopted, adapted and later tried to introduce into Russia.

Since *Alfred*, he had enlarged on the deficiency caused by recruiting officers from gentlemanly or factional infighters, and on captains having personal overall responsibility for purveyance, maintenance and payments. These, he proposed, should be passed to special shore committees, the prize system revised in favour of the actual participants, as against inactive seniors and bureaucrats taking their cut as one of the perks of office. Esek Hopkins had demanded one-twentieth of any prize money, whether or not he had fought.

Paul Jones did not, of course, neglect his own due. 'If my feeble voice is heard when I return to Philadelphia, our navy matters will assume a better face.' Slowly, very slowly, Congress began to hearken. The United States Navy was to conform very closely to his suggestions, though he never lived to see it. He did know a statement, made in 1788: 'I consider Jones as the principal hope for future American naval efforts. Thomas Jefferson.'

In 1783, therefore, Paul Jones proposed himself as a roving naval attaché, to inspect European naval procedures, voyaging in style on a frigate, though conceding, rather wistfully, that, despite some forfeiture of dignity, this was not totally essential. Congress, however, was grappling with civil adminis-tration, states' claims, institutional renovations, with shortages and inflation had neither money nor interest in a project surely needless in time of peace. Jones's belief that a time of peace made efficient armaments vital to preserve it was ignored or feared. This indifference, together with ill health, kept him gloomy and morose.

Prize money for *Ranger*, *Bonhomme Richard*, even *Alliance*, had yet to be collected and compensation sought from Denmark for the campaign prizes so wantonly sent to Bergen. Acknowledging this, Congress empowered Commodore Jones as prize agent extraordinary, general officer and special minister from Congress. It sounded more grandiose than its effects warranted. He was to sail to Europe, passenger under the trusted and genial Joshua Barney.

The Atlantic was mild. They halted in London for a brief visit, conducted without incident or official notice, for Jones to deliver dispatches to John Adams, while he endured with dignified reticence considerable social and official rebuffs from those still affronted by the Crown's loss.

In 2001, Raymond Seitz, former American ambassador to Great Britain, named Jefferson as the Pen of the American Revolution, Adams the Voice. With Abigail, forward-looking and perceptive, beside him, the soberly book-loving, learned, and industrious John Adams worked in London to reconcile the Republic with Britain, and to reassure monarchical Europe against considerable social and political odds. Later, he worked to retain, or restore, honesty in American politics and law, though his presidency was to be weakened by faction and intrigue, not least from the many-sided patrician, Thomas Jefferson.

Paul Jones spent some unsatisfactory weeks in Denmark and, despite his natural canniness and recent experiences, remained slow to recognise that royal amiability, ministerial flattery, clerkly wheedling and flunkeys' smiles were mere excuses to evade, procrastinate, obstruct interviews, audiences and serious discussion. All he achieved was the offer of a Danish pension for himself which, for the moment, he refused, 'through delicacy', a gesture lost upon the Danes. Jefferson himself was offered less, Congress having to pay the debts, decades later.

Returning not to America but to Paris, hopeful of new chances, Jones entered a darkly menacing atmosphere. Unstable cabinets, royal indecision, erratic financial projects and gambles, dubious interventions from speculators and self-styled experts, were all targets for street demonstrations by hired agitators – often employed by the Duke of Orleans, formerly Chartres – and inflammatory journalists. Utilitarian arguments caught from America and the returning volunteers also played their part. Men of the moment were Lafayette and, keenly observant, a forerunner of nineteenth-century technocracy, mechanical efficiency and meritocracy, the social philosopher Claude Henri, Comte de Saint-Simon (1760–1825), sometimes considered an influence on Louis-Napoleon, the modernising Emperor Napoleon III, seen by the historian Pierre de la Gorce in 1908 as a blend of Don Quixote and Machiavelli. As a young volunteer, then as French ruler, Louis-Napoleon fought for Italian freedom from Austria; Saint-Simon fought for American freedom from Britain, and he asserted in *Industrie*, 1817: 'It was not in France but in America that the French Revolution sprang to life. I felt that the American Revolution marked the start of a new political era. That this revolution would necessarily initiate an important movement in general civilisation, and that it would, before long, cause a great change in the social order then existing in Europe.'

The cries of Pym and the exceptionally wealthy Hampden against arbitrary 17th-century taxation had thrilled American radicals. In France, the case was not taxation but that the privileged orders claimed exemption. The nation was rich, the state was impoverished. Sensible reforms were continually obstructed or emasculated by sectional interests and economic charlatans, while Beaumarchais simultaneously mocked and amused the aristocracy and the king quarrelled with provincial legal assemblies and, when he could bring himself to a decision, it was too often a wrong one. Noble and clerical myopia was sapping the old, feudal France, enflaming bourgeois resentments, military disaffection, and the hacks, scandalmongers, mountebanks and buffoons assiduously stoking up a new social force, public opinion, whose influence was to pervade much of nineteenth-century France; the century reaching bloody climax of the disastrous Franco–Prussian War in 1870.

Yet, with 1789 approaching, no more than the young American politicians, were most Frenchmen desiring revolution. Mirabeau and Lafayette wanted accommodation with the court, scarcely reciprocated. Widespread distrust of the queen and contempt for courtiers had not demolished sympathy for the king and loyalty to a monarchy.

Paul Jones was received politely in governmental offices and flowery boudoirs, though compliments and assurances were mostly insincere. Never a sophisticated critic of courts and the *ton*, he may have been slow to recognise disquieting undertones in the king's ponderous indecision, the queen's make-believe rusticity. Versailles was less crowded, less fashionable, Paris journals and libels more venomous, the dossiers from secret police more discouraging.

In his routine protracted and intricate dealings with familiar sparring partners, Castries and Chaumont, Jones could rely, first, on Franklin, then on his successor, Thomas Jefferson. By 1784, he had collected necessary signatures for France's financial obligations, though payments were delayed two years. They were then delivered not to Jones but to Jefferson who, pending Treasury examination in America, was instructed to use them not in paying seamen but for diplomatic salaries, including his own. Only a minority of the sailors received lawful wages, descendants finally benefiting as late as 1861, in Lincoln's presidency, Paul Jones's own heirs receiving some 50,000 dollars. In Britain, in similar dispensation, David Hume, the philosopher, had payment for his work as a military advocate only after years of waiting.

Jones was usually less diplomatic than Franklin. Neither he nor the French had forgotten the grand invasion. He himself had at least stepped on soil and succeeded on waters which the invasion had failed even to sight. He ended one letter to Castries, otherwise devoted to financial claims: 'Permit me, my lord, to conclude by saying that no equal Expense in the War was made with so great effect, or had such good Consequences as that made by the ships I commanded in the Texel; since Holland was thereby drawn into the war, without which the World would not have been this day at Peace.'

He had learnt that honest dealings, like love, may require rhetoric: that the literate minority prospered by elaborating costume, deportment, hairstyle, by the manipulation of a snuffbox or the set of a cravat, by artificiality of style, personality, language, all that separated rulers from the ruled, an artificiality that, throughout Europe, was soon to be tested.

Paul Jones was also making private business ventures, none outstandingly profitable. In the nuances of commerce and law, the powers of subsidiary clauses and small print had never engrossed him, they were too far from the quarter-deck, the tricks of tide and current, the stimulus of command. He invested in schemes, not wild, but hazardous, of starting a fur and skin enterprise between North America and the Far East in partnership with John Ledyard, once an officer of James Cook's. He had a plan for the production of dyes, with Dr Bancroft, still safe in London with a British pension, and whose financial practices were, at best, unsatisfactory.

On a hurried return to America he at last finalised lengthy and bad-tempered disputes with the Treasury, and was granted 48,000 dollars for his accumulated expenses. Once, on a New York pavement, a shabby man spat after him, unnoticed – Pierre Landais, still pleading with Congress for prize monies, compensations and reappointment, a ghost among imaginary conquests and unfought battles.

Jones was ill at ease on the circuit of diplomacy, market speculation and business, chaffing at the restrictions and inner codes: 'I will not accept the half-confidence of any man living.' This adamantine resolution helps explain his failures, though also the loyalty and admiration of Richard Dale. On his own volition, he was soon back in Paris. He found himself no longer so in fashion but resumed a considerable social life in a capital ceasing to enjoy or afford its old luxuries and certainties. Franklin, Admiral d'Estaing, M Malesherbes, royal adviser, and M Genet, foreign minister, entertained him, though the Duke of Orleans – to whom the Houdon bust, now in the American Naval Academy Museum, was of special concern – was out of reach, immersed in political conspiracies and buying his way into popularity with the Paris poor and discontented. The duke was no favourite with historians – Alfred Cobban called him 'Scabrous' Philippe; like another duke, Monmouth, played with toys too big for him, encouraging those building for him and themselves a dreadful finish.

While the future Citizen Philippe Egalité chattered and pamphleteered, at court, among the Freemasons, in radical salons and obscure backrooms, for Liberty and Equality, his duchess fed the poor. The difference was forbidding. The duke, royal extremist, momentarily recalls Oscar Wilde who, more gifted, generous and witty than Louis-Philippe Joseph, was likewise tempted towards ruin, declaring of his grubby young rentboys and blackmailers, 'It was like feasting with panthers.'

Paul Jones feasted with another sort of animal, the British balloonist, John Jeffries, exchanging compliments, and instances of courage. Admiral Kenholm Digby, who had commanded in North America, sought his company. 'Delia' had faded, succeeded by 'Madame T', Aimée de Telison, or Théresa Townsend, widow of an Englishman. Little is remembered of Madame T; she may have borne him a son, child without a story; he helped her with money but continued to avoid marriage, and their relationship evaporated in disillusion, or the listlessness brought about by his inactivity or the ill-health of which 'the Fair Delia' had, in 1780, been 'in the greatest anxiety'. Paul Jones, though, whatever his sexual needs, was no Antony, neglecting an empire for a passionate flourish. In *The Corsair*, Byron shows insight into Jones's type:

> Love shows all changes – Hate, Ambition, Guile,
> Betray no further than the bitter smile.

Greying, tired, he could no longer absolutely rely on his body, and needed at least the companionship and domestic assistance of women. He was to inform Catherine the Great: 'I was formed for Love and Friendship, and not to be a Seaman or a Soldier; as it is, I have sacrificed my Natural Inclinations.'

This is disingenuous: he was scarcely suited to lifelong dedication to the study, the farm, or the salon. He may also have reflected on the natural inclinations of Mr and Mrs Patrick Henry: Dorothea now had nine children and six stepchildren, which could have been a depressing example of domestic bliss.

Meanwhile, he had to console himself with little more than the past, itself a dwindling asset, though, raised in ballad country, he himself was now a ballad.

> You have heard o' Paul Jones
> Have you not, have you not?
> How he came to Leith Pier and he filled the folks with fear,
> Did he not?
> He took the *Serapis*
> Did he not, did he not?
> He took the *Serapis*, and the Battle it was hot,
> But a Rogue ond a Vagabond
> Is he not?

Several years had passed since Flamborough Head, years of journeys often fruitless, of aborted plans and sterile loves, of waiting for the improbable and impossible, years of quarrels, false promises, talk without action. He was always about to visit his family in Scotland though unable to risk doing so, contenting himself with letters of advice on money, education and etiquette. Now he was the conductor without an orchestra, with days of mere correspondence, reliving rejections, of chances missed with one woman or accepted too eagerly by another; of plaudits dimming, friends going other ways; of ships denied him: 'When the *America* was taken from me I was deprived of my tenth command.' He was still fighting the Deanes, Langdons and Chaumonts, convinced that they had cheated and obstructed him; and suffering slaughter in the soul from Landais.

All that was left seemed his testimonials, notably the one from Robert Morris when relinquishing the Marine Office. 'I now take the last opportunity I shall ever have of expressing my sentiments officially, upon the zeal, activity, fortitude and intelligence which you have exhibited on so many occasions in the service of the United States.'

But it was not enough, nothing was ever quite enough. A hungry spirit demanded more than financial haggling, import-exporting, and political tittle-tattle of those who spoke bravely while protected by locked front doors. A Paul Jones, a Lafayette, a Nelson sought the exhilaration not of brandy, certainly not the torpor of opium, but of name, status and the ornate illusions that sustain society and the individual. In danger of being but one more shadowy civilian, he besought employment. Once again, the enormity of Barbary pirates was being debated not only in Paris and London but in Congress. Attacking foreign ships indiscriminately, Algiers also still held American sailors as slaves and hostages, willing to ransom them but at 3,000 dollars each and actually declaring war on America in 1785, angered by Congress's protests.

Ruminating in Paris, a lonely Jones envisaged an American admiral heading a United States–European Mediterranean expedition of retribution and rescue, and at last ending the international tribute, ransoms, protection money levied by the 'Barbary pirates of Algiers' already strenuously condemned by Thomas Jefferson and John Paul Jones. Not only would such an undertaking re-establish himself, it would also, as he lectured John Jay, unite the Americans in a single and righteous cause and lift them from their 'their ill-judged security, which the Intoxication of Success has produced since the Revolution'.

This got nowhere; he remained stranded. America, in its weakness, was preoccupied with constructing a complex federal constitution and administrative apparatus for the thirteen states. A career officer must yet again seek offers from France. In 1785, Paul Jones set himself to petition His Most Catholic Majesty, composing another elaborate, self-seeking, prospectus, incorporating the customary hyperbole of disinterest, honour, dignity, infusions of flattery, tempting proposals, selected testimonials, and even, with naive pathos, his beloved letter to Lady Selkirk. Very typical is: 'With the order of Military Merit, Your Majesty has conferred on me a Gold Sword – an honor which I presume no other Officer has received'; and, 'The Protector of the Rights of Human Nature will always find me ready to draw that Sword and expose Life for His Service.'

A later period, accustomed to daily dosages of sleaze, spin, jargon and showbiz clichés, does not have rights to condemn this as hypocritical sycophancy, though Paul Jones should have known its uselessness. French fleets were idle, anchored in poverty, neglect, defeat by Britain and acid politics. Admiral Kersaint was anxious to democratise the service, expel aristocratic officers and leaders – virtually everyone – without providing trained successors. State debts were about to topple the administration, successive ministers and quacks still disputed solutions. The rote of bad harvests, bread shortages and rising prices continued, and all departments shrank from an administrative overhaul as thorough as that to which Paul Jones would submit a ship. King Louis, by now glumly regretting the American alliance – 'I was dragged into the unhappy affair of America; advantage was taken on my youth' – was being deluged with remonstrances, panaceas, manifestos, petitions, usually imaginative, seldom practical. He was rapidly losing respect from the governing classes: aristocratic, bourgeois, ecclesiastical, and his cousin, Orleans, was implacably hostile. Like almost all the famous protagonists during the Revolution, he and his wife were still under 40, but he himself, save for hunting, lacked youthful vigour. He was not the last French ruler to be endangered by epigrams and ridicule. A street song was hummed:

> The fellow's never jealous, he's indifferent,
> Best able
> At stuffing himself like a swine,
> Swilling wine,
> Elbows on Table.

Paul Jones would soon see a placard: 'Palace for Sale. Ministers to be Hanged. Crown to be Given Away.'

In America, he was recovering some ground. Ceaseless requests – stronger terms could be used – for more concrete recognition were at last admitted. He had continued to hanker for an outsize medal and had already commissioned preliminary sketches from a French draughtsman. On 17 October 1787, Congress voted him its Gold Medal for valour, without dissent, instructing Jefferson to have it executed in France, and formally announce it to the king, together with a request to allow Jones a command in the royal fleet, to perfect his experience on behalf of the Republic.

Shared with Washington and several other generals, but with no sailor, the medal, inscribed 'To John Paul Jones, commander of the Fleet', depicts the *Serapis* saga, a copy now displayed in Paul Jones's more substantial memorial, the American Naval Academy.

He would not have been John Paul Jones had he been altogether satisfied. He was not yet an admiral, his debts had not yet been repaid, he had nothing very definite to do before, early in 1788, he received an astonishing offer that would surely metamorphose him into a European magnifico, perhaps a nobleman.

In Denmark, he had made earlier tentative inquiries about the Russian navy, now expanding, with the conquest of the Crimea and Black Sea ports. The fleets were very largely staffed by foreigners, particularly Scots, English and Germans. Now, on recommendations from Jefferson, and others, Catherine II sent him the suggestion that he join her service as a 'Captain of the Fleet'. This, though, was inadequate, he had waited long enough for more, so that, on 15 April the Empress sanctioned his appointment as Rear Admiral of the Black Sea Fleet, currently fighting the Turks.

His ego rose like a conning tower. Here must be a splendid notch on his tally, not only for its perquisites and scope but for that vital self-image. The great hat, the stars, gold-rimmed cuffs, ribbons, epaulettes, the grand sword and gleaming scabbard, the place in processions, even in music, all lit the trail winding from humble Kirkbean, West African slave heaps, the threat of the rope and rebuffs from petty scoundrels in office. All now dazzled, though he carefully assured Jefferson: 'I have not forsaken a country that has had many disinterested and difficult Proofs of my Steady Affection; and I can never Renounce the Glorious Title of a *Citizen of the United States.*'

The chances certainly appeared spectacular: no tiny squad with death or glory single combats and a few minor raids on unguarded ports, but a battle fleet of a notoriously susceptible ruler of an enormous, rapidly expanding empire. Hazards there might be, they existed only to be overcome.

George Washington wrote to Jefferson: 'I am glad our Commodore Paul Jones has got employment and heartily wish him success. His new situation may possibly render his talents and services more useful to us at some future day.' The commodore himself reflected happily on his address from the Russian minister in Copenhagen:

'The immortal Glory by which you have illuminated your Name cannot make you indifferent to the fresh laurels you must gather in the new career which opens to you. Under a Sovereign so magnanimous, in pursuing Glory, you need not doubt of the most distinguished Rewards, and that every advantage of Fortune will await you.'

12

The Most Distinguished Rewards

The Euxine, the Meotian waters felt thee next, and long-skirted Turk,
o Paul; and thy fiery soul has wasted itself in a thousand
contradictions – to no purpose. For, in far lands, with Scarlet Nassau-
Siegens, with sinful imperial Catherine, is not the heart broken, even
as at home among the mean?

Thomas Carlyle,
The French Revolution, 1837

Assure the Chevalier Jones that, as regards his entry into the Service,
I will do all in my power to place him comfortably and to advantage,
and that I will certainly procure opportunities for him to turn his
abilities and valour to account.

Alexander Potemkin, Prince of the Tauride

The Nation is not made for the Sovereign, but the Sovereign is made
for the Nation.

Catherine, Empress of all the Russias

The dark Intrigues and mean Subterfuges of Asiatic jealousy and malice.

John Paul Jones

St Petersburg was no organic growth loosely collecting at crossroads, river-
mouth, ford or hill, for trade, defence, worship but, like Versailles, the
upshot of a single will, dynamic and callous, that of Peter the Great
(1672–1725). Here, again as at Versailles, developed a regime of the
unearthly, the super-real, originating in the distant past and overwhelming
both reason and the senses, on the titanic scale of Egyptian and Mayan
pyramids, seeking the eternal, with ceremonies as intricate as those of

China and Byzantium. The Tsars surrounded themselves with images of power, some as weirdly animal as Sumerian reliefs and statuary, some as massive as the monuments, aqueducts, arches, forums, palaces of imperial Rome, erected as if for the giants or gods that some rulers imagined themselves to be. The Russian emperors, heirs of Byzantium, the Second Rome, headed a despotism all too visible yet in touch with the unseen and mystical. In towering architecture, lavish festivals and armies, akin to Incas, Aztecs and Moghuls, indifferent to lives and expenditure, they outspent even Habsburgs and Bourbons.

At a criminal cost to the serf labourers, Peter the Great created from the swamps miles of pale colonnaded mansions, spires and domes, Grecian porticoes, thrilling vistas and avenues, churches, theatres, barracks, prisons and squares. Always inescapable was Peter's massive monument, Pushkin's *Bronze Horseman*:

> The rearing steed and riding Tsar,
> Peter, joined with savage power,
> One arm outflung to proclaim
> 'All this, my work, I am master.'

Around it swarmed crested carriages, huge canopied sledges, operatic uniforms, ecclesiastical processions and choirs, imperial guards elongated by shakoes and majestic, gleaming topboots, soldiers transformed to the barely human by bearskins, wolf-pelts and polished leather gauntlets, which both stunned and exalted the imagination. The unconscious was jolted by reminders of a time when animals spoke, angels roamed steppe and forest, kings lived in magic, bards' tongues flickered with fire, the witch sat in a hut which moved on chickens' legs, princesses languished in paradisial greens and golds, and great ones died that the land might live.

Palaces of royalty, nobles, ambassadors, merchants, and favourites, 'temporary persons', stretching into the sky, might house those of Tartar brutality and repulsive habits, exotic tastes and attire, collecting the latest French, Italian, German and British music, dances, furniture, fashions in dress, gardens, phrases; also forming gentlemen's clubs on the London model. Freezing halls glowed with immense and opulent hangings and carpets, often filthy; they glistened with Old Masters and the latest rococo, with antique armour and weaponry, with ancestral or classical statuary and stuffed animal heads. Dreamlike galleries flickered with ill-paid servants, thieves, hungry petitioners and spies. Alcoves, passages, window seats, glimmering with the suspect and half-seen, were nests of gossip, whispers, conspiracy and fantasy.

The Winter Palace, marbled green and white, with 1,000 rooms,1,500 dignitaries, 600 gardeners, could blaze with 16,000 candles while in attics and screened-off corners lingered half-starved poor relations, nameless intruders, the superannuated and discarded. The currently unfashionable Sacheverell Sitwell, a connoisseur of the baroque and almost forgotten, wrote in *Valse des Fleurs*, 1942: 'This is the palace of the Caesars in its last travesty, beginning with the Golden House of Nero, and come down from Byzantium. Influenced by Le Roi Soleil and created in fleshy travesty of splendour by Catherine the Great. The ornate details of Alexander II's coronation filled a volume so weighty that two porters were needed to carry it.'

A pallid, neo-classical metropolis had components of opera and ballet, dosshouse, knacker's yard and hangman's shed, of violins, drums, bugles, of hurdy-gurdies, brawling fairgrounds, measured parades, international conferences, and an infinity of the diseased and derelict spewed from infernal hospitals, lodging houses, shanty-town stews. Bizarre Russian extravagance fascinated and shocked the Enlightenment, itself earnestly debating the usefulness of royal, clerical and seigneurial privileges. Royalty could display very particular oddities, exclusive of George III and Louis XVI. Emperor Francis I enjoyed making toffee and stamping sealing wax. Prince Henry of Russia loved to inspect the corpse of any recently deceased citizen; a Landgrave of Hesse composed 52,362 marches, on two fingers; Augustus the Virile, of Saxony and Poland, was hailed for fathering 300 bastards, rulers making love as frivolously as they made war.

Palaces, like the Tsar, were fairy tale, a genre in which Catherine herself wrote, with decor and themes of beauty and horror, penalties, rewards. Orthodox gorgeousness of music and ritual was streaked with refined superstition and the ruler's caprice. Peter the Great, determined to drag Russia from medieval backwardness, had survived perilous conspiracies and had always to protect himself, however brutally, while remaining so shy that he often conversed from behind his hand. Like many monarchs, he maintained a large troupe of dwarfs and fools, perhaps in the primitive tradition that believes excessive power and display invite the jealousy of Heaven and the impudent malice of demons, to be repulsed by the sight of the crippled and abnormal, stark injunctions against pride and vanity. Dwarfs jostled and tumbled, teased and conjured in a nether realm that still startles in Velasquez's scenes of the Spanish court. Emperor Rudolf II had a regiment of dwarfs; Frederick William I of Prussia one of giant grenadiers. A traditional connection between madness, deformity and spirituality was displayed by Philip II of Spain, whose dwarfs were largely recruited from the Zaragoza lunatic asylum.

The Russian God was held to especially favour not only the vast Orthodox empire but also the humble, the imperfect, the idiotic, granting them unusual virtue and insight. St Paul had written: 'God hath chosen the foolish things of the world to confound the wise; and God hath chosen the weak things of the world to confound the things that are mighty.' Thus mighty Lear learnt profound truths and personal guilt from his fool's candid simplicity and, in universal tales, the untutored peasant worsts the learned, the self-important, the powerful. Humour has no bounds, shrinks at nothing and no one, and laughter, as the distinguished academic Enid Welsford put it, melts the solidity of the world.

Periodically, society relieved the tensions of authority and order by saturnalia. In 1715, a Russian fool was installed as mock-patriarch amid hysterical mirth, ribald indecency, parodies of sacred and courtly rituals, giving substance to Wyndham Lewis's claim that the essence of comedy and tragedy is sadism.

Illiterate St Petersburg crowds, straining for survival like the agonised caryatides upholding gigantic palaces and mansions, would not for generations shatter the authoritarian fairy tale – more accurately translated as *fate tale*, with its initiations, tests, warnings against wrong choices, the fulfilment of personal self and destiny – though the metropolis, glistening with marble and water, gold and bronze, was breeding the criminals, obsessed dreamers and strange comedians that fill the pages of Dostoevsky. Religion was a potent consolation and hypnotic spectacle. Byzantine magnificence smothered dogma and dissent, a phenomenon that survived Leninist atheism, though in a way that would have appealed more to fools than to St Paul. A Russian poll, in 2002, disclosed that 60 per cent professed allegiance to the Orthodox Church, while only 30 per cent believed in God.

Tsarist theatre of power cost over ten per cent of the national income, outmatching all others save perhaps the Vatican, and rendering insignificant the sedate estates of Washington, Jefferson, Robert Morris, John Adam's book-lined offices and Paul Jones's 'small farm' idyll. The autocracy, however, was tempered by peasant rebellions, military coups, corruption, chicanery, Swedish aggression and fear and envy of Europe. Murder accounted for Catherine's husband, Peter III, and her son, Paul I. Peter, devoted to toy soldiers and military parades, and who once court-martialled and hanged a mutinous rat, was cruel to his wife, had scant interest in government, none in administration, though jealous of his prerogatives, and loved only his violin and black mistress. Palace troops and prominent nobles deposed him as a dangerous nuisance, replacing him with Catherine. She presumably connived at his strangulation by Prince Alexis Orloff, colluding with his brother Gregory, Catherine's lover and mentor, who had succeeded Stanislaus Poniatowski, himself tactfully consigned to be King of Poland; and preceding the stupendous, alarming Alexander Potemkin. Even into the twentieth century, Peter III was believed to wander Romania, as an incarnation of Christ.

The court to which Paul Jones was speeding was thus an apparition both splendid and monstrous, Olympian and Tartarean, entwined with viciously contrasting hues, like those in a cracked marble. Palaces which made grotesque and tragic backcloths for operas, poems, novels and movies. A Russian Macbeth, Boris Godunov, stalks halls of overwhelming forebodings, vast shadows, guilty fears, stupendous music. Always present were tales of the neurotic Ivan the Terrible, impaling birds and mice, as fearful as his victims, permitting a month-long massacre at Novgorod, having an archbishop sewn into a bearskin to be devoured by starving dogs, and ordering a boyar to be roasted alive in an iron pan, himself dying with laments for the son he had killed. Stories of an infant tsar imprisoned for life, in solitude, never learning to speak; stories of Empress Elizabeth's Tuesday transvestite balls. In such reports, greatness could attract spectacular wrath. In more tales, Empress Anna degraded Prince Galitzen to a court fool, and compelled him to marry a whore, for religious apostasy. Famously, a noble couple, for an unseemly marriage, were forced to spend their first, and last, night together, naked on an ice bed within a splendidly detailed ice palace. In her memoirs, Catherine recollected 'a victim of imperial displeasure made to squat in an anteroom for several days, mewing, clucking, and pecking food from the floor'. Among her own punishments was compulsory swallowing of ice-cold water accompanied by reading aloud of the long poem *Telemachida* (1766), noted for its excessive tedium.

Had he been more thoroughly versed in this compendium of truth and fantasy, Paul Jones might have travelled at a more leisurely pace, but he had probably heard that the Empress had exclaimed that she was expecting great things of him. This would have been sufficient. Urgent for the frontier, entrance to another New World, 500 miles away under winter skies and hazards, he was again the solitary wanderer, quest-seeker, corsair against fate, all considerations of prudence, business and diplomacy abandoned. He was excited as Charles Dickens climbing Vesuvius or seeing a mysterious shop. HV Morton has an imaginative inset:

> Ice blocked the Gulf of Bothnia. He decided on a mad enterprise that had never before been attempted, to cut through the ice, and enter the Baltic Sea. He set off in the dawn from Gresholdm in a thirty-foot boat and with a smaller boat to drag over the ice. His crew had no idea of the peril they were in. When, however, they understood the mad enterprise, Paul Jones had to cover them with a pistol, and urge them on with threats. All day he steered south along the coast of Sweden, picking his way between ice floes, and at night he sat, pistol in hand, facing his terrified crew and steering for the open sea. He hit a storm and for four days and nights he steered by the light of travelling lamp fixed over the compass. He finally crossed the Gulf of Finland and landed at Revel.

In Denmark, he had mentioned his 'inexpressible sufferings'. Of this escapade, 'I would not do it again for a thousand times the money I have.' Hurrying on, towards recognition, command, acclaim, he was soon undergoing sleeplessness and bronchial troubles but on 23 April 1788, he arrived at St Petersburg.

Eager to meet the Empress he was indifferent to her possessions: Winter Palace and Tsarskoe Selo, masterpieces of his compatriot Cameron, gardens that would have astounded his father, the Craiks, even the Selkirks; the 4,000 paintings – Rembrandt, Poussin, Rubens, Watteau, Tintoretto, Van Dyke, Caravaggio, Canaletto, Raphael, Murillo, Veronese, Domenichino, 10,000 drawings, collections of sculpture, porcelain, mirrors, candelabra taller than her black, turbaned giants and white and gold hussars, the golden statues, palm and orange trees, walls of amber, lapis lazuli, tinted marble, violet-stained glass... meant as little to him as spectral figures lurking in verminous, rotting tenements or the African slaves shackled beneath hatches.

In less haste, he might have sensed a Shakespearean dimension where fair was foul, much was 'gainst Nature, and welcome was equivocal, though, entering the outsize, with his bookish French, scanty German, lack of inches, he could also have felt sensibly diminished. Master of manipulative 'smoothness', he was about to meet past masters. He must surely have told himself of the need for caution.

An English traveller, Giles Fletcher, had reproached Russian rulers in

1590, for frustrating 'the natural wit' of their people. 'They are kept from travelling, that they might learn nothing, nor see the fashions of other countries abroad.' William Richardson, in 1784, was indignant that Russia had 'no trial by jury, no Habeas Corpus Act. A person accused of crimes may be kept in prison for ever.' Marx, no humanitarian, who wished Slavs to be exterminated as an inferior race, justly considered that history is made behind men's backs. Russian dissidents in his day, and ours, could be hidden in lunatic asylums.

Catherine was energetic, well informed and practical, with intellectual rigour, considerable learning and a fine regard for the possible. She disliked 'systems', which so easily induced the intolerance and persecution against which Voltaire 'my master' had often warned her. Of the philosopher Diderot, embodiment of the Enlightenment, she wrote: 'Diderot's proposals would make fine books but bad politics. He only wrote on paper, which submits to everything and opposes no obstacle to the imagination, but I, poor Empress as I am, work on the human skin, which is irritable and ticklish to a very different degree.'

It is fair to Diderot that he had observed that the first stage of philosophy is incredulity, with which the Empress, purposeful and hard-working, must have agreed.

Liberal by inclination, she deplored torture and the beating of children, and was merciless only in such a crisis as the dangerous Pugachev peasant rebellion (1773) – he is supposed to have had his beard torn out before execution. She resembled Augustus, reforming, teaching, controlling, more than Marcus Aurelius, wise though energetic Stoic. She desired the temperate, the broadening of human intelligence and faculties through instruction, rational government, unsensational but steady reforms. She had seen that wretched education, savagely enforced, had destroyed her husband, as much as had Orloff's unyielding hands. In private, she encouraged freedom of conversation and behaviour irrespective of rank, and for some years was progressive, within the limits prescribed by Sir Winston Churchill: 'All I wanted was compliance with my wishes, after reasonable discussion.'

She knew sufficient history to realise what the Diderots, Condorcets and young devotees of Rousseau did not, that idealists and philosophers in power can benevolently, witlessly preside over anarchy and dissolution. A Plato in Syracuse, Celestine V in the Vatican or a Savonarola in Florence, can swiftly create conditions worse than those they have been asked to solve. Rienzi and Jan van Leyden were catastrophic, and if St Francis were offered a seat on the board, the crooked and virtuous alike would best seek cover. Civilisation, like love, is provisional.

Revering 'natural man', passionate and humane adherents of the Enlightenment failed to realise that a state of nature is usually a state of chaos, and looked to Catherine for benefits they were unlikely to receive. She could make many mistakes for the best of reasons. For the education of her grandson, Alexander I, opponent of Napoleon, she selected a Swiss republican with ideals irrefutably generous, but with results decidedly muddled.

European wits, while acknowledging her intelligence, satirised her as hypocritical, a Messalina, imperial murderess, and mocked her many lovers as 'night emperors'. For millions at home, she was Saint Catherine, Little Mother, guardian of Holy Russia; for the intelligentsia throughout Europe and America, she might be the Northern Star, Minerva, patroness of wisdom, daughter of power, with precepts to be admired and accepted: 'Liberty, soul of everything, without you, all is dead.' 'Without popular trust, Power is futile.' She corresponded with the French Encyclopaedists, accepting their fulsome praise and scrutinising their advice; she enticed Diderot to visit her in Russia, though failing with Voltaire, who croaked a mordaunt sarcasm about the fate of husbands in Russia. Eventually, though her references to Liberty remained as frequent as those of Franklin, Jefferson, Camille Desmoulins and Paul Jones, her enthusiasm for reform was cooled by the shock of Pugachev and, while anxious to modify serfdom, like Washington, she shrank from the likely effects of abolition. Old age and the French Revolution completed her conviction that Enlightened Despotism was healthier than popular assemblies indebted to street fighting, demagogues and vicious factions. She once styled herself, 'By Profession, Aristocrat'. Like Plato, Thomas More, Erasmus, like Bertrand Russell, she thought civilisation, laboriously built institutions, culture and civilities, more important than justice, equality, chimerical notions of brotherhood.

Nevertheless, her *Instructions*, a massive compilation of suggested reforms, was sufficiently advanced to be banned in France as seditious, for recommending equality before the law, education even for serfs, the ending of undeserved privilege, the granting of more popular rights. This was not to be democracy, but an improvement. In religion, like Elizabeth of England, she 'sought no windows into men's souls', valuing the Church as support for social cohesion and docility, and was unconcerned with doctrinal niceties. She preferred to encourage medicine, importing Scottish, English, German practitioners and, like the French crowned pair, was an early volunteer for inoculation; libraries, music, theatres, gardens she saw as complementary to schools and hospitals. In her reign, some 300 new towns were founded; agriculture, mining, technology, public health and local government were better organised; she left Russia larger, perhaps more contented. She had no factional backing for much economic reform and little personal zest. She was never very self-satisfied: 'All I have done is but a drop in the Ocean.'

The title of Diderot's play *Is he good/Is he bad?* in 1781 suits a period of grandees and intellectuals doing good for varying reasons, some very devious, and often unscrupulous, while engaging in the useful, humanitarian and just. One can cite Beaumarchais, Arthur Lee, Mirabeau, Potemkin, Danton, Bonaparte.

Neither the Empress, rational in all save sexuality, nor her mercurial Prince Marshal, 'Serenissimus', would be much impressed by Paul Jones's acquired civilities, soft-spoken allusions, his knowledge of cosmetics and ladies' bathing routines, noted by Abigail Adams. The illustrious couple were busily extending and fortifying an empire, and would praise foreign hired hands only in proportion to the successes they provided.

In appointing John Paul Jones, Catherine had exclaimed: 'One more bull-dog for the Black Sea!' A promising start. He was presented by the French Ambassador, Comte de Ségur, a volunteer in the American Revolution, fellow member of the Cincinnati, on 25 April. Jones offered her, not a set of his verses, not his letter to Lady Selkirk, not even his memorial to Louis XVI, but, doubtless misled by her plaudits from liberal philanthropists, what was only slightly less tactless, an elaborately bound copy of the 1787 American Constitution, impeccably Republican.

Not quite a cynic, not wholly a romantic, a seasoned man of the world, he would have seen no sugar-plum ballet princess but a short, fleshy, free-speaking woman, who was, behind the necessary compliments, severely direct. For her, his small stature might belie his reputation for the fierce and extraordinary, as it had for Mrs Adams. Afterwards, he pronounced himself 'entirely captivated' by her friendliness and charm, but his written request, submitted almost at once, that she would never condemn him unheard, suggests misgivings. Catherine could tolerate elegant vacuity in youthful, do-nothing bedmates, but from corsairs she demanded results, swiftly accomplished, lavishly rewarded. Delicate degrees of achievement interested neither herself nor he whom she had named the most extraordinary man in world history.

Potemkin, Prince of the Tauride, a lord of New Russia, was field marshal, statesman, administrator, naval supremo, founder of cities and ports, sexual athlete, scholar, art connoisseur, linguist, lover of music and architecture, admirer of English culture and politics, collector of human curiosities. He was an Ovidian image of flux, the flowing liquidity of self, the disputable nature of personality. Grandiose in extravagance, veering between childish petulance, boredom, indolence, manic activity and delicious raptures, he was on a scale scarcely imaginable to one accustomed to the puritanical Franklin with his regular hours and regular homilies; to sober, reserved John Adams; Robert Morris with his dry columns of figures, and French officials single-minded in petty rapacities. In dealings with the Prince Marshal, Paul Jones could have profited from serious study of Pierre Landais. At one instant, Potemkin stood astride the world, smiling in a blaze of abnormal light, then abruptly had stepped into a mass of morbid shadows. Everywhere, on campaigns, pleasure jaunts, journeys to imperial conferences, he had a mistress, sometimes several; he had dancers, actors, singers, orchestra, specialised chefs, intimates and favourites, chance acquaintances and visitors from many lands attracted by incredible stories. Among his lovers were three of his nieces. At his private box – spectacular, loud, dangerous, martial – seated behind a parapet of unflawed crystal 'throwing a dazzling fire around the audience', he dominated the very stage.

Overbearing, secreting the melancholic, with one eye blinded and the rough facial cast of Mirabeau and Danton, he was, like them and Johnson, a fisher of men. Like Herman Goering, he loved display, the aura of power, yet with a self-absorption almost mystical. In bewildering turns, he was magnanimous and sulkily grudging, cultured and primitive, frequently slovenly, barely decent, despite capacious wardrobes filled with uniforms, costumes, startling robes, sashes and turbans. He was selfish, exacting, jocular or dully silent, liable to reckless affection and generosity, imaginative to a height of genius, yet with deviousness of a cunning scoundrel and prone to sudden abstinences as alarming as his excesses. Like some Shakespearean character, he could diagnose his enormities with a memorable phrase or renounce them with a gesture heroic or ironic. Difficult, though not quite impossible, to imagine in quiet deliberations with Washington or Jefferson, the Prince Marshal inhabited his stormy imagination like an impatient magician, capriciously transforming the visible from a rainbow pavilion to a dungish hovel, a jewelled pleasure-dome to an anchorite's cell.

Potemkin has now been justly restored to full stature by his latest biographer, Simon Sebag-Montefiore, who shows him alongside the most remarkable figures of the century, after, at least for English readers, a long period of neglect, ignorance or travesty.

Ambassador de Ségur saw much of him, and at close quarters, and, in his memoirs, remembered:

> He was colossal, like Russia itself. In his mind, as in that country, were uncultivated districts and desert plains. It also partook of the Asiatic and the European, of the Tartarean and the Cossack; the rudeness of the eleventh century and the corruption of the eighteenth; the polish of the arts and the ignorance of the cloisters; a civilised exterior and many marks of barbarism. Briefly, if so bold a metaphor can be ventured, even his two eyes, the one wide, the other closed, were reminders of the Euxine, always open, and the Northern Ocean, imprisoned for long periods in ice.

The witty, sophisticated and shrewd Austrian courtier and soldier Prince de Ligne wrote in his reports his estimate of Potemkin as a strong, perverse and mischievous child, whose promises and stories lacked the element of truth. 'What is the secret of his success? Genius – natural ability – an excellent memory – the art of conquering every heart in his good moments – the talent for guessing about things of which he knows nothing – and a consummate knowledge of mankind.'

For Jeremy Bentham, he was 'Prince of Princes'. Byron called him 'the spoiled child of the night'. Pushkin judged him 'touched by the hand of History'. The disparaged Sitwell described him as:

> ...a combination of Diaghilev and Peter the Great. His character partook of both, but in the Russian or Tartar canon. He was one-eyed, like the Cyclops; and, as in most giants, could be entranced by music...He had a wild, disordered fancy; and a personal quality, an attack or touch, which can only be described as a great hand in everything. One of the huge physiques of Russian history; to be ranked, though only for his follies, with the Tsar Peter, the Patriarch Nicon, or even with the great actor, Chaliapin.

Follies distorts the entirety of Potemkin's achievements: the prince's conquest of the Crimea, his construction of roads, harbours, vineyards, markets, of the Black Sea fleet, his founding or restoring of Kherson, Sebastopol, Odessa, Kerch, Simperpol, Balaklava, Theodosia and Yenikale.

He realised the necessities of trade and for warm waters, relished the expansive and visionary, though, unlike the American, was bored by details and could neglect to follow up a success. His letters to Catherine have been compared to exchanges between bear and lioness. For her, he was 'a raging lion', to him, she was 'my she-wolf'. Their relations began in passion, and slowly subsided into an enduring partnership, active, humorous and tolerant. As Hector, warrior hero, subtle and mocking Hermes, or as Poseidon the earth shaker, he kept the empress informed, amused and astonished, while never overlooking her prerogatives. Of her subsequent lovers, he might laugh at one, deplore another, recommend a third. When persuaded, or needing, to attend her council, he might appear in dressing gown and towel: he could lounge as an equal, book in hand, with Diderot, exchange anecdotes with Nassau-Siegen, throw insults at the pretentious or stolid, sit rapt over the latest concerto or sonata – particularly of Mozart – while his inward glance roamed continents. Sumptuously costumed, within an afternoon he might discuss technology with Samuel Bentham, question some illogicality in a Montesquieu thesis or ponder the siting for a defensive tower. For a novice, he was difficult to please; he had experienced too much to be easily surprised, shocked or gratified. Surfeited with palatial monotony, military bravado and with pageantry, he could still loathe unjustified boasts, lengthy excuses and explanations, the earnest, the pedantic, the self-righteous.

By 1788, long past his youth, he would toy with life through dejected or listless hours before, stung by a joke, caress, flake of music or sudden news, recover his hunger for movement and decision.

Such a man could be misread by Chevalier Jones, who was late in understanding that Potemkin preferred flamboyant disaster to niggling triumph, that he disliked any talk of moral rectitude, was swift to yawn or vanish, and was more protean even than Benjamin Franklin or Jefferson. Paul Jones had his own vanity, love of finery, unconventional exploits, his certainties and reserves. Like Byron's Conrad, like Potemkin himself, he preferred many questions to be unasked. 'Too close inquiry his stern glance would quell.' The match of Admiral against the Prince Marshal threatened to be unpropitious to the former. Potemkin was gargantuan in his appetites, captious in his moods, sybaritic, often dilatory in his arrangements and thoughtless in his judgements. His regard for the English must not have pleased. Paul Jones would have found him too outsize and complex for ballad simplicities; he was more akin to the giants in Gaelic or biblical legend. The American would have to adjust very quickly to a phenomenon so unexpected, otherwise he would be stymied by the other's shifts of mood and expression. Ill temper, surliness, absolute adherence to the small print, would give Potemkin inadequate challenge, like feeding a mighty orator or actor feeble lines. Such words as Honour, Dignity or Liberty would prove insufferably tedious.

Yet, at first, all appeared well. 'I was entirely charmed,' Jones wrote to Lafayette, 'he is a most amiable man, and no one can be more noble than Prince Potemkin.'

All might be for the best. Plans were exchanged, tactics devised, guarantees signed, mutual admiration was scattered like blossom in a May breeze.

At a distance, Americans could respect Russia as a naval power. Her ships were numerous, her officers dazzled, her seamen had worthy records. Slavonic sailors may have been charting the White Sea as early as the fourth century. Learning his craft in Dutch and English yards, Peter the Great, with impressive assiduity and disconcertingly bad manners, had built fleets to engage the aggressive Swedes – Semyan Dezhnev was claimed as first to sail across the Bering Strait in 1741, reaching North America, exploring the Aleutians, and supposedly forerunning Cook in the Pacific. Russian ships were now voyaging in all oceans, while the British Admiralty knew the worth of Russian timber, hemp and tar.

From the capital, Jones could view the naval situation with equanimity. Potemkin had ousted a Tartar khan under Turkish suzerainty, from the Crimea, but the conquest required finalising by the expulsion of all Turkish vessels from the Black Sea. Turkey was no longer the feared enemy of Christendom but retained its mastery of Greece and the Balkans, and its Black Sea fleet, if unwieldy, was reckoned equal to the Russian. It was commanded by 'the Crocodile', Capitan Ghazia Hassan-Pasha, already renowned in Turkish annals and tall stories, his most constant and loyal companion not a reptile but a lion.

Catherine had visited the Crimea, that large and vital addition to the empire, in full pomp, a theatrical progress stage-managed by Potemkin, who has also been compared not only to Peter the Great but to Cecil B de Mille. Like Antony and Cleopatra, ageing but victorious, accompanied by Emperor Joseph II, Marie Antoinette's brother, they passed through vast acclamations, glittering receptions, through the 'Potemkin villages', though attempts to disguise from the Empress a prevailing squalor, seem a libel from Georg von Hetbig, a Saxon diplomat who hated Potemkin. The story is more relevant to Mussolini, who used cardboard movie frontages to conceal decayed houses and mean streets during Hitler's 1938 state visit.

For generations the legend so diminished Potemkin's reputation that in places he is still remembered for nothing else. It assumes that Catherine the Great was a gullible fool, Potemkin a foolish knave, an unsustainable thesis about their natures and relationship.

Sporadic Turkish resistance was continuing, based upon the powerful fortress of Ochakov, within the Liman, a Black Sea estuary covering the mouths of the Bug and Dnieper. This overcome, from land and sea, Russia would be nearer the Tsars' long-held design, the capture of 'the Second Rome', Constantinople, and the toppling of the Muslim caliphate, thus redeeming the disgrace of Christian Orthodoxy falling to the Ottomans in 1453. Russia could then rival or overtake Britain in maritime supremacy from the Mediterranean and by defeating the Turkish Empire in Europe, assume world power.

The Liman was shallow, with shifting sands and accesible only through two Russian-fortified peninsulas, though, supported by Ochakov, Turkish ships were ready to oppose a detachment of Potemkin's Black Sea fleet, centred at Kherson and Sebastopol.

The prince himself, no longer an active fighter, had land forces to besiege and assault Ochakov, under another eccentric, Alexander Suvorov, a hero of the Seven Years' War, undefeated in two Polish and two Turkish wars. The plan required the elimination of the Crocodile's fighting and supply ships, though this was being delayed by the alternate lethargy and tantrums of the Russian admirals.

Paul Jones, 'Pavel Dzhones', in white, blue and gold admiral's uniform, proudly drove south for what he envisaged as total command. At St Petersburg, in etoliated salons and anterooms, his qualities were ineffective but, with ships and the sea, he could freely expand, resume true self, far from courtiers' sniggers about piracy, privateering and murder.

A series of shocks ensued on his arrival, and it can be maintained that he had been given no real chance. He needed what Washington and Nelson, Carnot and Wellington, would have expected: goodwill, workable materials, political co-operation and undisputed authority, none of which was available.

Since Peter I, the administration had largely been staffed by foreigners, indiscriminately called 'Germans', or 'heretics'. The British were very numerous, largely controlling the commerce. Superior among them were the famous brothers, Samuel and Jeremy Bentham, the former being Potemkin's leading expert in constructing the Black Sea fleet, with unusually heavy guns. As inspector general of the Royal Navy, he was to similarly assist Nelson. Already, the Scot, Admiral Samuel Grieg, and the British officers of the Baltic fleet had announced their refusal to meet or help the infamous traitor, Jones, and British sailors threatened mutiny at a rumour that he was to command them. Thus the Black Sea was his only option, and he trusted that conditions would be better.

They were not. The Benthams, and such Britons as Knowles and Fanshaw, were jealous or hostile, and Paul Jones was at once confronting a situation exemplifying Rousseau's dictum that everything is a matter of luck and, in adversity, any act of courage is considered a crime.

Always scared of conspiracy, Catherine herself having been enthroned by a coup, the autocracy was cautious about entrusting total military command and, neither in speech nor writing, had the Empress specifically promised it to Paul Jones. In such matters she usually deferred to Potemkin, who would never allow to a stranger an authority almost equal to his own. Moreover, Jones's Squadron, thirteen ships, was too heavily built to manoeuvre in shallows, thus needing an auxiliary smaller and lighter Flotilla, over which the Admiral had no direct authority, Potemkin leaving its commander responsible only to himself, an arrangement open to the comedy and drama he so relished.

The Flotilla leader, a favourite of the Empress and Prince Marshall, had been recommended not only by Jefferson, but by an exiled Scot, Lord Wemys; by the Virginian voyager, Lewis Littlepage, and by Baron Frederick Melchior von Grimm, encyclopaedist, friend of Rousseau, secretary to Chartres's father, the Duke of Orleans, literary and musical critic, French representative in Gotha; and later sent by Catherine to be Russian minister in Hamburg. The naval careerist he joined in supporting was the ubiquitous Prince Charles de Nassau-Siegen, frequenter of many courts.

This Dutch nobleman, already known to Paul Jones, had flair less for naval gallantry and expertise than for wit larded with innuendo. A hedonistic, sophisticated raconteur, he attracted Potemkin, for whom boredom was more dangerous than any Muslim Crocodile. His demand for unfailing admiration and compliance was more readily supplied by a socially adept Nassau-Siegen with a fluent tongue than by a truculent Scot unversed in Russian manners and customs. It could be said of Serenissimus Potemkin, as John Burns said of Lloyd George, that his conscience was as good as new because he never used it. John Paul Jones had been more Catherine's choice than Potemkin's, but to balance one rear-admiral against another and watch the outcome would provide entertainment, watched as if from that flashing theatre box. That Nassau-Siegen might prove a naval charlatan was less important than the probable conflict of opposites. The siege of Ochakov, important, actually all important, was, like most sieges, very tedious. However, Paul Jones, with his reputation and backing, must be allowed his chance, kept in play, lest he desert to the arch-enemy, Sweden.

Like Chartres, Nassau-Siegen hankered for naval distinction, but was hampered by fits of foolhardiness. These had guaranteed his failure to capture Jersey. His ineptitude, casual though stylish, was never impeded by methodical planning or attention to seasoned officers. He had already been so trounced by the British that his assumption of a Russian army command provoked sufficient uproar to have him transferred to the Black Sea fleet, as rear-admiral. Here, he was senior to Paul Jones, not in rank but in chronology, a technicality causing trouble from the start unless exceptional amiability could be mustered. This was unlikely, after that caustic remark from Jones that the prince was 'almost a sailor'.

Nassau-Siegen, who had Polish interests, was also an accredited French diplomat, at a time when both France and Britain were opposing Russian designs on Turkey, with both countries currently at war. This imbroglio might amuse Potemkin, particularly because of its awkwardness for everyone else. For Nassau-Siegen, however, it gave some extra importance, his Paris connections might become helpful, so that he must not be offended. He had also personal qualities much appreciated at any court, the charm, malice and the frivolity of aristocratic Europe. 'The nobles will ruin us,' lamented Marie Antoinette.

By freak of singularity, Nassau-Siegen had already acquired intimacy with Potemkin, connoisseur of human talents, frailties, oddities, seeker of novelties, lover of reckless, improvident Cossacks, of anything to relieve the lassitudes of monotony. The philistine seriousness and social disadvantages of a wandering Scot had no spontaneous appeal to the Russian nobleman who relished the gossip, anecdotes, the thrusts and parries of wit which accompanied the hours spent with the adroit, cosmopolitan Dutch prince. Such was Nassau-Siegen's rooted superficiality that Potemkin might eventually tire of the friendship but, with him, almost nothing was predictable, even to himself.

One more profound encounter was to be denied him. But for the Revolution, with insufficient aristocratic quarterings or connections to rise high in the French royal army, Bonaparte might have entered Turkish or Russian service. A hypothetical match between the mercurial Prince of the Tauride and the keen-witted, sceptical, future Emperor of the French, could challenge the wit, and the wits, of a major dramatist.

Excluded from Potemkin's inner councils and refulgent court, Paul Jones was uncovering the worst. At Kherson, Admiral Mordinov, with English training and English wife, angrily rejected the Scot's position. On his own flagship, *Vladimir*, primed by Captain Panaitto Alexiano, all ranks were unwelcoming. More outrageous still was the divided command, despite Nassau-Siegen behaving as pleasantly as he had a few years previously. 'You know my esteem and friendship. It will end only at my death.' An unprofitable assurance, identical with that which Robespierre made to his victim, Danton, a few years hence.

Whatever qualms Paul Jones had developed about Potemkin in his glory and condescension were trivial compared to his feelings about the naval scene. Despite Samuel Bentham's modern guns, the ships were barely seaworthy: hulls needed caulking, guns were unpolished, masts and woodwork unvarnished, the decks strewn with garbage, the Russian crew fractious, with hostile gestures and cheapjack invective. Signalling was mere bawling in several languages, an unnerving process of bargaining, or a despairing appeal for help. His technical expertise elicited pained incredulity or dissent from officers, incomprehension below deck. Meticulous discipline, thorough marksmanship, rigorous cleanliness, precise tactics, were all unknown, though Jones himself was remembered by Ivak, a Cossack sailor: 'He looked very impressive and brave. It was at once obvious that he was an expert. As soon as he stepped on board he began to arrange everything as he wanted, examining sails, guns, ammunition.'

In mobility and numbers, and on some ships in guns, the Squadron was inferior to the Turks, and because of this, several Russians had already refused its command. The Flotilla had adequate guns and marines but Nassau-Siegen, on his private yacht, was lapsing into envy of Jones on his large *Vladimir*. Yet their unity was vital: one defeat, of themselves on sea or Suvorov on land, could endanger Russian occupation of the still volatile Crimea.

To ease the siege of Ochakov, Jones determined to tempt the Crocodile into battle with the combined Squadron and Flotilla strung across the Liman, covering all salients. On the south shore were waiting battalions under the ruthless, effective Suvorov, who liked to write his dispatches to Catherine in verse and, allegedly, to address his troops naked. He accepted Jones's suggestion of planting guns – always guns – on the Kinburn peninsula, over the most slender Liman ingress. These speedily inflicted harsh damage on reconnoitring Turks, not wholly pleasing Potemkin, always suspicious of intelligent moves made independently.

For Paul Jones, the flimsy fairy tale was rapidly shrivelling, and the well-disposed though erratic Suvorov, advised him: 'You must adapt yourself, like me. Pay homage to the powerful, bow to each in turn. Then, none will be jealous of you. Cultivate as many eccentricities as you see fit. The more they think you mad, the less you will scare them.'

The start of the first Battle of the Liman was unpropitious. A contrary off-shore wind handicapped the cumbersome Squadron while, in calmer waters, the Flotilla was able to advance, until, with the wind slackening, Jones broke free, to join up with Nassau-Siegen.

Full co-operation between the two, together with Suvorov and Mordinov at Sebastopol, could soon have settled the Turks, who, despite greater numbers and much individual bravery, were inferior in gunmanship. Such mutual assistance, however, seldom occurred; the lack of it was disastrous for the Russian armies as late as 1914. Potemkin's orders to reinforce Jones with quick-moving gunboats were ignored or sabotaged. He promised to order Suvorov to advance in concert with Jones's movements, but did nothing but interfere with contradictory or garbled instructions.

The Crocodile cheerfully accepted the challenge, sending forward ships, not very skilfully handled, on 18 June. Paul Jones prudently assessed his own resources and, with the wind still not wholly satisfactory, chose to force the Turks into the shallows, grounding them, to be destroyed at leisure with cannon and grenades, caught in crossfire between the ships and the Kinburn battery. Strategically. this excelled, though Nassau-Siegen disregarded it in an impetuous frontal attack, against advice or orders, and was soon meshed in a confusion from which Jones had to waste time extricating him, making sure that his own ships suffered least.

The Turks fought as he had anticipated, with spirit but no overall capacity. Twice he broke their line and, manipulating his fire with the better accuracy, forced them back with considerable losses, pursuing them in doubtful alliance with the Flotilla. Sebag-Montefiore judges this more stalemate than rout, for, though encouraging, Ochakov remained intact, the Crocodile's force, severely mauled, could yet regroup, and his lion had survived, as important for popular morale as Prince Rupert's poodle, 'Boy', a mascot for the royalists whose assurance suffered when the animal was killed at Marston Moor.

Russian losses had been negligible, but Paul Jones's plan had relied too much on others' support; Alexiano had been dilatory and complete Turkish entrapment in the shallows was foiled by Nassau-Siegen's attempt at a personal set piece, the speed of pursuit being vitiated by unnecessary delay and resistance to orders.

Depleted, the Turks withdrew to the safety of Ochakov. Although Paul Jones was dissatisfied with partial victory, he knew that sovereign and supremo, looking for more, would be unlikely to accept that any blame attached to their friend the prince, though he had shown both recklessness and timidity, was inexperienced in tackling changes of wind and currents, was ignorant of the shoals, and unconcerned with signals. The slower Squadron had prevailed through Jones's deployments, and his skill with guns.

A victory *Te Deum* was sung on *Vladimir*, but such rituals, theologically unsound, do not axiomatically promote humility and unity. Nassau-Siegen was soon assuring Potemkin that the day had been won by himself alone, a claim forwarded to Catherine, to Warsaw and Versailles and, with the effrontery of the young John Paul himself, pronouncing himself master of the Liman, dismissing Jones as an amateurish privateer: 'My Name will travel into the Future.' In this, he was not altogether mistaken.

Jones had to change tack. He was ill and despondent and recognised that he must establish himself more securely with the Prince Marshal; with a daring, but misplaced, acumen he judged it tactful to praise his associate: 'I did my best to help the Prince with the necessary manoeuvres.' Unwontedly, restrained, against all his natural grain, he allowed himself to add, incredibly to all who had known him, that Nassau-Siegen had shown great coolness and intelligence. Then, as if seeking self-destruction, totally oblivious to the psychology of his employers, he had to add: 'I had the Honor to act as his aide-de-camp, and he took all my suggestions in good part.'

Anything ironic or sardonic was lost in an apparent servility which the Prince Marshal could only despise. Potemkin admired Cossack ribaldry, obscenity, swagger and, what Paul Jones might consider subtle or politic, he despised, even though in another part of his self which so swerved between extremes, he might have suspected the truth, and been the more entertained. He then sent grandiloquent congratulations to both men, while committing himself to neither, like a supple drama critic.

In the contest between giant and dwarf, folk tales mislead. Giants often prevail. In the realm of politics and war, SE Morison is forthright about the Russian giant: 'What Potemkin did was to toss Paul Jones into a pack of sea-wolves.' This may insufficiently acknowledge Potemkin's complexity. Tired of the Ochakov Siege, victim of many impulses, he could not yet collect himself for total involvement. In such a man, in history itself, the effects of boredom, caprice, mischief – and music – can be overlooked. Potemkin embraced so vigorously many disparate histrionic parts and scenes that connections between them could be temporarily mislaid. Thus promises, contracts and arrangements could be left disregarded, causing grievance, wretchedness and accusations of bad faith which could actually amaze or bewilder him, reinforcing his convictions about human absurdity, while his imagination lurched elsewhere and he rejected, in anger and puzzled incredulity, those who dared inform him of the disturbances he had provoked.

Paul Jones had no time to ponder the imponderable. The Crocodile was regrouping, still with numerical advantage. He too needed a swift victory. The Sublime Porte, the government at Constantinople, ruthlessly discarded losers, and even the famed *capitan* could expect poison or strangulation should he return with the Black Sea lost.

Spies would have reported Russian divisions and recriminations. Outside Ochakov, the siege commanders waited; within, the Turkish governor waited; Suvorov, at Kinburn or wherever his fancy took him, waited. The Crocodile arranged his line. On shore, two glistening rear-admirals disputed with comic-opera panache, like rival tenors singing vulgar songs in discordant harmonies, the libretto unoriginal, the finale ludicrous.

Nassau-Siegen was temperamentally dazzled by visions of the breakthrough, the ecstatic charge, irrespective of strategy, resources or casualties. For Paul Jones, all battles were special circumstances requiring foresight, grasp of detail, overall design, yet allowing for generous improvisation during the conflict itself. In the days ahead, any insistence on Nassau-Siegen's compliance would be mere bluster or token authority without urgent support from Potemkin, which would never arrive.

Jones must do as best he could. Without Nassau-Siegen's impetuosity, he too valued the memorable gesture. On 27 June, he and Ivak sailed out at sundown in a small boat to assess the Turkish warships at close quarters, inspect their formations, overhear their watchwords, sense something of the Turkish mood, while pretending to be peasants selling salt. 'We kept moving among the ships like a seagull,' Ivak remembered. Afterwards, many saw, chalked on the stern of the Turkish flagship: *To be Burnt, Paul Jones. 27/8 June.*

The second Battle of the Liman, for overture, offered another quarrel between Dutchman and American, guaranteeing imperfect co-operation of Squadron and Flotilla. Following early skirmishes, two large Turkish battleships and five frigates, attempting to avoid Suvorov's shore guns, tacked badly and ran into the shoals, stranding themselves. The Crocodile ordered the general advance, as Jones hoped, of warships, fire ships and light craft in general line, the flagship almost at once crashing onto a sand bank, dislocating those around it. A strong wind prevented immediate counter advance, Nassau-Siegen blaming not this but Jones's irresolution. Two more Turkish ships, paying for poor charts and careless planning, grounded themselves in the shallows; then, at a sudden favourable slant of the wind, Jones could signal attack on an enemy floundering in almost total confusion. The Flotilla, however, chose to move too slowly and, reluctant to close upon the impotent Turks, bombarded them from safe distance, many balls falling short. On the Squadron, Bentham's guns were making havoc and Jones, shouting from an open craft, ordered the Crocodile's motionless flagship to be boarded by marines from *Vladimir*. In this, he was frustrated by Alexiano. Hitherto effective, the Greek, from jealousy or, as he later excused himself, fearing the shallows, commanded absolute halt, which would have left Jones isolated and unprotected had he not contrived to regain safety by dextrous steering. An oncoming tide refloated the Turk, only for it to hit another sandbank. On this, its gunners courageously resisted until, with atrocious noise, fire and pandemonium, it blew up. This did not complete Jones's victory, for the sheer bulk of the Turkish vessels, many still unable to free themselves, delayed, then prevented him reaching Ochakov. Also, too many of his own ships contravened orders and paused to burn rather than capture. This had the further result of preventing the valuable addition of Turkish ships to Potemkin's Black Sea fleet.

Nassau-Siegen, till now content with firing without personal danger, wavered between loss of nerve and prospects of complete Turkish disaster, and decided against allowing any ships to leave in support of Paul Jones's efforts. The Crocodile, barely destructible in battle, had survived explosions, cannonballs, bullets, fire, together with the lion. Briefly, with Nassau-Siegen ignoring Jones's appeals for auxiliaries, the Turks rallied until Jones, re-forming his line, swept them back. Suvorov at least was not failing him; his Kinburn artillery was so vicious that nine enemy ships were left shattered, easy prey for the light Flotilla and, at this, the prince signalled his intention of directing his entire strength against them. Not now holding himself as an aide-de-camp, Paul Jones retorted that this was unnecessary and that, to deliver the knockout, to clear the Black Sea and to deprive Ochakov of supplies and reinforcements, he needed all ships available. Piqued by threats to his own chance of personal glamour, Nassau-Siegen raged, then, urged by some of his officers, grandly consented to release some ships. In their later dispute, he taunted Jones for usurping a reputation and for begging protection when he least needed it. Paul Jones, to whom 'A man's first Duty is to protect his own Honor,' exclaimed that his reputation had resulted from actual fighting against the British, a telling reminder of the Dutchman's failures against that nation.

Seven of the stranded Turks were needlessly burned, two were captured, the prince again applauding himself as conquerer of the Liman. A replica of Landais, in language and attitude, though, in the prince's favour, less so in personality.) 'It was seemly that I won great succes.s. I always acted against the advice of the Squadron Leader, who has achieved nothing. Paul Jones has learnt the difference between commanding a privateer and a squadron.'

In his journal, Paul Jones reported the loss of one frigate, 18 dead, some 90 wounded. Turkish losses were 15 ships, including 10 frigates, 3,000 dead or wounded, 2,000 prisoners. The Liman, if not completely Russian, was now sufficiently open to allow forces to cross the Bug and redouble the strength poised against Ochakov.

The second victory was more decisive than the first, though less so than Paul Jones could have wished. Potemkin, Nassau-Siegen, and staff officers dined with him on *Vladimir* on an occasion which could never have rollicked in good fellowship. What should have been an unarmed truce almost ended in a general brawl. Toasts were soon being ignored, jokes rebounded like poisoned boomerangs, recriminations were invisible fireworks. Potemkin alone was unperturbed, the playful giant, until at last roused by Nassau-Siegen's expletives and ordering him to apologise to Paul Jones, though perhaps with an inward chuckle at hearing the American ridiculed as 'the pirate'.

Still in lethargic ill-health, Potemkin announced the immediate assault on Ochakov; postponed it, for a banquet; delayed it for a fishing jaunt; then lost interest, with reassurance to Suvorov, made an effort to reconcile the two admirals, an effort for which the Dutchman was eager to take the credit; a grab for attention, which perhaps succeeded with the weary Prince Marshal, grateful for anything at which to smile.

In all this, some guesswork pervades: accounts vary, often written in heat or remembered inaccurately, chronology wobbles, prejudice abounds, some episodes seem improbable. Undeniably, however, the aftermath was unsatisfactory for Paul Jones. As if affected by northern airs or a Russian wizard, he was still shedding habitual caution and good sense, confusing obsequiousness with diplomacy, accepting courteously worded insults as rewards. This miasma was dispersed when orders, roubles and estates were distributed for victory in the Liman, the largest share awarded to the Prince Marshal, already overflowing with all three. Nassau-Siegen and his officers did well. For Paul Jones, the Order of St Anna, useful but not first class, unaccompanied by an extra star, ceremonial coat or substantial money grant. Of his officers, only Alexiano, who deserved nothing, received anything. Then, worst of all, Charles de Nassau-Siegen was promoted Vice-Admiral, senior to the baffled, incredulous Paul Jones who listed six reasons for refusing to acknowledge his flag: 'I will say this in the Face of the Universe, that he is Unworthy of it.'

Still misjudging Potemkin, who preferred outright opposition to smothered resentment and muttered curses, Paul Jones publicly expressed gratitude, and in private, sunk into futile anger, emotion without action.

The Crocodile had retired with his survivors into the comparative safety of Ochakov, trusting, with some realism, that internecine enemy feuds and jostles for attention from almighty Serenissimus would save the fortress.

On 12 July Suvorov was allowed another mobilisation, though by early autumn it had not been fully realised. Paul Jones was ordered to strengthen the blockade of Ochakov and destroy or neutralise any Turkish ships still at large. This remained difficult, for Potemkin's querulous complaints, extravagant demands and wilful interference prolonged Turkish resistance and allowed supply ships to reach Ochakov from Constantinople.

Jones retained some sparkling initiative, sailing into gunfire, striving to induce discipline and pride and, demonstrating the possible, once leapt onto a Turkish gunboat, captured the crew and, in silent goad to land action, left it in a bay facing the Prince Marshal's headquarters. He was forced to rescue Nassau-Siegen from a confusion after having mishandled a simple diversionary attack. Yet his ill luck persisted. Nassau-Siegen was providentially watched by Potemkin when damaging Turkish ships on foreshore waters too shallow for heavier craft, with Paul Jones directing operations further away and unseen. Afterwards, steering *Vladimir* alone through enemy galleys, Jones captured the first galley, scaled another at the head of marines and won its surrender, together with several more. During this, behind Jones's back and without orders, Alexiano, who had not endangered himself, commanded the destruction of four captive vessels, with some 3,000 sailors and rowers, chained convicts or serfs burning to death, unnoticed by higher authority and to Jones's appalled fury.

Suvorov's assault was permitted to dwindle to a reinforced siege, foreign to the general's excitable temperament. All continued to be impeded by preposterous orders from Potemkin. He was distracted not only by sickness and moodiness but by messages from Catherine, coping with the complexities of the entire empire at home and abroad. He had no time to spare for Paul Jones's repeated requests for more ships, the unification of Flotilla and Squadron under a single command, and the translation into Russian, French and German of his signalling codes. Serenissimus lingered with his entourage of women, musicians, diplomats, courtiers and cosmopolitan socialites, his presence denying the initiatives natural to Suvorov and Jones. This protracted the siege, at agonising cost to the soldiers, a tableau perennial and seldom excusable. Like others of the great – Alcibiades, Henry II, Tolstoy, Victor Hugo, Bernard Shaw – the Prince Marshal's compound included streaks of irresponsible perversity and silliness. Also, some admiration for physical and mental cruelty, a defect common among intellectuals.

Paul Jones was now literally and figuratively at sea; he struggled to maintain the blockade while temperatures lowered, skies darkened and seas heaved more fiercely. Dependent on such as Alexiano and Nassau-Siegen, he must have envied the technical proficiencies and traditions of the British he so condemned. To rebuffs and refusals from headquarters, he replied with terse correctness, annotating and storing all correspondence and signed witness from officers, a precaution against trouble ahead, while sending candid reports to Catherine, to whom the Prince of Princes was simultaneously confiding stories of Nassau-Siegen's tireless cleverness and of Jones's unpopularity, negligence and 'sleepiness'.

Periodically, Jones's restraint faltered, 'as I have not come here as an Adventurer nor as a mountebank to repair a ruined Fortune...I hope henceforward to experience no Humiliation, and to reach the Position promised me.'

Protests can engender shrillness, never an agreeable sound, and seldom successful. Jones was unable to feel or acquire the affection, curiosity or imaginative artistry requisite to confront Potemkin, skills which, in more momentous issues, Roosevelt and Churchill imagined was theirs when associating with Stalin.

That autumn, Jones failed to disperse the Crocodile's defence, Nassau-Siegen also, though more miserably. The prince then quarrelled and lost favour with Potemkin, who belatedly divulged awareness of discrepancies between the vice-admiral's bombastic dispatches and the facts. Feeling his genius slurred, the prince huffily announced his departure to Poland, where virtual anarchy might provide spectacular opportunities. Responsibility for a naval onslaught on Ochakov was then transferred from both antagonists to a posse of Potemkin's beloved Cossacks who, fortified by drink, with berserk courage and the wind behind them, scattered the

Turkish ships, enabling Potemkin to join Suvorov in plans to mount the decisive land assault.

Disgusted by Potemkin's behaviour, Lewis Littlepage, a Virginian who had served under Paul Jones, resigned his commission, having repeated to his fellow-American the essentials of Suvorov's advice: 'Remember, you have to sustain here a political as well as a military character, and that your part is now rather that of a courtier than of a soldier.' Dourly, sadly, Paul Jones replied that he was never made for that part.

It was a part familiar in discussions and pleas with Franklin, Adams, Morris and the French marine, but here, combating not only corruption and inefficiency but the incalculable, even mysterious, he had endured enough. In a last interview, in which his loyalty, competence, and courage were questioned, he sturdily, then angrily, faced the Prince Marshal, his pride unshaken but still with plain misunderstanding of the other's nature, flourishing his testimonials and commendations, his written objections to Nassau-Seigen's artful devices, and notes of his own correctness and others' refusal to enact his stratagems.

Nothing could have been more mistaken. Signatures, correctly phrased documents, lengthy explanations and logical argument would enflame Potemkin to unreachable proportions. Criticism of Nassau-Siegen was criticism of himself and of Catherine, both of them, by their status, irreproachable. He listened, he was affable, he was charming, gave purrs of assent: yes, the divided command had been an unfortunate error; certainly, the campaign had been all but the finest; without question, the esteemed admiral deserved a post even more distinguished, perhaps on the Baltic, where honoured Grieg had, by convenient mischance, recently died. Those Swedes, as so often, deserved the best of enemies. And was not the Taganrog squadron in need of the very special talents now under discussion?

In this pernicious climax, Jones, while no nimble Lord Nelson, kept a hard core of personal identity, pushing his case to the utmost. Hating unfinished work, he desired to be in at the kill when Ochakov fell, and deliver lasting defeat to the Ottomans, while Potemkin was equally determined to be rid of him and from Catherine orders swiftly arrived, for Jones to depart for St Petersburg.

He did not quite realise its import, and with new expectations outweighing his dissatisfactions, he made another hectic journey north, confident in the effect of his own dispatches. These, to avoid spies and thieving officials, he had entrusted to de Ségur for delivery to the

Empress. Ignoring her devotion to Potemkin, her regard for Nassau-Siegen, he might have fared better had he sent nothing.

While awaiting private audience, he worked devotedly on plans to drive Swedish interlopers back to port; to organise a Russo–American expedition against the damnable Barbary pirates, he himself in the van, granted five warships and a free hand; then a commercial alliance, using his own business adroitness. He had a scheme for recruiting Americans for imperial service in return for American access to the Black Sea, another for refurbishing the Baltic and Black Sea fleets.

One recipient of his letters was Thomas Jefferson, though only one escaped the vigilance of censors and secret police. They were optimistic, though temperate in admiration of things Russian.

Catherine, however, had her own plans. She was harried by accounts of English and Scottish enmity to Jones, complaints of his rigour and doubts of his capacity. Potemkin had fluently described ill discipline on his ships, dissension with his officers, a bad example set to the vivacious Cossacks. A decision was necessary, was easy, was at once made. The Scot had been a bad investment and now, from Poland, reappeared as diplomat, financial adviser, delightful companion, was none other than Charles de Nassau-Siegen, privileged in possession of the imperial entrée, and at once given the Baltic command, the sovereign pledging him: 'I will never permit whatever I had ordered and found satisfactory on military affairs to be allowed revision by any man on earth.' This was an obvious thrust at Admiral Jones, followed by an assertion of Germanic and Russian dynastic heritage: 'You are right, because I myself consider you right. This is, no doubt, the logic of aristocracy, but so it must be, unless common sense is to be wholly disregarded.'

The Swedish Admiralty rejoiced at the new appointment: by the end of 1790, the Russian professionals were cursing.

On 6 December 1788, Ochakov was at last taken, settling the future of the Crimea, and further chastening Ottoman fortunes. In Cossack and Asiatic tradition, the Prince Marshal, indifferent to soldiers, his own or the enemy's, allowed pillage and massacre, atrocities even on children. Then, in his pomp, with spendthrift insignia, banners and drums, baggage wagons and attendants, he prepared his spectacular, triumphant progress towards she whom he loved, teased; joined in mirth, madcap pranks, statecraft, domination over a quarter of the known world.

While still dangling hopes, Paul Jones considered a Swedish offer, then declared that such a switch of allegiance would impair his 'honor'.

Catherine's silence he excused as due to fatigue and overwork, Potemkin's aloofness must be caused by labours even more arduous. In a fantastic city, Jones was being intoxicated by his own fantasies. The winter was painful, he succumbed to pneumonia and left damp St Petersburg to breathe better in windy Kherson. Recovering, he heard of Nassau-Siegen's return and judged it essential to be seen again in the capital.

At first, all appeared well. Though still ignored by the highest, actually welcomed only at the French embassy, he found apparent cordiality elsewhere, before realising, as he had at Versailles, that smiles could be grins, murmurs unfriendly, embraces vicious.

The outcome still needs conclusive clarification. At its simplest, he fell deep into an ancient trap. Disconsolate admiral without a fleet, American hero without a commission, Briton without a country, chevalier of a French regime nearing disintegration, he still had to linger in Russia, keeping up appearances despite chest pains, a fraying temper and unpleasant rumours. One rumour had it that an offer was being prepared, then scandal intervened, perhaps engineered, perhaps accidental, possibly neither.

His sexual magnetism, which had so markedly failed with the Empress, was now used against him, by those never positively identified: Potemkin, Nassau-Siegen, Britons and Americans, have been suspected, never verified. What is undeniable is that John Paul Jones was accused of raping a ten-year-old, half-German girl, Stepanova Gottwast. on the testimony of her mother who, he wrote to Potemkin, 'lives here in a brothel leading a debauched and adulterous life'.

The charge he furiously denied. Seduction was an exercise from which he did not instinctively shrink, no more than did Nassau-Siegen or Potemkin, but rape and children were scarcely his style. Hastening to his defence, he was soon dismayed to find no lawyer willing to undertake his case. This was not strange, it was all too obvious, enemies as usual had been active, he was surrounded by malefactors, spies, the envious and mischievous. Everywhere, save by de Ségur, he was ostracised. Threats came of a humiliating public trial, or secret and indefinite imprisonment, with no trial whatsoever. Stories were released as if on kites, luridly tinted. In Scotland he had murdered his own nephew; the English wanted to hang him as killer, traitor, bandit, thief. He was down in the shadows, with Mungo Maxwell and the Tobagan 'Ringleader'.

Arrest was deferred, while he collected and distributed evidence and wrote letters to Paris and America. His one unflinching defender was de Ségur who, though a friend of his graceful fellow diplomat, Nassau-Siegen, was loyal to the American Revolution and those who had risked life and fortune to accomplish it. He reported Jones's innocence to Thomas Jefferson, he informed the Prince Marshal that the chevalier had been wantonly libelled by a woman certified by her own husband as a procuress and, in this instance, prompted by Nassau-Siegen. Paul Jones too counterattacked, recovering his old vehemence. A mere plea was inadequate. He admitted sexual relations with the girl, but anyone with eyes and ears could confirm that she was not ten but at least fourteen, performing as a regular waitress and whore at his own hotel, more than willingly. 'I always gave her money.' Her mother regularly traded young girls, proof was copious; colluding with the daughter, she admitted lying about her age.

The charge was withdrawn, without arrest or trial. An unknown potentate was whispered to have masterminded or protected a design to overthrow the American: Nassau-Siegen was never exonerated, never condemned; Jones's German servant was understood to have pocketed covert payments in return for false testimony. Nothing was certain. One political faction might have wanted to disgrace Paul Jones, in attempt to placate Britain, always suspicious of Russian anti-Turk policies and desire to become a Mediterranean power. Russian neutrality was also needed, in case of rupture with Sweden.

Paul Jones was probably framed, but in circumstances largely of his own making. Like so much in his life, distortion, slander, subterfuge, the human disposition to embroider, had fabricated another accusation which may yet have enclosd a tiny sliver of truth.

In the final event, few had wanted a courtroom drama with angry exchanges, tainted evidence, and aspersions, unspoken yet obvious, directed at imperial favourites. The plan, if plan there had been, had succeeded sufficiently to discredit the foreigner. By consorting with bad company, he had sawn off the branch on which he had been sitting.

The British responded with unexpected generosity. At home, they mostly refrained from exploiting their old enemy's plight, and at St Petersburg many unfroze, offering sympathy, advice and hospitality. Although often ridiculed for prudery, the English and Scots were willing to use the sexual imprudence of a Parnell, a Dilke, for political manoeuvres, in dram shop, coffeehouse and on the streets, but often applauded such libertines as Wilkes and Fox. Edward IV had long ago been rebuked for his womanising, but this, a chronicler added, 'not greatly grieved the people'. Henry VIII, with his stack of maltreated ladies, remains popular:

> Bluff King Hal, full of Beans,
> Married half a dozen Queens.

The maraudings of a Palmerston, an Edward VII, the 'dalliance' of Pretty Nelly, and the Jersey Lily, seldom furtive, elicited much popular jocularity, understanding and envy.

Ambassador de Ségur published his official support for the Chevalier, and was joined by an influential diplomat, the younger de Genêt, subsequently to be over-embroiled in American politics as Minister of the French Republic from 1793 to 1794. Jefferson affirmed his continuing trust in Paul Jones, together with that of George Washington, who, next year, fateful 1789, was unanimously elected President of the United States.

Paul Jones was allowed two years' 'leave', a Russian euphemism. He left Russia, behaving as if nothing untoward had occurred and, braving out everything, from Warsaw, Amsterdam, Vienna, Paris, continually sent Catherine and 'My Prince' packages of his latest schemes, naval, commercial, political. He recommended a novel warship designed by himself and Franklin, suggested a stratagem against 'Turkish Arabia', included a design to disrupt British India, outlined a programme for wholesale reform of the Russian navy. In character, he would enclose more testimonials, justifications and demands for a more distinguished decoration. His manner 'of injured pride and misunderstood virtue', SE Morison compares to that of Columbus in a similar position. 'Since I am proved too candid,' Jones wrote, 'and too sincere to make my way at the Russian Court without creating powerful Enemies, I have sufficient Philosophy to withdraw into the peaceful Bosom of Friendship'.

His gift for friendship had never been remarkable, he was incapable of withdrawal, save as a breathing space to return, and almost to the end persisted in his claims for attention. He had to convince the world, convince himself, of his singularity. Also, he was to remind the English that 'I was known to have given more alarm to their Three Kingdoms than any other Individual had done...in short, I am pleased with myself.'

To Grimm, the Empress wrote: 'Tell him to go and mind his own business in America.'

Paul Jones would have attempted to mind his own business anywhere, given half a chance, and in Russia, this was all he was ever given. EM Almedingen, born in St Petersburg in 1898, concluded that Catherine would have had fewer reverses 'had she trusted to the genius of John Paul

Jones, whose treatment at her hands was both shabby and foolish'. With allowance made for Jones's temperamental flaws, posterity might respect the Cossack, Ivak, who declared that he had never seen such a man as the Admiral. 'Sweet like a vine when he wished, but, if necessary, like a rock. And how we gave him our trust! A mere gesture we would obey like the actual Voice of Authority itself. Some men seem to be born to give orders.'

Catherine the Great, and Alexander, Prince of Princes, great in themselves, possess names still resonant. Despite world wars, Russian and German death camps and revolutions, much of their work – their homes, gardens, collections – remains. However, doubtless necessarily in the magnitude of their accomplishment they inflicted much pain, injustice and sorrow. Power neglects the individual, overlooks the personal. A reader today might find Scott Fitzgerald's summing up the far from illustrious Tom and Daisy Buchanan, in *The Great Gatsby* in part apposite:

'They were careless people, they smashed up things and creatures and then retreated back into their money, or their vast carelessness, or whatever it was that held them together, and let other people clear up the mess they had made.'

13

Decline

The trumpet shakes with great discord. An agreement broken: a face raised to heaven; the bleeding mouth will swim in blood; the face anointed with milk and honey lies in the dust. Before long, all will be organised; we await a very evil century. The state of the masked and solitary greatly transformed: few will find desire to retain their ranks.

Michel de Notredame,
Centuries, 1555

The absence of a King is more desirable than his presence, and he is not only a political superfluity, but a grievous burden, pressing hard on the whole nation...Let France, then arrived at the age of reason, no longer be deluded by the sound of words, and let her deliberately examine if a king, however insignificant and contemptible in himself, may not at the same time be extremely dangerous.

Tom Paine,
Common Sense, 1776

> Too firm to yield, and far too proud to stoop,
> Doomed by his very virtues for a dupe,
> He cursed those virtues as the cause of ill,
> And not the traitors who betray'd him still.

Lord Byron,
The Corsair, 1812

Of thee too, for country's sake, o chevalier John Paul, be a word spent or misspent! In faded naval uniform, Paul Jones lingers visible here, like a wine-skin from which the wine is drawn. Like the ghost of himself! Low is his once loud bruit; scarcely audible, save with extreme tedium, in ministerial ante-chambers; in this or the other charitable dining-room, mindful of the past! What changes, culminations and declinings!

Thomas Carlyle,
The French Revolution, 1837

The French Crown, for the first time in over a century, in an effort to stabilise the Treasury and effect administrative reform, had summoned the Estates-General, where progressive nobles – Mirabeau, Orleans – joined with advanced bishops, such as Talleyrand, and middle-class professional men – Brissot, Danton, Robespierre. Led by the nobles themselves, feudal privileges had been enthusiastically abolished. The storming of the Bastille, partly to capture its arsenal, and the defection of many royal troops, had roused extraordinary expectations of plenty, though the king had already meditated its demolition. The towering fortress-prison was found to contain only a dissipated young nobleman, four forgers, and a couple of lunatics, one convinced that he was God. This was not publicised, so as not to detract from the symbolism of the event. 'From this moment, we may regard France as a free country,' reported Lord Dorset, devotee of Marie Antoinette, who had been frustrated by the Bastille tumult in his plan to introduce cricket to Paris. Madame de Genlis was now wearing in her corsage a chip of the Bastille, embedded in jewels.

Liberal sentiments were rampant. The American, Gouverneur Morris, declaimed 'the whole conspiracy against Freedom is blown to the moon,' and Lafayette was assured by Tom Paine that he would become the French George Washington. That the Bastille's governor had surrendered on promise of a safe conduct, only to be butchered, and that two ministers were then lynched, was disregarded, or excused. Paine traced such outrages not to new principles but to the degraded example for so long exemplified by kings, priests and aristocrats. These would now be purged by the virtuous, the fearless, the high-minded. Thomas Jefferson, in the spirit of Mussolini, Lenin, Franco, Castro – who praised and desired a Robespierre – and Bernard Shaw, inquired:

'What country before ever existed a century and a half without a rebellion? And what country can preserve its liberties if their rulers are not warned from time to time? Let them take arms. The remedy is to set them right as to facts, pardon and pacify them. What signify a few lives lost in a century or two? The tree of liberty must be refreshed from time to time with the blood of patriots and tyrants. It is its natural manure. What signify a few lives?'

These lines summarise the flaw in the French Revolution, which periodically convulsed the nineteenth century and contaminated the twentieth. Momentous issues were directed by careless, over-cerebral, or impatient people, who were then shocked by outside pressures and internal fears into self-righteousness, massacre, one-party despotism.

Jefferson himself, like Robespierre, cherished smallholders who subscribed to 'Virtue, civic responsibility, concern for the well-being of the virtuous, obedience to the laws.'

In Britain – revered as the home of Cromwell and Locke, Newton and Hume, Blake, Joseph Priestley, Richard Price – the younger Pitt, himself not disdaining the use of spies, provocateurs, stool-pigeons and informers against radicals, republicans and Irish malcontents, was presiding over recovery from the American War. He was striving to transform setbacks to assets, but he had no regard for 'natural manure' as spiritual or political sustenance. Not so Charles James Fox, witty, charming, much loved. 'How much the greatest event it is that has ever happened,' he reflected on the fall of the Bastille, 'and how much the best!' British Whigs, scientists, intellectuals, poets – Byron, Wordsworth, Shelley, Blake, Burns, Southey, Coleridge – turned from applauding the American Revolution to idolising the French. David Williams, Sir James Mackintosh and Tom Paine accepted honorary French citizenship and assisted in designing the revolutionary manifestos, declarations and constitutions. Mackintosh published, 'with reasoned dullness,' as a critic commented, a defence of the Revolution translated by Paul Jones's old acquaintance, the Duke of Orleans, in reply to Burke's Tory diatribe. Wordsworth rejoiced at what he saw as the rebirth of Human Nature in France. *The Times*, on 20 July 1789, boomed: 'We have no period of history affording so striking an example of a distracted government and the bloodshed of civil war as that which France now exhibits... the concurrent Voice of the Nation demands a new Constitution, nor do we forsee that any power can resist it.'

All movements, evolving their distinct morality, plead the necessity for violence and amorality. Oliver Cromwell, who was a virtuous husband and loving father, was convinced that in exterminating Irish Catholics he was doing the Lord's Work. The French Revolutionaries, covering themselves with such clarion calls as 'The Country is in Danger', but imprisoned in spiritual pride, dogma, or simple bewilderment, would, like any monarchy, break treaties, kill opponents, invade and pillage, on behalf of the People, Liberty and Virtue, mesmerising themselves not with the sense but the music of words. Politics became anthems or requiems. Conviction of their own virtue was less dishonest than corrupt. Himmler was probably honest in believing the Final Solution was 'an act of hygiene'.

Dr Johnson's notion that political liberty is justified only if it produces private liberty was unlikely to prevail in the France of 1789. In St Petersburg, Catherine was rightly blaming Louis XVI for incomprehension of dire events and, wrongly, for over-drinking. Her experience of politics and human nature made her inimical to the Revolution, so far from the disciplined reforms and intellectually reasoned discussions for which she had earlier hoped, and the execution of the royal pair profoundly shocked her, surely provoking grim recollections of Pugachev. Also, and more coarse in her motives, she was preoccupied with troubles and opportunities in Poland, where aristocratic freedom was unbounded, discipline unknown, and misery almost universal, for want of a strong arm.

Montesquieu had taught, though citing very little evidence, that knowledge induces gentleness and reason reconciles people with humanity. The test for the American and French Revolutions would be whether they fulfilled the Enlightenment or rejected it: whether they remained optimistic about human nature; whether they slumped into the immoderate and vindictive, into the academic and utopian, into dictatorship.

Americans were already facing what Alexis de Tocqueville was to assert about their democracy, that you can have equality of opportunity, or you can have equality, but that you cannot have both. Sydney Smith was foretelling 'a bloody, servile war', within the states, caused by slavery. Pitt was to condemn 'the vain and false philosophy which refers all things to theology, nothing to practice – which refutes experience, which substitutes visionary hypothesis for the solid test of experience, and bewilders the human mind in a maze of opinions when it should be employed in directing to actions.'

This, though not exceptional to France, was there to be heard at its most drastic. To the ailing citizen of the world, John Paul Jones, the street cries and salon jargon about Liberty, Equality and Fraternity, meant as little as the thesis, 'Hunger as a Philosophical Concept' would have upon a starving crew. In London, more hopefully, George Canning and JH Frere would soon reflect on Mrs Brownrigg, who beat two girl apprentices to death, hiding the cadavers in a coal hole:

> For this act
> Did Brownrigg swing! Harsh Laws. But time shall come
> When France shall reign, and laws be all repealed.

Versailles, that symbol of unearthly, unassailable grandeur, but rotting within, was abandoned, the king relinquishing it on the insistence of hungry and threatening crowds from Paris. He and his family were escorted to their capital by the commander of the new and enigmatic National Guard, the Marquis de Lafayette, inscrutable beneath forms of deference. The court now inhabited the decayed, disorganised Tuileries, under the eyes of a Paris seething and inflammable. G Lenôtre wrote:

> The Parisians, who had, for nearly a century, lost sight of and forgotten the manner in which a Court was conducted, beheld with amazement the arrival in their town of the army of courtiers and servants which the Royal Family dragged in its train. These thousands of functionaries whose titles seemed comical and superannuated, had no longer any prestige for this people, who imagined itself to have made a revolution.

Louis could trust neither Mirabeau nor Lafayette, nor his ministers, his nobles, his own relatives. Fellow monarchs could actually welcome a temporary weakening of haughty France, for long so aggressive to the German lands. Headed by his two brothers, aristocrats were emigrating, joining in foreign threats to the National Assembly which had replaced the Estates-General, top heavy with noble and clerical privilege. To prove his radical credentials, Louis's cousin, Orleans, was styling himself 'Egalité', and would soon join the Jacobin extremists, though his convictions were shallower than his ambitions. On election to the Estates-General, he had remarked: 'I don't give a damn about what the Estates-General do, as long as I'm present when they set about individual liberty, so that I can support some law which guarantees that, should I wish to sleep at Raincy, I cannot be forced to sleep at Villers-Cotterets.'

The pace of moderate reform was quickening into actual revolution. The atrocious and salacious murder of the queen's intimate, the Princess de Lamballe. by what even Wilkes, with recollections of the wild Gordon Riots in London, was calling 'mobocracy', extracted from Orleans only a languid injunction to some horrified English friends not to be late for dinner. In *A History of Modern France* (1953) the historian, Alfred Cobban, reflected on the egalitarian royal prince: 'He was quite prepared to be a patriot king if Louis XVI could be eliminated, and would shrink from no means, however despicable, of achieving his ambition.'

Orleans remains a telling reminder of a particular human type, that can hate its class, its country, ultimately perhaps itself, while proclaiming faith in a nebulous chimera: the Republic, the Workers' State, the Perfect Society, the People's Society, the Kingdom of Heaven. Boredom, debts, self-destructive forces, spurts of genuine social sympathies, desire to experiment, all have place in such figures. Orleans may have had kinship with Catiline, that amoral political incendiary, bankrupt young Roman aristocrat, conspiring to ransack Rome; with Russian millionaires, hating their country, class, perhaps themselves, assisting the founding of *Pravda*, the revolutionary newspaper; with wealthy or prominent whites subscribing to Black Panthers' pledges to destroy them.

Serious reformers trusted Mirabeau, but he was soon to die, and Lafayette, hero, marquis, liberal, though the two men disliked and distrusted each other. Many assumed that from the medley of disputing would-be saviours would emerge a Fox, a Washington, a Jefferson or Franklin to guide the king into an era of peaceful change. Dazzled by the rational precepts of the Enlightenment and the examples of liberty-loving England and America, popular assemblies, clubs and café intellectuals still relied on the natural goodness of mankind, forgetting the bullies, sneaks, toadies and gangsters visible in the nearest schoolyard. Despotism was as natural as charity and tolerance.

The reformers under-estimated the irrational, perverse and the dotty. Some were doomed for rapid extinction, intoxicated not only with Rousseau, but with Rabelais and his injunction to abandon themselves to Nature's truth and to let nothing in this world be unknown to them. For a number of Frenchmen, the shocks were too often fatal, so that eventually Jacques René Hébert, about to be pulled before the Revolutionary Tribunal by his fellow Jacobins, exclaimed in despair: 'To be safe, we must kill everyone.'

In 1790, Paul Jones was living quietly in rue de Tournon, the house on which his memorial plaque is still to be seen. The problematic Madame T and the suppositious son had gone or were seldom seen. Even his enthusiasm for didactic letterwriting had diminished for, by 1792, Thomas Jefferson, now Secretary of the Navy, was wondering whether he was still alive. His Russian 'leave' ended in silence. Forced to reconsider the Danish offer of a pension, he made a belated acceptance, but without avail. On a short trip to London for unsatisfactory conference with Dr Bancroft, he was threatened at Harwich by an angry crowd shouting at him as a rapist and a pirate.

The Russian Baltic fleet was routed by the Swedes in July 1790, losing some 50 ships, with hundreds of men and guns captured or lost, the admiral in blind flight, the Empress's heart, she confided to Potemkin, almost broken. The admiral? His Highness Prince Charles de Nassau-Siegen. In Paris, a disappointed man must have allowed himself an understandably vulgar grin.

Physically depleted, with lungs and kidneys strained by his career, he was not yet seeking the small farm and the noble sunset of a Cincinnatus. Still he had projects for improving naval design, succouring the Americans rotting in Algeria and, by exploiting the British flag, capturing the British East Indian squadron off St Helena. Bruised and scarred, he refused to surrender, though he could scarcely claim not having yet begun to fight. In 1793, after the September Massacres, the overthrow of the monarchy and the outbreak of war with England and the European coalition, Paine, whom Gouverneur Morris considered 'inflated to the eyes, and big with a litter of revolutions', recommended the St Helena plan to Robespierre, giving credit to 'the late Captain Jones'.

He had not yet finished wrangling with the indigent and unconcerned American Naval Office about *Bonhomme Richard* dues and advising upon the needs of the French fleet. Loyal to Louis XVI, he suggested, through Lafayette, that he should visit him in full admiral's uniform, as if this apparition might reassure the helpless monarch. On 10 July 1790, he led an unofficial American delegation to praise the achievements of the Assembly, to which Robespierre replied at inordinate length, disregarding periodic discouragement from the chair. That Jones himself remained silent is often attributed to his ill health, or to his command of French, which was unsuited for oratory. He might simply have been wavering between old sympathy for the king, 'Protector of Fair Freedom's Rights', and his oft-repeated devotion to Liberty, Philanthropy and Human Dignity, the chevalier at odds with the republican. Equally, he may have had nothing to say.

At a reception at the American Legation, he had a more poignant encounter with a youthful son of Lord Selkirk, who, after so long, passed him the noble family's appreciation for his return of the silver and the celebrated teapot, assuring him that his orders against plundering had been strictly obeyed. Writing home, the junior Selkirk declared: 'He seems a very sensible little fellow.'

His verses, like his loves, had dried up. Ladies, from Avignon, from Trévoux, urged him to visit, but he pleaded sickness. He wrote to his sisters, advising and moralising, but never promised to return. HV Morton considered that the greatest fault for his reputation was in being a Scot who never expressed any affection for his native land.

He still had business projects and contacts with which to tinker, Masonic gatherings to attend and, more doubtfully, philosophy and poetry to study. He would visit Jefferson's successor as minister, Gouverneur Morris, who had been a financial adviser and entrepreneur under Robert Morris. A wooden-legged, alert, verbose witness of the Revolution, he is recorded in the *Oxford Companion of American History* as a brilliant debater and keen observer of human weakness. He liked the Chevalier well enough, in a condescending way, but deplored his too frequent appearances, suspecting that they were only the desultory occupation of an unemployed Scot, scarcely comparable to the attentions of an English milord or the dinners with one of the new, exciting French celebrities: 'Paul Jones calls on me. He has nothing to say but is so kind as to bestow on me the Hours that hang heavy on his hands.' Always an intriguer, Morris has been suspected of some responsibility in influencing Robespierre and the Committee of Public Safety against Tom Paine, leading to his arrest.

Thomas Carlyle glimpses Jones amid the passions and hugger-mugger of Paris. 'Poor Paul! hunger and disappointment track thy sinking footsteps; once or at most twice in this Revolution-tumult the figure of thee emerges; mute, ghost-like, as 'with stars dim-twinkling through.'

Morris, something of an adventurer, more of a philanderer, would have better appreciated the earlier Paul Jones, corsair and warrior. His own particular distinction, the wooden leg, is controversial. In his biography of Talleyrand in 1932, Duff Cooper, discussing Morris, avers: 'On one occasion he found himself at the centre of a hostile mob in favour of hanging him on the nearest lamp-post as an Englishman and a spy. He unfastened his wooden leg, and proclaimed himself an American who had lost a limb fighting for Liberty. The mob's suspicions melted into enthusiastic cheers, but, as a matter of fact, he had never fought for Liberty or anything else, and had lost his leg as the result of a carriage accident.'

The second Viscount Palmerston, who thought Morris 'a gentleman-like, sensible man of property and estimation in America', maintained that he had maimed himself by jumping from a window 'in an affair of gallantry'.

Letters show Jones still brooding over the small, faraway estate or farm in America, where now famed captains, Barry, McNeill, Dale, had never lost respect for him but, lacking full purpose and with an unforgiving nature, he trusted few. 'Sad Experience generally shows that where we expect to find a Friend we have only been treacherously deluded by appearances.' The happiness of sharing had never for long been his. Minor rhetoric, sham philosophy, self-bluff, were now rather too easy. 'It may be,' he wrote to Catherine, 'that I have been Unfortunate, but it cannot be made to appear that I have ever, even in the weakest moments of my life, been capable of a Base or Mean Action.'

Certainly he could remember sailing into Brest triumphant, his long hours with Franklin, excitements with Ivak, praise from ladies, but now the silences were prolonged, the praises fainter. He had a Name. but nowhere to put it, he awaited orders that did not come. Did he know of Columbus's last letter?

'I trust Your Highnesses will believe that at no time did I crave personal health...so that I might serve them and display my experience and navigational skill...These unfortunate days and other anguishes which I have suffered have placed me in great extremity, so that I have been unable to approach Your Highnesses.'

Some figures – Elizabeth Tudor, Robespierre, Louis Napoleon, Lincoln, Kitchener, Shaw, Virginia Woolf, Hitler – even when surrounded by crowds and family, seem always alone. Angus Wilson stresses the loneliness of Kipling's heroes, of Kipling himself, his 'agonising sense of personal isolation, of Man's lonely futile-seeming journey from childhood's wonder to death's eclipse.' This seems relevant to Paul Jones also, though SE Morrison, an admirer, squarely blames his undeniable loneliness on 'his colossal egotism'.

Not short of company, he never appears to have forgone a loneliness of spirit, both hateful and, for long, fortifying. His womanising seems mostly expediency, letters suggesting no very profound desire for vital companionship or sense of the mystery of other people. He required 'dalliance', comforts, periodic furious couplings, but not the delights of shared discoveries, long talks, the private vocabulary of generous and developing mutual understanding. A Delia, a Madame T, could not disturb his inner silence, perhaps his innate indifference. An Abigail Adams was perhaps what he needed, but such a woman, companionable, vivacious, sensitive, inquiring, was rare and scarcely attainable. He mentions no desire to procreate, a name would suffice.

The decade was one of fleeting reputations, Time stumbling over itself, prodded by young men and women in a hurry to overturn the outmoded, the superstitious. the absurd. His own certainties were crumbling. What use were royal decorations and swords of honour in a dispensation where crowns were mocked, aristocratic values reviled, and a Duke of Orleans hastened to become Citizen Egalité? Franklin, 'my fosterfather', died in 1790, and his well-known sayings, 'So it goes,' 'It'll get done,' were adapted to a favourite tune of the queen's and was now whistled in parks and arcades, squares and back alleys, in the lively but sinister famous revolutionary *Ca'ira*, which would have scandalised him:

> We'll get it done, done done,
> The aristos, string 'em up,
> So it goes.
> The aristos be hanged,
> Freedom lasts for ever
> Despite the tyrants,
> So it goes.

The Prince Marshal was dead, dying by the roadside, exhausted at 52. The Soviet governments attempted to expunge his memory save as a wasteful, degenerate ponce, or class enemy. After many vicissitudes, his massive Tauride Palace is now a museum. One sees him as if in a cracked mirror, hideously distorted, one detail grotesquely swollen, another absurdly shrunken, yet with an alarming but thrilling presence seeping through all. His marvellous partner still lived, triumphant in Poland, baffled by the French Terror.

Maria Theresa, Joseph II, Frederick the Great, were gone. France was about to fight foreign and civil wars, invasion, political paranoia, Terror masquerading as Virtue, and, as diseased ideals lapsed into denunciations, betrayals and a general passivity, a paralysis of the nerve to resist; dramatic irony overhung the nation like an immense head jigging at carnival. On many walls was daubed a staring eye, surmounting a single word: *Supervision.*

During an invasion of the Tuileries, 'the Protector of the Rights of Human Nature', Louis XVI, had been forced to don the red cap of Liberty, liberty which he had now lost. International enthusiasm for liberty faltered, crowned heads and French émigrés were threatening the National Assembly and mobilising troops. In June 1791, the royal family, attempting flight to join supporters on the frontier, was arrested and, ignominiously, brought back to a silent but unforgiving Paris, guarded by their defender and jailer, Lafayette.

The Hero of Two Continents was riding high, too high to remember Paul Jones, though he had given a Bastille key to Tom Paine, requesting him to forward it to George Washington. He was also riding too high for his own capabilities. Gallant on the battlefield, he was indecisive against rioters. A mass demonstration occurred in July 1791, demanding the king's abdication, at once dubbed 'the massacre of Champ de Mars'. Two men had been murdered and, attempting to restore order, Lafayette's National Guard shot down about 50 rioters. This stimulated republicanism, destroyed the king's last hopes and discredited the moderates. The popular idol, Lafayette, was execrated. In America he had led, in France merely drifted, and has been recently assessed, by Robert Harvey, as 'sycophantic'. He always needed acclaim, from contradictory elements: from generals and those wishing to supplant them, from kings and republicans, from crowds and statesmen. Each new crisis, he understood too late. Believing himself a leader, he no longer knew who or where to lead. He had not the nature of a dictator, yet in 1791 to 1792, he had to be that, or nothing. To an insult from Robespierre he could find no effective retort. He was unable to wholeheartedly demand the abolition of the monarchy or the heroic proclamation of the Republic. 'He is brave and chivalrous,' Paul Jones commented from rue de Tournon, 'but he has not the heart or brain needed in this crisis. He shrinks from the *ultima ratio regum*.'

Gouverneur Morris reported, not quite accurately, that Lafayette's sun had set for ever. British historians have largely regarded him more as a soldier than a statesman, French wits joked about a hero in search of a pedestal. He had kissed the queen's hand after savage crowds had swarmed into the Tuileries, having slaughtered the Swiss Guards whom the king, supine or good-hearted, had forbidden to fire on 'the People'. One young man, contemptuously watching, was Bonaparte, who had declared that Louis need only to have shown himself on horseback to have won. He, like Jones, would have added guns, placed in strategic positions. Lafayette's responsibility was to protect the royal family, but he had been asleep almost throughout, and was caricatured as 'General Morpheus'. Soon replaced as commander of the National Guard, he accepted a senior army post, attempted a march on Paris on behalf of the king, but failed to enthuse his troops, and fled abroad, Danton, not him, rallying the Republic against foreign invasion. General panic provoked the September Massacres, which were ignored by Danton, as another instance of the manure thought necessary for the Tree of Liberty. The 'Kingdom had become the Nation'.

Lafayette represented 'that being which, of all on earth, Danton thought most dangerous, the epitome of all the faults he attacked to the day of his death, the weak man in power.' Hilaire Belloc's words (1899), though Jones would have agreed, and Bonaparte might have been thinking of Lafayette, among others, when remarking that Vanity had caused the Revolution, Liberty only the pretext.

Lafayette survived foreign prison, exile and near oblivion during the Bonaparte empire. Under the Restoration he was a deputy. In 1824, he revisited America, where, acclaimed everywhere as saviour and hero, he revived old glories. Congress voted him land, money, full American citizenship, an honour shared with Sir Winston Churchill. In the poignancies of time he again rode through Paris during the 1830 Revolution which ousted Louis XVI's brother and, banner in hand, proclaimed the Orleans monarchy of Louis Philippe, 'Citizen King', Egalité's son, reigning not as the seigneurial 'King of France' but the more democratic 'King of the French'.

When Lafayette lay dying, in 1834, his doctor addressed him as 'Father of the French People'. The old man murmured: 'That is true – to the extent that they never do what I tell them to.'

The Oxford historian of the First Revolution, JM Thompson, supplies a postscript. During Hitler's onslaught on France in 1940, in the French Senate only one man rose in protest against the surrender of the Republic. He was the great-grandson of the Marquis de Lafayette, and 'the last defender of the Rights of Man'.

Gouverneur Morris asserted that Paul Jones detested the Revolution and its participants. No doubt that while Mirabeau, Lafayette and Orleans, declaimed about Liberty and Universal Brotherhood, Jones was disillusioned with France, Europe, perhaps life itself. He had realised, none better, the imperfections of mankind, dramatised in the Bible, classical history, and the ballads, blatant on ships, in offices, daily visible in revolutionary and wartime Paris, and in the rowdy hurly-burly of the Assembly. Far more than Brissot, Vergniaud, Manon, Roland or Robespierre, he had experienced humanity in all its variety: Scots peasants and fishermen, West Indians, African slaves, Virginian gentry, French, American, Russian, German, Dutch statesmen, bureaucrats, craftsmen, knaves, politicians. He had suffered extremes unknown to most respectable lawyers and journalists now legislating the Perfect State, inspired by the goodness of human nature. No ship's captain had evidence of such goodness, and could expect the modification of ambition, violence, greed and envy by sensible laws, pious hopes, exhortations about reason, virtue, sacrifice. No gardener's son could vouch for the benevolence of nature. Mirabeau, more realistic, potential saviour of society, died in 1791, and the passionate eloquence of a Brissot, Desmoulins or a Saint-Just, could convince a weary American of very little, save that good intentions would not achieve human regeneration, and that the Revolution was capsizing from clear principles and honest debate into factional vendettas and mumbo-jumbo. *Sublime*, much favoured by Robespierre, was usually followed by the malicious or silly. 'Sublime People', sublime Virtue' were synonyms of the anarchic or inane. In forbidding his guards to fire on 'the people', the king guaranteed their massacre. Paul Jones knew in his blood the gaunt distance between the professional at the wheel and the philosopher descanting on the sublimity of storms, the majesty of fire. He himself was a trimmer, adjusting his sails to the wind but trusting few others with the wheel, the compass or the map. He had no eagerness to destroy institutions, though incessantly critical of their administration and profuse with remedies. The overthrow of officers by crews and sea lawyers was as intolerable as the privileges of gentlemen captains. His objections to Catherine and Potemkin were not egalitarian or anti-aristocracy, though he would have preferred American, Benthamite or Napoleonic utilitarianism and meritocracy. Yet he could not have heartily supported Jeremy Bentham's hopes of a league of nations. He objected to the abuses of aristocracy: negligence, wastefulness, sloth, though he would not have contested Johnson's, 'Your Levellers wish to level down as far as themselves; but they cannot bear levelling up to themselves.' On that formal visit to the Assembly he could have seen no working-class member.

As the months passed in turmoil, calls to arms, cat-calls at royalty, shouts for a Republic and some sensible legislation couched in idealistic language, he would also have been aware, perhaps more with dour interest than humanitarian protest, that the Rights of Man were increasingly excluding those of women, children, servants, of provincial assemblies, universities, labour unions, religious groups, literary and financial associations, guilds. Probably he was more absorbed with the rights of Jones.

His health never recovered, so that he never saw the Jacobin, one-party committees execute France's finest poet, Chénier, and its foremost scientist, Lavoissier, Robespierre declaring that the Revolution had no need of science. The Jacobin leaders would soon be ordaining that all resistance to the State was criminal, a maxim that helped destroy them when they themselves were outlawed by the Assembly in 1794. Nor would Paul Jones have known that Condorcet, with his beliefs in sexual equality, birth control, reason, liberal constitutions, was to kill himself in prison. A friend of Jefferson's, a veteran mathematician and philosopher, Condorcet had been arrested for 'betraying the People', after he had been identified by publicly carrying a volume of Horace, an indisputable classic, impeccably leather bound.

The practical and reforming John Paul Jones would have approved of the new centralisation, the mathematical, technological and scientific boys' schools, the decimal coinage, internal free trade, the museums, help for Jews, price controls, the abolition of unearned privilege, the imposition of general conscription in the face of invasion.

John Adams, 'Mr Roundface', 'His Rotundity', whom Jefferson called the Colossus of Independence, held that though government should be sanctified by the People, in practice a democracy should be guided by the rich and well born, those with a stake in the ground, as well as by the able, a conviction earlier maintained by Oliver Cromwell, to the disgust of Levellers in his New Model Army, whom he had no hesitation in shooting for proposals which he deemed anarchic or unprincipled, certainly breaching military regulations. Paul Jones reserved his respect only for the able. Among the rich and well born were the irresponsible Potemkin, the deplorable Nassau-Siegen, the outrageous George III, and the go-getting Lees, the Family Compact. The People were not only Dale, Meijer. Barry, Ivak; but Landais, Silas Deane, Thomas Simpson, Mungo Maxwell and 'the Ringleader'. He could never have endorsed Robespierre's sentimental plaudits: 'The People are never wrong...the People are just, good and magnanimous.' Anyone with memories of West African slave pits, Caribbean fever ports, the holds of oceanic ships and indeed of Poland Street irregularities was entitled to demur.

Ill and fatigued, with his last illusions vanishing, he had not relinquished letterwriting and daydreaming of future projects. These were not for the abolition of navies in the interests of universal philanthropy and liberty, but still for root and branch reforms to assist revolutionary America becoming a Great Power. This would advance peace and liberty as much as conquest disguised as Liberation, wholesale arrests masquerading as equality, and politicians clucking Brotherhood while protected by secret police from those they spiritually ennobled. Republican America could check and surpass monarchical Europe and the Spanish–Portuguese empires south of the border. He was not, like Condorcet and the Paris intellectuals, seeking Utopia, merely better administration: honest ministers, useful officials, less corruption, fewer slogans. The Citizens of the World had been, not a baleful conspiracy, but an elitist club which buckled beneath the realities of hunger, war and revolution. Restless, he was never anarchic. Were there a ship there must be a crew, officers were needed, a captain required. Such an essential hierarchy was sustained by discipline, common interest, morale and by personal flair. He admitted only the criticism of example. His reaction to an assertion of Tom Paine is easily imaginable. The Englishman, mighty in his obdurate beliefs, insisted: 'The instant the form of government was changed in France, the republican principles of peace and domestic prosperity rose with the new government; and the same consequences would follow in the case of all other nations.'

It did not, it has not, and France, envisaged as a ship, was not safe in the hands of Lafayette, Brissot, Marat or Madame Roland. The slogans were inadequate: Liberty incited Mutiny, Equality placed cabin boy alongside the captain, Fraternity envisaged Landais and Dale pulling together. No revolution extinguishes greed, envy, malice and intrigue. Nassau-Siegen had drowned hundreds, through conceit, incompetence and influence. The Prince of Princes, in all his magnificence and intelligence, was negligent in his concern for others. Jones had little reason to praise the Old Regime, but he saw it being replaced by Orleans and his friends who, forgoing wigs and knee-breeches for dirty hair and patched trousers, were simultaneously flattering the People and spitting on them. No major transformation there, for a man who remembered the bloodshot mutineer towering above him, who had also conferred with John Adams and Benjamin Franklin, men whose repute would probably outlast that of Danton and Desmoulins. He could not admire eloquent prophets seeking to ruin France in order to save it from ruin. Public opinion could be a valuable check on erratic authority but a fearful platform from which to rule. Platforms quickly became scaffolds. In Eldridge Cleaver's words, gadflies are needed to gad, not to govern.

Paul Jones had never been negative or politically apathetic. From Russia, he had written to Lafayette, recommending the American Constitution. 'I hope, however, they will alter some parts of it; and particularly that they will divest the President of all military Rank and Command; for though George Washington might be safely entrusted with such tempting power as the Chief Command of the Fleet and army, yet depend on it, in some other hands, it could not fail to overset the Liberties of America. The President should be only the First Civil Magistrate.'

In some other hands . . . He may have been thinking only of Arthur Lee, Sam Adams, Silas Deane, though within a few years France was thinking of Bonaparte: General, First Consul then Emperor. By 1792, the French Republic was, in the great towns, as phantasmagoric as the Winter Palace or the now abandoned Versailles. Parisians had seen a king in a red cap, an atheist bishop presiding at a populist festival, a republican duke, and heard Madame Roland assuring the world from her respectable salon: 'Peace is retrograde. Rebirth is possible only through bloodshed.' *La Patrie* was replacing *Père Louis*.

This she was given full opportunity to test, with her Girondin friends orating for the war that, by their failures in conducting it, destroyed them and herself. Marat clamoured for 263,000 heads, the guillotine making this technically possible.

Tyrants were to be overthrown, peoples liberated, the ghettoes opened, cruel and oligarchic Britain defied. Meanwhile, to defend the Republic from enemies without and within, extremist committees assumed powers almost total, to shouts of 'Hang Lafayette', 'The Country in Danger', 'Liberty or Death', 'The Despotism of Liberty'. Russia, Austria and Prussia were dismembering Poland, where Tadeusz Kosciusko, who had befriended Paul Jones in Warsaw, was bravely, hopelessly resisting.

In America, France was seen to be either imitating its own marvellous overthrow of George III, or falling apart, perhaps with most of vicious, degenerate Europe. Paul Jones would be informed of French naval commissions being cancelled and competent royalists ejected, the commissions then distributed to the politically correct; experienced gunners being replaced by enthusiastic novices, discipline denounced as counter-revolutionary until drastically enforced by Jacobin commissars, 'representatives on mission'.

With the crowds absorbing slogans as if they were blotting paper, Gouverneur Morris wrote to Jefferson: 'We stand on the edge of a vast volcano.' In the turmoil of war and fear, Paul Jones was forgotten, along with *Alfred*, *Ranger*, *Ariel* and *Bonhomme Richard*. His self-respect was ebbing. Resentment can weaken initiative, gaiety and hope, and was inducing lassitude. He had always harboured the self-righteous, the self-pitying, and now his very body was treacherous, afflicted with jaundice, nephritis, dropsy, recurrent pneumonia.

Tell me how you die, goes the Mexican saying, and I will tell you who you are. Paul Jones was dying, morose, silent, at 45, apparently with nothing achieved, without a name, without honour. Gouverneur Morris, on 18 July 1792, informed of the Chevalier's condition, was kind enough to visit him, together with Jones's attentive American friend, Colonel Blackden. They found him ill but able to stand, though anxious to make his will, leaving all to his sisters, Janet and Mary. In this, Morris assisted and formally witnessed, though declining to join Robert Morris as executor. Then he departed, to dine with an English nobleman. Later, he returned, with his mistress, in whom he had rivals, both Talleyrand and a former royal physician Dr Vic d'Azyr. They found the admiral dead, not like Nelson, in full regalia during the din of battle, but in an almost deserted house, face downwards on the bed, feet touching the floor.

Morris informed his namesake, Robert: 'Before I quit for Jones, I must tell you that some people here, who like rare shows, wished him to have a pompous funeral . . . but as I had no right to spend on such follies either the money of his heirs or that of the United States, I desired that he might be buried in a private and economical manner. I have since had reason to be glad that I did not agree to waste money of which he had no great abundance and for which his relatives entertain a tender regard.'

Despite Mr Morris's conscientious scruples, and objection to follies, both Colonel Blackden, addressing the Assembly, and a local official, Pierre-François Simmoneau, wanted more than the private and economical, if necessary at their own expense. Despite the tensions throughout Paris, they gathered a cortège, scarcely pompous, but dignified. French grenadiers paraded, with twelve delegates from the Assembly, Masons from the Nine Sisters Lodge, and a number of French and Americans. The American Legation was represented by a minor official, the minister again being entertained by British personages of title.

The body, buried in the Protestant cemetery, was soaked in spirits, to preserve it should some future removal ever be contemplated. 'On a permanent jag, they say,' naval cadets were to sing, in irreverent, though affectionate, memory of John Paul Jones. A French pastor delivered the oration, with several unconscious ironies as he saluted 'One of the first champions of Liberty in America . . . unwilling to breathe the pestilential air of Despotism in Russia,' and 'preferring the sweetness of a private life in France, now Free, to the éclat of titles and honours which, from a usurped throne, were showered upon him by Catherine.' The good man concluded:

Let his Example instruct Posterity in the efforts which noble souls are capable of achieving when stimulated by hatred of oppression. Associate yourselves with the glory of Paul Jones by imitating him in his contempt of Danger, in his patriotic Devotion, in his noble heroism, which, having astonished the Present, will continue to be the immortal object of veneration for the Future. What more flattering Homage can we pay to the shades of Paul Jones than to swear on his tomb to live or to die in Freedom?

Afterwards, when grander folk had dispersed, a few ragged seamen might have spoken of the commodore 'losing the number of his Mess', told a few stories, mostly untrue, swore a little, not in the manner commended by the pastor, perhaps briefly kept silence, remembering a few humble symbols: the colours on *Serapis*, the scribble on the Crocodile's warship, as potent in their way as Gouverneur Morris's wooden leg.

Several days later, after so long a silence, a letter arrived for Admiral John Paul Jones, from George Washington and Thomas Jefferson:

'The President of the United States, having thought it proper to appoint you Commissioner for treating with the Dey and Government of Algiers...' and instructed him to employ all his experience to list all local details that would be essential, if demanded by 'the necessity of coercion by cruises on their coasts.' They concluded by affirming their 'special trust and confidence in the integrity, prudence and abilities of John Paul Jones.'

Between 1790 and 1800, the United States paid two million dollars, almost a quarter of its revenue, in ransoms, tribute or blackmail, to Algiers and its satellites. Finally, incensed by more exorbitant demands, Jefferson ordered a squadron against the Barbary pirates, an effort only partially successful. In Europe, the Congress of Vienna decided that the pirates must be eliminated. An Anglo–Dutch bombardment of Algiers, in 1816, rescued 1,200 Europeans and Americans, imposed an indemnity and ordered a cessation of piracy. A resumption caused French intervention, the deposition of the Dey, the suppression of piracy, and one excuse for the French conquest of Algeria.

Paul Jones, 'pickled in alcohol,' on his permanent jag – the dead Nelson was borne home from Trafalgar in 1805 soused in brandy, preserved for the state funeral – remained ignored in Paris, though never forgotten in America. Inspired, inventive, though negligible, biographies appeared regularly, together with letters, absurd falsehoods – his hectic love affair with the Duchess of Orleans, his barnstorming theatrical performances – and grandiose, patriotic legends. Herman Melville and Walt Whitman particularly goaded the public awareness, then an increasing curiosity and uneasy national conscience, fanned further by a widely read protest in a New York newspaper against 'the spectacle of a hero whose fame once covered two continents and whose name is still an inspiration to a world-famed navy, lying for more than a century in a forgotten grave, like an obscure outcast relegated to oblivion in a squalid corner of a distant foreign city.'

General Horace Porter, American ambassador to France, made insistent efforts to restore the status of John Paul Jones and finally, in 1905, American and French sailors were marching down the Champs-Elysées bearing his draped coffin. Speeches were declaimed, flags unfurled, salutes fired, then warships carried him back to America. At the Naval Academy,

Annapolis, the sight of which would have given him some self-congratulatory delight, he was laid in the Napoleonic sarcophagus, for which he would not have bowed low in humble gratitude but accepted as his right, rather overdue. It was not his small estate, his little farm, more his own great house, emblazoned with the names of his warships. Tributes were given him by the French ambassador and by Theodore Roosevelt, twenty-sixth President of the United States.

14

John Paul Jones

Though Jones had it in him to he a great naval strategist, he found opportunity to prove himself only on the tactical level. There he was magnificent. Recall how he made prompt and sure decisions in emergenciess. perfectly adapting his tactics to suddenly confronted facts, as in those first audacious cruises on *Providence* and *Alfred*, and in the battles of *Ranger v Drake*, *Bonhomme Richard v Serapis*, and *Ariel v Triumph*. That sort of thing is the sure mark of a master in warfare. Of the quality of his seamanship, one needs no more evidence than those early escapes from faster and more powerful ships, and the saving of *Ariel* from crashing on the Penmarch rocks. His battle with *Serapis*, as an example of how a man, through sheer guts, refusing to admit the possibility of defeat, can emerge victorious, is an inspiration to every sailor.

Samuel Eliot Morison,
John Paul Jones: A Sailor's Biography, 1959

He always contemplated...in fury to the enemy, not prize money, primarily. This expresses decisively the career that Jones, throughout the Revolutionary War, proposed to follow – to pursue the enemy, not in occasional merchant ships, but where great interests were concentrated and inadequately protected; and to do so not with a single ship, seeking to snatch a hasty morsel, but with a squadron capable of deliberately insuring the destruction of the enemy rather than its own profit. Such a conception places its author far above the level of the mere prize seeker, as well as in loftiness of purpose as in breadth of view.

Admiral Alfred Thayer Mahan,
John Paul Jones in the Revolution, 1898

235

I should do injustice to my own feelings, as well as to my country, if I did not warmly recommend this gentleman to the notice of Congress, whose favour he has certainly merited by the most signal services and sacrifices.

Congressman Robert Morris,
To Congress, 1788

Those who most loudly clamour for liberty do not most liberally grant it.

Samuel Johnson,
The Lives of The Poets, 1779–81

We desire to substitute morality for egoism, honesty for honour, principles for customs, duty for charity.

Robespierre,
Speech to National Assembly

By 1800, Napoleon had remarked that the romance of the Revolution was over, it was time to begin its history. The age of Bonapartism, Stephenson, Faraday, Edison, Galvini, Darwin and Curie, held eighteenth-century reputations in a more sceptical grip. Some were soon forgotten, others remembered for reasons misleading or distorted; few remained intact.

Among Paul Jones's contemporaries, Egalité Orleans coldly contemplated his cousin, the king, on trial, through his exquisite lorgnon, then voted for his death: 'I am heartbroken, but for the sake of France, I consider it my duty.' Within a year, he was condemned by the Revolutionary Tribunal he had helped establish and, befuddled with factional paranoia, literally losing his head, dying with some dignity, belated tribute to his heritage. He had trivialised aristocracy and shown that the great Revolution was as much the product of ambition as of good sense, idealism and impersonal economic forces.

Catherine the Great considered the Revolution a betrayal of liberty, justice and fraternity, and denounced Franklin and Mirabeau as energetically as she did in joining Prussia and Austria in destroying the liberties of Poland. Out of tune with the new age, with young men accepting her favours like tips, the mighty Prince Marshal ridiculed or faded, she died in 1796, with Bonaparte on the first rungs of power. She left the empire to Paul I, mentally unstable, devotee of the national enemy, Bonaparte, devotee too of himself – he once informed a courtier of venerable lineage that he was a nobleman only whenever the Tsar deigned to notice him. Unsurprisingly he was assassinated, in 1801, and succeeded by his son, Alexander I, who had ambiguous mystical traits and who, as a victor over Napoleon, became, with Wellington and Metternich, an arbiter of Europe at the Vienna Congress.

Replying to Burke's denunciation of the Revolution, scourging Jacobin women for presuming to confer 'Certificates of Correct Thinking', Tom Paine early demanded whether the Assembly had brought anyone to the scaffold. This was soon answered, himself escaping only by the revolt against Robespierre and Saint-Just, finally abandoned by the People in 1794: upholders of reason, they were victims of their own unreason, ignoring the unconscious and perverse. So violently against kings, Paine nevertheless courageously argued for Louis XVI's life, pleading that the French, having been the first to abolish royalty – he overlooked Switzerland and America – should be first to abolish capital punishment.

'He whom we have condemned to death is considered in the United States as their best friend, the Founder of their Freedom . . . Do not give the Despot of England the pleasure of seeing on the scaffold the man who delivered our American brothers from Tyranny.'

Admiral d'Estaing, who had fought 'Foul-weather Jack' Byron in the Atlantic and praised Paul Jones's courtesy to Lady Selkirk, who supported the early Revolution and proposed mitigating the hardships and aristocratic perks of the fleet, was destroyed for his sympathy for the queen. The Duke de la Rochefoucauld was murdered. Lord Dorset never recovered from Marie Antoinette's execution. Back in England, while Britain warred with France and supported civil war in Brittany, he would sit alone, 'listening to distant violins', dying mad, in 1799.

Richard Dale was a respected captain by 1794. Always loyal to Paul Jones's memory, through Robert Morris, John Barry, and perhaps – accounts vary – Janet Paul, he gained possession of his old chief's French sword of honour, his descendants presenting it to the Naval Academy in 1938. A nephew of Paul Jones, whom the Russians alleged he had killed, settled in Charleston in 1800, served in the American navy, sired twelve children, and returned to Kirkcudbright, dying in 1846.

Pierre Landais fought with some vigour for revolutionary France against Sardinia, was promoted rear-admiral, though compelled to resign in 1793, after several mutinies. Back in New York, in 1797, he at once began claiming prize money owing to *Alliance* and received some, though without restitution of rank. He died in poverty, supposedly buried 'in a potter's field', probably a poetic symbolism, near Washington Square. He had previously arranged for a memorial tablet to be placed in old St Patrick's: 'To the Memory of Pierre de Landais, formerly Rear-Admiral, in service of the United States, who vanished June 1818 at the age of 87.'

Jefferson's status as Founding Father, president, statesman, educator, remains scarcely questioned, though humanitarians have noticed that the great upholder of The Rights of Man never freed his slaves, not even Sally Hemmings, thought to have borne him children.

Even after death, Paul Jones suffered further letdown, for Robert Morris, in financial stress, had small time to spare as executor, though Janet Paul sent him her gratitude for whatever he did do.

If her brother had, on the whole, deserved well of America, he must sometimes have wondered whether he deserved well of himself? His life had petered out ingloriously. America had triumphed, but he himself had failed. He had a name, but it had already faded: he had established nothing, invented nothing, he had dominated no significant changes, his raids had contributed little. No more than Charles James Fox could he be identified with anything but personality, and his was equivocal.

John A Alden estimated, in 1969: 'Neither the flamboyant and redoubtable Jones nor any of his fellow-officers could offer battle to British ships of the Line, nor could they disrupt the British blockade of American ports.' Admittedly, Lord Acton, in a lecture in 1901, maintained that, not the land forces but the French and American ships had won independence.

History, though, traces the contest of rhythms: the fortunes of class, gender, commerce, climate, empires, reputations. Deaths are not always final, the last word is often the. preliminary to energetic disputes, torrents of words: resurrections occur. Something about Paul Jones quickened the imagination of Scott, Melville, Fenimore Cooper, Thackeray, and many others, and had never been lost by the American people. They slowly began recognising the genius of Whitman, stylistically iconoclastic as America itself, tossing 'A Song of Myself' like a clattering can into a literary market for so long almost monopolised by European traditions, imagery and metre. Readers could see the tempestuous captain ramming the *Serapis*, heard a tale of the scared master-gunner imploring 'For God's sake, Captain. strike,' and Jones's 'No. I will not strike. I will never strike.'

Thackeray's Denis Duval muses: 'No doubt many of us youngsters vapoured about the courage with which we would engage him, and make certain, if we could only meet him, of seeing him hanging from his own yard-arm. Traitor, if you will, was Monsieur John Paul Jones, afterwards knight of his most Christian Majesty's Order of Merit; but a braver traitor never wore sword.'

Scott, in *Redgauntlet*, has a possible caricature of him as Nanty Ewart, ageing master pilot ready to support an argument with a cudgel, 'a human shipwreck, pirate, smuggler, drunken son of the manse, in shabby-genteel costume... with the hue of death on his cheek and the fire of vengeance glancing from his eye.'

Paul Jones might have gloomed over rebuffs to his 'Honor and Dignity' more than he rejoiced over scaring one nation and thrilling two others, but he always had defenders. Like Washington and Jefferson, John Jay, a negotiator of the Versailles Treaty, first Chief Justice of the United States, disregarded the Russian accusations and believed that America would again need 'this officer as the principal hope of our future efforts on the ocean'. A London journal admitted, in 1799, that 'Justice requires that while we execrate the principles of him who fights against his country, we should not rob him of those merits which we see him possess as a man, in a very eminent degree.' Admiral Mahan judged the *Serapis* victory 'was wholly and solely due to the immovable courage of Paul Jones; the *Richard* was beaten more than once, but the spirit of Jones could not he overcome.' Isaac Asimov. in his survey of Amencan history, rated him the most successful of the Revolutionary captains.

He was always fertile with schemes. almost always feasible, often unexpected, but dependent on unworthy ships and subordinates. His flaw was in lack of interest in others for their own sake, which in part induced his failure with Simpson, Landais and Potemkin. If he demanded love, it was seldom on equal terms. Though he could inspire affection, and possibly sought some lasting union, within 'Calm Contemplation and Poetic Ease', he was as mueh in love with horizons, work, and himself. When horizons narrowed and work lapsed, his spirit lapsed. Yet his regard for the few he respected was emphatic. After losing his chance of the ship *America*, he wrote to Franklin: 'You are beloved; and will be ever while Virtue is honorable, be revered as a Father and Savior of our Country.'

Like Drake, Nelson, Bligh, Jefferson, Lafayette and Catherine, he was self-regarding: the curiosity and moments of humility of the artist were not in him; he was the dedicated technician, anxious to improve design, organisation, discipline.

Posterity will not be fulsome in praise of his writings. To his old Tobagan acquaintance, Thomas Scott, who had sent a message of support, he replied that he wished to observe the good opinions of the good men in England, by his wartime record as 'A Man of Honor and principle; not serving America from pique or ill-nature towards England, nor from views of Profit for myself but acting from the Noblest of all principles, Gratitude for unmerited favors received from America.'

This, though it is not the eighteenth century at its most honest, is what America enjoyed hearing. Talleyrand, a more candid pragmatist, liked to say that whenever a man spoke to him of 'principle', he recognised an enemy. Jones would boost himself like a prima donna, movie star or footballer, more verbosely. 'I pledge myself to that generous Public that it shall be my first Care and my Heart's supremist wish, to meet the continuance of its Approbation.'

While exhibiting himself a fall guy or bad guy, by his moralising and masculinity, his Kiplingesque admiration for professional elites, he must repel current upholders of political correctness. No more than Cochrane, Nelson, Patton, Moshe Dayan, or Orde Wingate, can he be claimed, by party or sect. He was independent and, though from 'the People', despised populism. Neither 'regular guy' nor 'decent chap', he was not in Dickensian sense, a 'character'. His social grace he wore like a cravat arranged not quite to perfection. Crews and officials found him braggardly, interfering, ungiving. Morison avers that his resemblance to Columbus includes reluctance to share credit with others. Franklin, trying to maintain balance between him and Landais, once sent a rebuke which could scarcely fail to rankle:

'If you should observe on this occasion to give your officers a little more praise than is their due, and confess more fault than you can justly be charged with, you will only become the sooner for it, a great captain. Criticising and censoring almost everyone you have to deal with, will diminish friends, increase enemies, and thereby hurt your affairs.'

Paul Jones is comparable to another noteworthy Scottish American, Alexander Hamilton, illegitimate son of a merchant, born in the West Indies, wartime confidant of Washington, later Treasury Chief and founder of the National Bank: ambitious, gifted, solitary, suspicious, pugnacious and self-righteous. In such emigrants can often be the complacent 'I Did It My Way' of the Sinatra song. Gentleness. modesty, restraint, compromise do not always promote success, even survival, in unfamiliar territory. The sensitivity of the physically small can tempt them to aggression. Jones needed to control his own pugnacity, though without it, he might have remained a minor trader. When out of action, he let anger fester in quarrels and brooding, leaving him the boxer unfairly counted-out and spoiling for the next bout. He would have been startled by Wilde's quip that to do nothing is the most difficult thing in the world and quite the most intelligent.

The Dictionary of American Biography admits Paul Jones's superiority to most rivals, his considerable literary facility, frequent financial disinterest, 'though he could also promote his own interests', his indomitable courage, unfaltering faith in himself, his ability to conceive daring schemes and execute them with insufficient means. It also mentions defects in taste and character, caused by 'insufficient breeding and education . . . His chief fault was vanity: often obsequious to those above him, he sometimes forgot what was due to those below him, and to his own character as an officer.'

When his will and health faltered, he could be left victim of intrigue. Mutineers could be slammed down, officialdom countered, but shadowy cabals could not. Disappointments he bore as personal insults. Self-absorption could impair his sense of reality, prevent his understanding that Catherine was not susceptible to all comers, that Chartres was drifting towards ruin, that Madame T was only a social sham, and that Washington and Franklin had duties not exclusively naval. He knew well enough that others, sometimes unknowable, contained cruelty and malice, or, like Landais, abnormal fixations, but these he might sometimes exaggerate, as with bumbling, decent enough old Hopkins. He was swift to detect a bad cause, but not always pausing to discover its causes. He would certainly have rejected any supposition that his setbacks were partially self-induced. His attitude of injured innocence might have unconsciously acknowledged his own limitations. For him, a Paul Jones devises a plan and a Silas Deane steals it: he breaks the battle line, and a Nassau-Siegen wins promotion. Others arrive too late for the battle and complain of the mess. Absentees win profits. HV Morton considered:

> There were some men, I think, who in spite of their courage and abilities, are dogged all their lives by envy, slander and misfortune. He was one of them. He seems to have been a man with a deep-seated grudge. There may have been some idea of 'getting his own back' when he raided the scene of his childhood. He was a brooding creature, one of those men who, even in success, brood on imaginary failure, and no doubt the fact that he was always being 'let down' developed this habit, deepening his melancholy and sense of injustice. There is a modern term for this attitude: persecution complex. He shared with Nelson many of the traits of genius. He was wildly ambitious and he had a childish love of honours. Action stimulated

him, inaction flung him into ill-health and melancholy. Both men were ruthless in love, both adored not wealth but fame. Few men have been more abused than Paul Jones; and he writhed under this. He wanted, above everything, to be popular and praised: and he was detested and slandered.

Nelson was accused of allowing, or ignoring, the killing of some hundred prisoners during a vengeful suppression of Neapolitan Jacobins. He did not disdain to publicise his exploits in the press. He too was unpopular with superiors, many admirals and senior officers vainly attempting to resist the public demand for his state funeral.

Paul Jones was no Alexander or Napoleon craving to change society, to devour the world; he was not one of those praised by Goethe for seeking the impossible. He made a one-man cult of the possible and immediate, needing not posthumous glory but tangible results. He would have agreed with another unpopular figure, AL Rowse, in preferring even the animal to the inane. He lacked the cultural range of Jefferson and Adams, Catherine and Potemkin, of Burgoyne: of TE Lawrence, Saint-Exupéry and Malraux. Of other great captains, he had some affinities with Francis Drake. They were outstanding navigators, daring fighters, but less effective as diplomats and reconcilers. They could be generous to prisoners, drove hard bargains, were 'upwardly mobile' perfectionists, clumsy in personal relationships. Jones sworded the mutineer, Drake gave his brother officer, 'Thomas Doughty, dinner, Holy Communion, then personally beheaded him for treachery on voyage.

Morison aligns Jones not only with Nelson but with Columbus. The latter too was independent, largely self-educated, badly served by his men and by his employers, and died sadly, though with a prophetic vision and no under-rating of his achievements. The three were professionals, contending against wealthy dilettantes, outdated veterans, useless place-seekers and enigmatic ruffians.

Robert Harvey in 2001 was concise and objective about John Paul Jones. 'No Naval Commander has been so lionised for such a brief career. But he was independent America's only naval hero, and he undoubtedly carried out his spectacular raids with great flair, courage and determination. His exploits – appropriately inflated – gave new heart to the American cause.'

Eventually, he climbed into myth, as Whitman's 'Little Captain' standing supreme. Herman Melville (*Israel Potter*, 1855) saw a figure real yet not quite earthly:

Paul Jones, in his small craft, went forth in single-armed champion-ship against the English host. It is not easy in the present day, to conceive the hardihood of the enterprise. It was a marching up to the muzzle; the act of one who made no compromise with the cannonadings of danger or death; such a scheme as only could have inspired a heart which held at nothing all the prescribed prudence of war... The vengeful indignation and bitter ambition of an outraged hero, with the uncompunctious desperation of a renegade. In one view, a Coriolanus of the Sea, in another a cross between the gentle-man and the wolf.

Some British, generous even when angry, compared him to Robin Hood, outlaw, bandit, thief, yet memorably enduring.

In any life, however well documented, there can remain the unsaid, barely suspected by contemporaries, later detected, however inaccurately, by poets. The half-mythical John Paul Jones, and his impact upon the Romantic imagination, can be pushed a little further in applying to him some of André Maurois's dissection of Byron's *The Corsair* in 1963: 'Conrad – A fierce, outlandish solitary man driven by some inner fatality, a hurricane let loose upon the world... No one knows whence he came, nor whither he goes. He is wrapped in mystery. His past always contains a crime which is kept dark from us.'

A Lowland outsider, socially and professionally ambitious, unflinching in action, with Calvinist self-confidence and poetic undercurrents, needing external success but learning its disappointments, unsubtle with women, he would have fitted into a romance by John Buchan, who noted a sentimental Scottish attachment to heroic failure.

We know from where Paul Jones came and whither he went. Much else has necessitated *perhaps, possibly, allegedly*, while remembering 'Kung', in Ezra Pound's Canto 13, wistfully reflecting:

> And even I can remember
> A day when historians left blanks in their writings,
> I mean for things they did not know.

John Paul Jones came from a definite place, had solid objectives, retired involuntarily, his pledged work unfinished, scarcely begun. Later, he was etherealised into something of a folk hero, more creative than Pretty Boy Floyd, Billy the Kid, Jesse James, at least more appealing than Bonnie and

Clyde. He had helped define ingredients for an American image, mean, tough, self-reliant, independent, capable, disrespectful, also an unadmitted snobbishness. His attempts to stride into new, sometimes incompatible milieus, would have intrigued both Balzac and Brecht. He had Joseph Conrad's belief in personal responsibility founded upon physical and moral courage. Like Lord Jim, his own flaws endangered his substance, his wholeness. He was, to paraphrase VS Pritchett, one of Conrad's uprooted men, a wanderer. In a complicated career, he was not exceptionally complex, was conventional in many tastes and values; an improver, not a destroyer. Fretful, often unappealing, he was part of a universe that, from boyhood, appeared to him the interplay of random forces, overcome only by the unscrupulous and unremitting will. Success and failure could be no more than temporary illusions: finery concealed corruption, sin and crime were condoned, or punished too late. Sickness, mischance, treachery destroyed the just and the unjust. Ambition could be ruinous, the mediocre survived. He himself wished to escape petty villages and small crafts, and by some 'brilliant action' enlarge his name. This he achieved, but gained little. As in a fate tale, he was the younger son who entered a palace but the jewels and golden promises never came and the princess was a youthful hag; his romances were sterile; in victory, his own ship foundered, the convoy escaped, the traitor sailed from the dark to stab his back.

At this distance, nevertheless, more zest than glumness is evoked by 'John Paul Jones'. The mighty individualist, Walt Whitman, sat down on Broadway to eat a watermelon, forcing carriages and wagons to divide around him. While onlookers hooted, Walt smiled: 'They laugh at me. But – I have the watermelon.' Paul Jones too prized the watermelon and, in general, presumed he possessed it.

Founder of the American navy? That is how he must have regarded himself, and certainly, more than any other, he spent years demanding and outlining innovations and reforms in education, technological training, ship design, administration that, over half a century after his death, helped all else to crystallise into his central proposal, the American Naval Academy.

In brute fact he founded nothing but, along with his professional recommendations, his personality gave inspiration to the navy he sought. He was only a shadowy admiral, the order of St Anna is trash: 'Chevalier' means nothing in America and Britain, 'commodore' is insufficient. No last word, however is inevitably final. For the moment, he remains John Paul Jones, tilting against the elements, himself somewhat elemental, a harsh man yet hoping to be remembered with affection when he was no more.

Appendix 1

From Byron's *The Corsair*, 1814.

Unlike the heroes of each ancient race,
Demons in act, but Gods at least in face,
In Conrad's form seems little to admire,
Though his dark eyebrow shades a glance of fire.
Robust, but not Herculean – to the sight
No giant frame sets forth his common height;
Yet, in the whole, who paused to look again,
Saw more than mocks the crowd of vulgar men;
They gaze and marvel how – and still confess
That thus it is, but why they cannot guess.
Sunburnt his cheek, his forehead high and pale,
The sable curls in wild profusion veil;
The haughtier thought it curbs, but scarce conceals.
Though smooth his voice and calm his general mien,
Still seems there something he would not have seen:
His features' deepening lines and varying hue
At times attracted, yet perplex'd the view,
As if within that murkiness of mind
Work'd feelings fearful, and yet undefined;
Such might it be – that none could truly tell –
Too close inquiry his stern glance would quell.

Appendix 2

A letter from John Paul, about the Maxwell affair, 24 September 1772.

My dear Mother and Sisters,

I only arrived here last night, from the Grenadas. I have had but poor health during the voyage; and my success in it, not having equalled my first sanguine expectations, has added very much to the asperity of my mis-fortunes, and, I am well assured, was the cause of my loss of health. I am now, however, better; and I trust Providence will soon put me in a way to get bread, and, which is by far my greatest happiness, be serviceable to my poor, but much valued, friends. I am able to give no account of my future proceed-ings, as they depend upon circumstances which are not fully determined.

I have enclosed you a copy of an affidavit made before Governor Young, by the judge of the court of Vice-admiralty of Tobago, by which you will see with how little reason my life has been thirsted after, and, which is much dearer to me, my honour, by maliciously loading me with obloquy and vile aspersions. I believe there are few who are hard-hearted enough to think I have not long since given the world every satisfaction in my power, being conscious of my innocence before Heaven, which will one day judge even my judges. I staked my honour, life, and fortune for six long months on the verdict of a British jury, notwithstanding I was sensible of the general prejudices which ran against me; but, after all, none of my accusers had the courage to confront me. Yet I am willing to convince the world, if reasons and facts will do it, that they have had no foundation for their harsh treatment. I mean to send Mr Craik a copy properly proved, as his nice feelings will not, perhaps, be otherwise satisfied; in the mean time, if you please, you may show him that enclosed. His ungracious conduct to me, before I left Scotland, I have not yet been able to get the better of. Every person of feeling must think meanly of adding to the load of the afflicted. It is true I bore it with seeming unconcern, but Heaven can witness for me that I suffered more on that account. But enough of this.

Appendix 3

Text of Lady Selkirk's letter to William Craik, Esquire, Arbigland, from St Mary's Isle, 25 April 1778.

Sir, Mr Jeffrey being abroad when your letter came, I was desired to open it, and believe, upon perusing it, an answer by my own hand will be full as satisfactory. The visit we had on Thursday was by no means desirable, but I have the satisfaction to be able to assure my friend that I neither was alarmed at the time, nor have suffered in the least degree since. They took pains to make themselves be understood a pressgang, till they had surrounded the house and the principal one had asked for me. I went down without scruple, they informed me what they were, said their orders were to take my Lord prisoner, or, if he was absent, to demand the plate. I was so sensible of the mercy it was that my Lord was absent that I never hesitated about the other. I apprehended the consequences of a refusal or a search to be so much worse that I would not permit the servants to conceal, as they meant to do. I must confess I now regret that, as I might have saved some of the best, for it came afterwards to be firmly believed that they were much alarmed, but at the time that was not observed, and could not otherwise be learned, as nobody was permitted to leave the house. They asked nothing but the plate, and I find more of that is left than I at first supposed, but, unluckily, it is either the least useful, or what is useful happens to be the worse of its kind. The value of it I never suffered to give me a thought till last night, after the bustle was over, my spirits did fail me, and I began to reckon what I might have saved, and consider what better might have been done; but I revived with daylight, and am resolved, if possible, not to let myself sink again. I am sure I behaved at the time with the most perfect composure, I may even say indifference, and did what I then thought best, if I had done otherwise, it might have turned out worse, I shall therefore allow no more reflections, and as few regrets as possible. The only real concern which I cannot remove is to think how my Lord must be affected if he hears this before he hears from me, and that is most likely, for though I wrote and enclosed in the packet that was sent off express to London on Thursday evening, yet I have no reason to think it will find him there, for on Sunday last I had a letter telling me I need not write again, as he meant to leave town before he could get any letter I should write after that. If you hear we have gone to England do not apprehend we have run away, for in that letter my Lord said he would tell me in his next when and where to meet him on the road, and the letter I expect every post. The people really behaved very civilly. The men who surrounded the house never offered to come in nor even ask for anything, they were well armed, each a musket and bayonet, two large pistols and a hanger, their number I cannot tell, they were called at first forty, afterwards fifteen. I reckon they were not near the first, but am persuaded more than the last. The youngest of the officers was a civil-looking lad, in American uniform, but it seems had had a blue great coat as a disguise. He meddled little, the other dressed in blue behaved civilly, but with so confident a look and so saucy a manner, that I daresay he could have been very rough had he deemed it necessary. They told me they were of the *Ranger* frigate, belonging to the States of America, commanded by Captain Paul Jones, Esq., whom, I understand, you know better than me, being John Paul, who they say was born in your ground, and was once a gardener of yours, and afterwards had the command of a training vessel in this place, and is understood to have deserved the gallows oftener than once. It seems it is known this is the name he takes, and he was seen on the Isle, though the tenderness of his heart, they said, would not allow him to come to the house. The frigate was at a good distance before the boat reached it, and were seen to make all the sail they could till they passed the Burrowhead, and a cutter from Whitehaven dogged them all day, but lost them in the dark, about the Mull of Galloway. As we have not yet heard of them, I fear they have escaped. The alarm still continued so a watch was placed, on the Isle all night of a great many men, a good deal of arms, also on two points of the Bay. I never did apprehend their return, which would have been a very foolish undertaking, as they were then so well known; so I would not leave the house, but I let Mrs Wood take my two girls to Dumfries with her, and part of the younger children being at Carlinwork, I sent another after them. But I was not left alone, for my good friend, Miss Elliot, who is as tenderly attached to me as ever friend could be, has never been ten yards from me since, and had they taken me on board, or even to America, was resolved to be of the party. We are all settled now as before, and I expect the girls home to-night. This has proved a very long letter, much more so than I thought of or than was necessary; but may I beg you will send it to Mrs Maxwell of Kirkconnell, I daresay I shall hear from her, and if I do before this reaches her, she will be so kind as to take this for an answer, for I have a great deal of writing and it is rather fatiguing. Mrs Maxwell will be pleased to understand that I sent her letter to my Lord, which I hope he would get before he left London. I once thought of writing north myself, in the expectation mine might reach first, but expecting a letter on Tuesday to bid us set out to meet my Lord on Wednesday, put it out of my head one post, and the next I was so engaged with my American friends, she will not be surprised I forgot it, so much time has now elapsed I hope my Lord's may reach us soon, if he thinks it can be of use. I beg my compliments to all your family, and am, sir, with sincere regard, your very humble servant,

H Selkirk

Appendix 4

Text of Paul Jones's letter to the Countess of Selkirk, from *Ranger*, 8 May 1778.

Madam, It cannot be too much lamented that, in the profession of arms, the officer of fine feelings and real sensibility should be under the necessity of winking at any action of persons under his command which his heart cannot approve; but the reflection is doubly severe when he finds himself obliged, in appearance, to countenance such acts by his authority. This hard case was mine, when, on the 23rd of April last, I landed on St Mary's Isle. Knowing Lord Selkirk's interest with the King, and esteeming, as I do, his private character, I wished to make him the happy instrument of alleviating the horrors of hopeless activity, when the brave are overpowered and made prisoners of war. It was, perhaps, fortunate for you, madam, that he was from home; for it was my intention to have taken him on board the *Ranger*, and to have detained him until, through his means, a general and fair exchange of prisoners, as well in Europe as in America, had been effected. When I was informed by some men whom I met at landing that his Lordship was absent, I walked back to my boat, determined to leave the island. By the way, however, some officers, who were with me, could not forbear expressing their discontent, observing that, in America, no delicacy was shown by the English, who took away all sorts of movable property, setting fire, not only to towns and to the houses of the rich, without distinction, but not even sparing the wretched hamlets and milch cows of the poor and helpless at the approach of an inclement winter. That party had been with me the same morning at Whitehaven; some complaisance, therefore, was their due. I had but a moment to think how I might gratify them and at the same time do your ladyship the least injury. I charged the officers to permit none of the seamen to enter the house, or to hurt anything about it; to treat you, madam, with the utmost respect; to accept of the plate which was offered, and to come away without making a search, or demanding anything else. I am induced to believe that I was punctually obeyed, since I am informed that the plate which they brought away is far short of the quantity expressed in the inventory which accompanied it. I have gratified my men; and when the plate is sold, I shall become the purchaser, and will gratify my own feelings by restoring it to you by such conveyance as you shall please to direct. Had the Earl been on board the *Ranger* the following evening, he would have seen the awful pomp and dreadful carnage of a sea engagement; both affording ample subject for the pencil as well as melancholy reflection for the contemplative mind. Humanity starts back from such scenes of horror, and cannot sufficiently execrate the vile promoters of this detestable war –

> For they, 'twas they unsheathed the ruthless blade,
> And Heaven shall ask the havoc it has made.

The British ship of war, *Drake*, mounting 20 guns with more than her full complement of officers and men, was our opponent. The ships met, and the advantage was disputed with great fortitude on each side for an hour and four minutes, when the gallant commander of the *Drake* fell, and victory declared in favour of the *Ranger*. The amiable lieutenant lay mortally wounded, besides near 40 of the inferior officers and crew killed and wounded – a melancholy demonstration of the uncertainty of human prospects and of the sad reverse of fortune which an hour can produce. I buried them in a spacious grave, with the honours due to the memory of the brave. Though I have drawn my sword in the present generous struggle for the rights of men, yet I am not in arms as an American, nor am I in pursuit of riches. My fortune is liberal enough, having no wife nor family, and having lived long enough to know that riches cannot ensure happiness. I profess myself a citizen of the world, totally unfettered by the little, mean distinctions of climate or of country, which diminish the benevolence of the heart and set bounds to philanthropy. Before this war began, I had at the early time of life withdrawn from the sea service in favour of 'calm contemplation and poetic ease.' I have sacrificed not only my favourite scheme of life, but the softer affections of the heart and my prospects of domestic happiness, and I am ready to sacrifice my life also with cheerfulness if that forfeiture could restore peace and goodwill among mankind. As the feelings of your gentle bosom cannot but be congenial with mine, let me entreat you, madam, to use your persuasive art with your husband's to endeavour to stop this cruel and destructive war, in which Britain can never succeed. Heaven can never countenance the barbarous and unmanly practice of the Britons in America, which savages would blush at, and which, if not discontinued, will soon be retaliated on Britain by a justly enraged people. Should you fail in this (for I am persuaded that you will attempt it, and who can resist the power of such an advocate?) your endeavours to effect a general exchange of prisoners will be an act of humanity which will afford you golden feelings on a death-bed. I hope this cruel contest will soon be closed; but should it continue, I wage no war with the fair. I acknowledge their force and bend before it with submission. Let not, therefore, the amiable Countess of Selkirk regard me as an enemy; I am ambitious of their esteem and friendship, and would do anything consistent with my duty, to merit it. The honour of a line from your hand in answer to this will lay me under a singular obligation; and if I can render you any acceptable service in France or elsewhere, I hope you see into my character so far as to command me without the least grain of reserve. I wish to know exactly the behaviour of my people, as I am determined to punish them if they have exceeded their liberty. I have the honour to be, with much esteem and with profound respect, madam, etc., etc.,

John Paul Jones
To the Countess of Selkirk

Appendix 5

From Paul Jones's letter to Lord Selkirk, 12 February 1784.

The long delay that has happened to the restoration of your plate has given me much concern, and I now feel a proportionate pleasure in fulfilling what was my first intention. My motive for landing at your estate in Scotland was to take you as an hostage for the lives and liberty of a number of the citizens of America, who had been taken in war on the ocean and committed to British prisons, under an Act of Parliament, as traitors, pirates, and felons. You observed to Mr Alexander that my idea was a mistaken one because you were not (as I had supposed) in favour with the British Ministry, who knew that you favoured the cause of liberty. On that account I am glad that you were absent from your estate when I landed there, as I bore no personal enmity, but the contrary towards you. I afterwards had the happiness to redeem my fellow-citizens from Britain by means far more glorious than through the medium of any single hostage.

Lord Selkirk replied from London, 4 August 1785:

Sir, I received the letter you wrote me at the time you sent off my plate in order for restoring it. Had I known where to direct a letter to you at the time it arrived in Scotland I would then have wrote to you, but not knowing it, nor finding any of my acquaintances at Edinburgh knew it, I was obliged to delay writing till I came here, when by means of a gentleman connected with America, I was told Mr Le Grand was your banker in Paris, and would take proper care of a letter for you. Therefore I enclose this to him. Notwithstanding all the precautions you took for the easy and uninterrupted conveyance of the plate, yet it met with considerable delays, first at Calais, next at Dover, then at London. However, it at last arrived at Dumfries, and I daresay quite safe, though as yet I have not seen it, being then at Edinburgh. I intended to have put an article in the newspapers about your having returned it, but before I was informed of its being arrived, some of your friends, I suppose, had put it in the Dumfries newspaper, whence it was immediately copied into the Edinburgh papers, and thence into the London ones. Since that time I have mentioned it to many people of fashion, and on all occasions, sir, both now and formerly. I have done you the justice to tell you that you made an offer of returning the plate very soon after your return to Brest, and although you yourself were not at my house, but remained at the shore with your boat, that yet you had your officers and men in such extraordinary good discipline that you, having given them the strictest orders to behave well, to do no injury of any kind, to make no search, but only to bring off what plate was given them, that in reality they did exactly as you ordered, and not one man offered to stir from his post on the outside of the house, nor entered the doors, nor said an uncivil word, that the two officers stood not a quarter of an hour in the parlour and butler's pantry, while the butler got the plate together, behaved politely, and asked for nothing but the plate, and instantly marched their men off in regular order, and that both officers and men behaved in all respects so well that it would have done credit to the best disciplined troops whatever. Some of the English newspapers at that time having put in confused accounts of your expedition to Whitehaven and Scotland, I ordered a proper one of what happened in Scotland to be put in the London newspapers by a gentleman who was then at my house, by which the good conduct and civil behaviour of your officers and men were done justice to, and attributed to your orders and the good discipline you maintained over your people. – I am, sir, your most humble servant,

Selkirk

Appendix 6

Perhaps understandably, Captain Pearson's account of the great fight off Flamborough Head, on 23 September 1779, between Paul Jones's *Bonhomme Richard* and Pearson's *Serapis* and Thomas Piercy's *Countess of Scarborough*, does not exactly tally with American versions, and seems to give more credit to Landais or Cottineau than is generally allowed.

> We dropt alongside of each other head and stern, when the fluke of our spare anchor hooking his quarter, we became so close, fore and aft, that the muzzles of our guns touched each other's sides. In this position we engaged from half-past eight till half-past ten; during which time, from the great quantity and variety of combustible matter which they threw in upon our decks, chains, and, in short, every part of the ship, we were on fire no less than ten or twelve times in different parts of the ship, and it was with the greatest difficulty and exertion imaginable at times that we were able to get it extinguished. At the same time the largest of the two frigates kept sailing around us the whole action and raking us fore and aft, by which means she killed or wounded almost every man on the quarter and main decks. About half-past nine, a cartridge of powder was set on fire, which, running from cartridge to cartridge all the way aft, blew up the whole of the people and officers that were quartered abaft the mainmast... At ten o'clock they called for quarter from the ship alongside; hearing this, I called for the boarders and ordered them to board her, which they did; but at the moment they were on board her, they discovered a superior number laying under cover with pikes in their hands ready to receive them; our people retreated instantly into our own ship, and returned to their guns till past ten, when the frigate coming across our stern and pouring her broadside into us again, without our being able to bring a gun to bear on her, I found in vain, and, in short, impracticable, from the situation we were in, to stand to any longer with the least prospect of success. I therefore struck. Our main mast at the same time went by the board.

Appendix 7

A Yorkshire ballad, 1779.

An American frigate, call'd the *Richard* by name
Mounted guns forty-four, from New York she came,
To cruise in the channel of Old England's fame,
With a noble commander, Paul Jones was his name.

We had not cruised long, before two sails we espied,
A large forty-four and a twenty likewise,
With fifty bright shipping, well loaded with stores,
And the convoy stood in for Old Yorkshire's shores.

'Bout the hour of twelve, we came alongside,
With a long speaking trumpet, 'When came you? he cried,
Come answer me quickly, or I'll hail you no more,
Or else a broadside into you I will pour.'

We fought them four glasses, four glasses so hot.
Till forty bold seamen lay dead on the spot
And fifty-five more lay bleeding in gore,
While the thund'ring large cannons of Paul Jones did pour.

Our carpenter being frightened, to Paul Jones did say,
Our ship leaks water, since fighting today,
Paul Jones made answer, in the height of his pride,
If we can do no better we'll sink alongside.

Paul Jones he then smiled and to his men did say
Let every man stand the best of his play,
For broadside for broadside they fought on the main,
Like true British heroes we return'd it again.

The *Serapis* wore round our ship for to rake,
Which made the proud hearts of the English to ache,
The shot flew so hot we could not stand it for long,
Till the bold British colours from the English came down.

Oh now my brave boys we have taken a rich prize,
A large forty-four and a twenty likewise,
Help the poor mothers that have reason to weep
At the loss of their sons in the unfathomed deep.

Appendix 8

Paul Jones to Anna Dumas, aged 13, November 1779.

Were I, Paul Jones, dear maid, 'the king of sea',
I find such merit in thy virgin song,
A coral crown with bays I'd give to thee.
A car which on the waves should smoothly glide along.
The nereids all about thy side should wait,
And gladly sing a triumph of thy state
'Vivat, vivat, the happy virgin muse!
Of liberty the friend, who tyrant power pursues!'

Or happier lot! were fair Columbia free
From British tyranny – and youth still mine,
I'd tell a tender tale to one like thee
With artless looks and breast as pure as thine
If she approved my flame, distrust apart.
Like faithful turtles we'd have but one heart;
Together then we'd tune the silver lyre,
As love or sacred freedom should our lays inspire.

But since, alas! the rage of war prevails,
And cruel Britons desolate our land,
For freedom still I spread my willing sails,
My unsheathed sword my injured country shall command.
Go on, bright maid! the muses all attend
Genius like thine, and wish to be its friend,
Trust me, although conveyed through this poor shift,
My New Year's thoughts are grateful for thy gift.

Bibliography

The best biography of John Paul Jones is *John Paul Jones: a Sailor's Biography*, by Samuel Eliot Morison, (see below), followed by *John Paul Jones: Fighter for Freedom and Glory*, by Lincoln Lorenz, United States Naval Institute, 1943.

Simon Sebag-Montefiore's *Prince of Princes: the Life of Potemkin* is unrivalled as a biography of Potemkin in English. For an objective survey of the American Revolution, disposing of some misunderstandings and legends, I recommend Robert Harvey's *A Few Bloody Noses: the American War of Independence*, John Murray, 2001.

Others I have found useful are:

Alden, John R. *History of the American Revolution*. Macdonald, 1969.

Alexander, John R. *Catherine the Great*. Oxford, 1989.

Almedingen, EM. *The Romanovs*. Bodley Head, 1966.

Anderson, JRL. *The Ulysses Factor*. Hodder and Stoughton, 1970.

Aslmo, Isaac. *The Birth of the United States 1763–1816*. Dobson, 1974.

Ayer, AJ. *Tom Paine*. Secker and Warburg, 1988.

Bickford, Richard F. *The Story of John Paul Jones*. Tarton Edge, Dumfries, 1993.

Buckman, Peter. *Lafayette*. Addington Press, 1977.

Cobba, Alfred. *A History of Modern France*. Vol. 1. Pelican, 1953.

Coleman, Terry. *Nelson: the Man and the Legend*. Bloomsbury, 2001.

Deacon, Richard. *The Silent War: a History of Western Naval Intelligence*. David and Charles, 1978.

Franklin, Benjamin. *Autobiographical Writings*. ed. C van Doren, Cressett, Press, 1946.

Fuller. JFC. *The Decisive Battles of the Western World*. Eyre and Spottiswoode, 1954.

Gorer, Geoffrey. *The Americans*. Cresset Presss, 1948.

Hough, Richard. *Fighting Ships*. Michael Joseph, 1969.

Kemp, Peter. *The Oxford Companion of Ships and the Sea*. Oxford, 1976.

de Koven, Mrs Reginald. *The Life and Letters of John Paul Jones*. Scribners, 1913.

Longford, Elizabeth. *Wellington: Pillar of State*. Weidenfeld and Nicolson, 1972.

Lorenz, Lincoln. *John Paul Jones: Fighter for Freedom and Glory*. United states Naval Institute, 1943

McCollough, David. *John Adams*. Simon and Schuster, 2001.

Mackesy, Peter. *The War for America 1775–1783*. Longmans, 1964.

Mahan, AT. *John Paul Jones in the Revolution*. Scribners Magazine, 1898.

Morison, SE. *John Paul Jones: A Sailor's Biography*. Faber, 1959.

Morris, Gouverneur. *A Diary of the French Revolution*. Boston, 1939.

Morton, HV. *In Scotland Again*. Methuen, 1933.

Norton, William. *John Paul Jones*, University of Virginia, 1954.

Plumb, JH. *Men and Places*. Cresset Press, 1963.

Pole, JR. *The Decision for American Independence*. Edward Arnold, 1975.

Randier, Jean. *Men and Ships Around Cape Horn 1616–1939*. Barker, 1968.

Russell, Phillips. *John Paul Jones: Man of Action*. Brentano, 1927.

Sands, RC. *The Life and Correspondence of John Paul Jones*. New York, 1830.

Sitwell, Sachaverel. *Valse des Fleurs*. Faber, 1942.

Smout, TC. *History of the Scottish People*. Fontana, 1972.

Thompson, JM. *The French Revolution*. Blackwell, 1944.

Trevelyan, GO. *The American Revolution*. Longmans, 1965.

Index